AESTHETIC NERVOUSNESS

AESTHETIC NERVOUSNESS

Disability and the
Crisis of Representation

Ato Quayson

COLUMBIA UNIVERSITY PRESS NEW YORK

Columbia University Press
Publishers Since 1893
New York   Chichester, West Sussex

Copyright © 2007 Columbia University Press

Library of Congress Cataloging-in-Publication Data

Quayson, Ato.
    Aesthetic nervousness : disability and the crisis of representation / Ato Quayson.
        p. cm.
    Includes bibliographical references and index.
    ISBN 13: 978–0–231–13902–1 (cloth : acid-free paper)
    ISBN 13: 978–0–231–13903–8 (pbk. : acid-free paper)
    ISBN 13: 978–0–231–51117–9 (e-book)
    1. People with disabilities in literature.   2. English literature—English-speaking countries—
History and criticism.   3. Abnormalities, Human, in literature.   4. People with disabilities—
Social conditions.   5. Diseases and literature.   6. Beckett, Samuel, 1906–1989—Criticism and
interpretation.   7. Morrison, Toni—Criticism and interpretation.   8. Soyinka, Wole–Criticism
and interpretation.   9. Coetzee, J.M., 1940– —Criticism and interpretation.   I. Title.

PR 9080.Q38   2007
809′. 933527—dc22

To the memory of my father,
Emmanuel Laud Quayson,
a man with a limp and many stories to tell

CONTENTS

PREFACE

WHEN I WAS ABOUT NINE OR TEN YEARS OLD, MY BLIND grandfather on my father's side came to live with us. I recall him as a tall man who always walked with his back straight despite his blindness. From time to time, Nana would scream that soldiers were coming to get him, and my father would reply that he had soldiers stationed at the gate and at all four corners of the house. Nana was calmed by this reassurance for a while, but it didn't take long for the entire ritual of alarm and reassurance to have to be repeated. With time, my siblings and I were put in charge of what we then thought was a fun game. We ran out of the house each time Nana had his anxiety attacks and came back with elaborate descriptions of what the guardian soldiers were wearing and what they told us to tell him.

Nana stayed with us for the better part of two years before returning to the coastal fishing village in which he had spent much of his life. He spoke of the sea with much fondness. Some time after his return to the village, a distraught messenger came bearing tragic news. Nana had been found hanging from a beam in his dark room. He had taken his own life.

It was only some twenty-five years later that I came to understand a little bit of what Nana must have been going through. I recalled that in those days, whenever he was in a good mood he would gather the children together and tell us stories. Often in telling them he broke spontaneously into song, his favorite of which we mistook for something from a folktale:

> Hisafrica we shall go,
> We fear nobody,
> Hisafrica we shall go,
> We fear nobody.

> *Refrain:* Hisafrica we shall go, Hisafrica we shall go-o,
> Hisafrica we shall go-ooo, we fear no-booody.

This with energetic swinging of his arms interspersed with booming commands to turn left, turn right, about turn, and stand at ease. My sisters and I marched delightedly to the song. It was only many years later that I realized that Nana had fought for the British in World War II and been sent to East Africa. When he came to live with us, and apparently from a long way back, he had been suffering from post–traumatic stress disorder. Being a mere soldier in the colonial army, Nana, like most other such soldiers, did not have the benefit of the diagnosis and treatment that European soldiers received. Rehabilitation for colonial war veterans was practically unheard of, and most veterans ended up being the responsibility of their families. Thus Nana's anxiety attacks were not just brought on by his blindness but by the fact that his darkened world was populated with traumatic images from the war.

It is my father, however, who provides the more complex enigma and trigger for my interest in literature and disability. His right leg was shorter than his left, and when he walked, his body leaned sharply to his right side and back. It was never clear to us what the cause of the limp might have been, and being from a culture that never discussed impairments for fear of causing offence, we never spoke about it. He never told us about it either, but we learned from other members of the family that he had suffered a nasty accident in his childhood and broken a bone in his thigh, which had set badly. This accounted for his unusual gait.

My father was unusual in other respects too. After the breakup of his marriage to my mother when I was about seven years old, he became a fugitive from matrimony, a condition that several women tried to cure him of with no appreciable success. He was universally acknowledged to be a strange man. He had a ferocious temper that often flared up unpredictably. He was also the only man I know of his generation who regularly went out to the market to buy foodstuffs for cooking at home. He was an indifferent cook, but he took the feeding of his children very seriously. Many a time my two sisters and I were roped into the kitchen to be engaged in collective attempts at divining whether the food was actually cooked or merely edible without causing food poisoning. The debates were often inconclusive, the idea being that the proof of the cooking had to be in the eating itself. My own love of cooking dates from this period, when I often saw my father "steering" fufu with one hand while trying desperately to keep the soup placed precariously on the coal fire from boiling over. Yet it was really my father's incredible flair for storytelling that defined for good or ill the way in which I was to remember him. Often, on a Saturday evening, he would invite the children on our street for a meal of fufu and fish or meat soup, after which would follow the most amazing and colorful stories. Many of these featured Ananse, the trickster spider of Akan folktales, along with ghostly *sasabonsam* tales and a variety of stories from other traditions. He leavened all his stories with a good number of parables, jokes, and moral puzzles. Later on, we children came to realize that his diehard optimism sometimes led him to confuse fact with fiction in real life, thus making it difficult to know whether he was really serious or just making things up. With time I came to see him as existing in his own fantastic story, in which he was sometimes the epic hero and sometimes the victim of others' machinations.

Sometimes, the stories provided him the opportunity to give us a memorable take on what passed for the ordinary. One such instance that I remember quite clearly occurred when I was about eleven or twelve years old, just before I began attending secondary school. He often took us on walks. Sometimes we all went together, but at other times he took one or the other of us three for a treat. This time it was my turn. We started kicking a particular stone. He kicked it, and I kicked it; he kicked it, and I kicked it. After about ten minutes of this, he asked me, quite unexpectedly, "How old do you think that little stone is?" I was taken completely by surprise, having never thought of a stone as having an age before. But then followed the most breathtaking story of the formation of the earth, of volcanoes and avalanches, of magma and igneous rocks. The lesson:

every stone you kick has come a very long way, both geographically and in terms of time. I have never looked at a stone the same way since.

My father was also an avid reader of all things written. These included newspapers, Buddhist texts, novels, women's magazines, refrigerator manuals, and Shakespeare. There was no knowing what he would be found reading next. This meant that reading became a natural part of the domestic environment in which we grew up and also that our early reading was completely eclectic. I used to spend many secret afternoons after school in his bedroom, rifling through his books and documents. He also had a peculiar talent for picking quarrels, both on his own behalf and on behalf of others. This frequently led to impassioned letters to various civil-service departments. Being a civil servant himself, he had mastered what I later came to recognize as a peculiar form of "bureaucratese," but one which he often personalized with the odd literary inflection from his varied reading. For a while, he was with the Ghanaian Foreign Service, having to leave it as part of the purge of the service that was undertaken by the government in the late 1960s and early 1970s. A period of uncertainty followed, during which he launched a massive and ultimately successful challenge to his dismissal. He was reinstated after five or so years, but to a different branch of the civil service, and he spent many years as a dutiful upholder of its values. He was a model of efficiency and also highly competitive by nature. Dad took early retirement in the late 1980s and relocated to Brazil, where he had enjoyed a pleasant Foreign Service posting earlier on and where I had spent a part of my childhood with my very young siblings. He spoke impeccable Brazilian Portuguese and had so fallen in love with the country that he decided to spend the rest of his productive life among the people he so loved and admired.

The first immediate trigger for my interest in representations of disability in writing and culture came with an innocent question asked by Jo Emeney, a student taking a set of supervisions (tutorials) with me on postcolonial literature at Cambridge. This was in the 1995–1996 academic year. After six weeks of supervisions, she mused aloud as to why nearly all the texts I had assigned for discussion had disabled characters in them. Her question came to me as a complete surprise, for the simple reason that I had not noticed the disabled characters myself. I reread the texts, and sure as anything, they were populated with disabled figures in casual and not-so-casual roles. Moreover, figures that did not initially appear as disabled suddenly took on a more significant hue when read through a prism of disability. This fascinated me greatly. I had been trained in a tradition of close reading, so the obvious question that struck me was what could account for my blindness to the presence of these characters. As I began research for the project, I also began to think more and more about my father and grandfather. My interest at this time was not so much to learn how they got their impairments as it was in finding out how they felt being persons with disability in a culture that did not speak about disability as such. This was even more pertinent to understanding my father than my grandfather. Several questions I wanted to ask him pressed themselves on my mind: What was it like growing up in a coastal fishing village where a particular form of masculinity and masculine prowess was the norm (swimming, fishing, weaving nets, and so on) when, as far as I could ascertain, he did not even know how to swim? What was it like going to school in the 1940s and 1950s and imagining oneself as one of the inheritors of the independent nation when there were so many subtle and not-so-subtle prejudices against people with disability? Why was he so absolutely driven and such a perfectionist in all things? And why did he sometimes surrender to sputtering anger when he felt himself contradicted on what seemed to everyone else quite minor details? And what about women? What did he think women thought about him that made him such a difficult person to please? In short, what did it feel like to be a highly intelligent and articulate man with a physical impairment in a postcolonial African setting that promised opportunities to its elites but that implicitly conceived of these elites as "perfect" beings without physical blemishes?

Unfortunately, I never had the opportunity to ask my father the many questions that swirled through my mind. He suffered a massive heart attack and died in Rio de Janeiro in May 1996. This was during my first year as a Lecturer in English at the University of Cambridge. The impulse behind writing this book is to pose to the universe the inchoate but pressing questions I had wanted to ask him. To answer them, I have had to go through a diverse and varied corpus of texts and ideas, for even though I see my father in every person with disability I meet, I also know that each person perfects their own inflections of how to negotiate the fact of impairment; they each bear the "slings and arrows of outrageous fortune" (one of my father's favorite lines) within the world that shapes and often misunderstands them.

This book is dedicated to Nana, to Emmanuel, and to all those like them.

ACKNOWLEDGMENTS

T HERE ARE MANY PEOPLE I WISH TO NUMBER IN MY SONG of thanks, starting with the following for their help and comments on different incarnations of various chapters in the book: Anjali Prabhu, Ananya Kabir, Stuart Murray, Tejumola Olaniyan, Abiola Irele, Mark Wormald, Drew Milne, Mary Jacobus, Simon Baron-Cohen, Joanna Lewis, Graham Pechey, Harriet Deacon, Benita Parry, Dickson Eyoh, Alissa Trotz, Sara Abraham, and Fiifi Jehu-Appiah. Brian Corman was an interlocutor and facilitator without even knowing it.

I wish also to number my many students at Pembroke College and the Faculty of English at Cambridge, on whom many of the ideas expressed here were first tried out. Special thanks are due to Henry Louis Gates Jr. and the staff of the W. E. B. Du Bois Institute for African American Research at Harvard University for a very pleasant sabbatical year in 2004. The institute's regular Wednesday colloquium was the first place I tried out my notion of aesthetic nervousness. Abiola Irele (again), Emmanuel Akyeampong, and John Mugane were great hosts and companions and made my stay an enjoyable and productive one.

A very special thanks to Sunil Agnani, for the opportunity to present an early version of the chapter on J. M. Coetzee at the University of Michigan, and to David Theo Goldberg and Philomena Essed, for inviting me to make a presentation drawing on the first chapter at the Cloning Cultures conference in 2005. To the Ghana Academy of Arts and Sciences, I express warm gratitude for the opportunity to present the central points of my research as my inaugural lecture to the Academy in May 2006 (and to Agya Appiah, for the timely cufflinks on the day of the inaugural lecture). Boafo-Gyimah and Abdul Wahab Musah of the Ghana Center for Democratic Development (CDD) I also thank, for arranging for me to meet with advocacy groups and other interested parties on the historic passing of the Ghana Persons with Disabilities Act.

The anonymous readers of Columbia University Press did an amazing job of joining the dots between the suspension marks in my thought and pushing me to examine much further the questions raised in the manuscript. Their comments were both critical and highly productive. I want to thank them and also my editor, Jennifer Crewe, whose gentle but persistent pressure brought this project to a happy and timely conclusion.

I swell to full-throated thanks when turning to Valentina for her forbearance in a time of transition; to Barry Rosen for conversation, conviviality, and great friendship; and also to Antonella Rosen for her hospitality.

Jijo, Abena, and Kamau sing with me on all my daily rounds, but I wish to number them especially for providing me with the primary audience for my storytelling impulses, something that I use to join my own childhood to theirs and to that of my parents. Hopefully, they will continue the song.

AESTHETIC NERVOUSNESS

I'm disabled. Not someone to look straight through.

Time to get equal.

Please don't see me as the invisible man. See me as John. John who loves playing chess. John who likes going down the pub. John who has a degree. John who's really just like you. See me for who I am...and treat me as an equal. **Thanks.**

Pledge your support to disabled people achieving equality
Visit: www.timetogetequal.org.uk Phone: 0845 355 0700
Text: Equality Pledge (Your Name) to 60003*

scope

About cerebral palsy.
For disabled people achieving equality.

1

INTRODUCTION

Aesthetic Nervousness

I N 2004, SCOPE, A BRITISH ORGANIZATION FOCUSING ON people with cerebral palsy, launched a campaign called "Time to Get Equal," in which they highlighted the various forms of discrimination that people with cerebral palsy were exposed to by care professionals, the various care institutions, and the general public. A Web site, www .timetogetequal.org.uk, provided personal accounts of some of the ways in which such people had been negotiating their day-to-day lives. One of the supporting images (figure 1) used to launch the campaign is fascinating in its suggestive use of literary echoes. To the right hand side of the frame, we see a man with a round hole in the center of his face, through which is visible the blue wall behind him. Just above him and to his left are the words: "I'm disabled. Not someone to look straight through." The words are placed to act like a speech or thought bubble similar to those used in cartoons, but with the contours of the bubble removed. The picture has been taken in such a way as to cast a shadow on the blue background against which he stands. Whereas the man clearly has a hole in his face, the shadow of his face looks like that of a man screaming. There is an optical illusion at play in the picture that suggests a double speech act. The subtle literariness of the way the words are placed and the screaming penumbral projection behind the man are further augmented by the first sentence of the printed text right below the picture: "Please do not see me as the invisible man." The kinship evoked between the person in this picture and the narrator of Ralph Ellison's classic novel is telling, because as in *Invisible Man*, the problem is not one of not being seen, but of being framed within a discourse of stereotypes and expectations that serve to efface a person's identity. While people routinely "look straight through him," the person with cerebral palsy, like the Invisible Man, constantly wants to scream. I shall have more to say about Ellison's novel in the next chapter, particularly in relation to his own ironic treatment of Brother Jack, the leader of the Brotherhood and who happens to have a concealed disability.

The Scope poster and Web site serve to highlight in a highly succinct and effective way some central features of disability studies. From at least the 1980s, the main interest of scholars in this field has been to shift the discussion of disability away from the medical discourse that had dominated such discussion previously and to see disability as woven out of a range of problems connected to the architectural environment, the public-transport system, and most important, to the often ill-concealed social attitudes that attend people with disabilities. In this regard, the term disability is no longer taken as referencing the notion of a reduced ability deriving from an impairment, but speaks to the built and social environments that generate difficulties for the disabled person's capacity to live a full and fulfilled life (Corker and French 1999; Linton 1998; Davis 2002, 33–46). Once viewed from this angle, disability can no longer be seen as the product of tragic circumstances and thus be understood simply as the presumed sad fate of the individual (Oliver 1990). The notion of disability as personal tragedy places people with disabilities within a narrative in which accommodation to the impairment is squarely their own responsibility or that of their families. The medical and social systems are then tasked with corrective, ameliorative, or reprimanding roles, reminding the person with disability to "get a grip" and take charge of the process of his or her self-improvement and adjustment. Indeed, in the medical model, the person with disability is placed under an obligation to want to get well, his or her multiple social roles of parent, worker, spouse, and so on being suspended temporarily in exchange for a sign of strenuous effort toward improvement. (Murphy 1990; Wendell 1996, 87–109). Shifting the focus of disability to see it as primarily the product of social circumstances complicates even the notion of impairment. As the sociologist Oliver notes, the dominance and indeed proliferation of certain impairments can be directly linked to social systems. Thus in Africa there is a direct correlation between poverty and such diseases as polio. Additionally, it is not uncommon to see people with physical impairments reduced to begging on street corners or living a generally twilight existence, concealed from the eyes of the public. And it is not idle to note that the many civil wars that have blighted the continent, from Angola and Mozambique to Rwanda, Sierra Leone, and Liberia, have served to greatly increase the number of people with impairments. All these wars may be directly attributed to incoherent political and social structures that, for some, have made the instrumentalization of disorder an attractive option for the resolution of social conflicts.[1]

In the contemporary West, on the other hand, noncongenital impairments such as spinal-cord injury and various workplace-related impairments derive directly from the relations of production within capitalism. Certain injuries and impairments are more likely to be sustained by factory and construction workers than by those who spend their time in an office, for example. If we recall the effect of disasters such as the chemical leakage at the Union Carbide plant in Bhopal in 1984 and the terrible impairments incurred among the local population because of it, we see a worrisome link between global capitalism and local disabilities. And to render matters even more complicated, it could be argued that the landmines sown into the land in Angola and elsewhere are a direct product of cold-war politics and therefore an extension of the cynical underside of the West's military-industrial complex. "Long cited as one of the most heavily mined countries in the world, the early UN estimate of 10 to 15 million landmines contaminating Angolan soil is still widely cited." These are the words of the *Landmine Monitor Report* (1999, 117) on Angola. Viewed through a wider lens of social structures and international formations, disability ceases being an individual affliction to be borne silently by the person with an impairment. However, when the intricate links between social or international systems and such impairments are exposed, the response is often a mixture of guilt, bewilderment, and denial on the part of the nondisabled. I will be using the terms "impairment" and "disability" interchangeably, even though "impairment" refers to the specific physical or cognitive deficiency that leads to a reduced capacity to fully actualize all aspects of one's life and "disability" to the socially regulated parameters that exacerbate the effect of the impairment.

In practice, it is almost impossible to keep the two separate, since "impairment" is automatically placed within a social discourse that interprets it and "disability" is produced by the interaction of impairment and a spectrum of social discourses on normality that serve to stipulate what counts as disability in the first place.

It is not only the oppositions between impairment and disability that are rendered unstable once we begin to see disability within a social as opposed to a medical discourse. Various other oppositions are also destabilized, such as those that might be discerned in the distinctions between congenital and adventitious disability, between disease as causative factor and impairment as effect of disease, between physical deformity and madness, and between the material consequences of blindness or deafness and that of nonvisible disabilities. The central reason for this instability is that though different kinds of disability can be shown to have historically followed different rhythms and patterns of institutional evolution in the West and elsewhere, viewed from the perspective of what Rosemarie Garland Thomson (1997) calls the normate, disability has always been the object of a negative comparison to what is typically construed as corporeal normality. The attitudes that have historically attended people with disabilities have varied over time, but reiterated in all epochs is the idea that they carry an excess of meaning and therefore offer an insistent invitation to a series of interpretative and institutional framings. Thomson (1996, 1) puts it succinctly when writing in the context of the display of freaks: "By its very presence, the exceptional body seems to compel explanation, inspire representation, and incite regulation." Seen from the perspective of the normate, the boundaries that might be taken to differentiate and divide various disabilities are frequently blurred. The disabled body has historically invited, compelled, and incited a variety of responses in spite of whatever specific impairments may be at issue. Even as different impairments become the touchstones or focal points for intensified social processes of corporeal hierarchization in different historical periods, certain symbolic representations and social attitudes were regularly transferred across disabled groups. As Stiker (1997, 72) puts it, writing of the Middle Ages: "Beyond these figures, so important in the Middle Ages—the beggar, the monster, the criminal—lies the silhouette of the disabled, borrowing features from the other three all at the same time or successively, and yet sharply contoured, taking us down into the depths of as yet unthought social ideas." Even though in Western societies the disabled are no longer directly linked in the social imaginary to monsters and criminals, the point of Stiker's remark is that persons with disabilities, located on the margins of society as they are, have historically taken on the coloration of whatever else is perceived to also lie on the social margins of society. It is this that allows Scope to invoke the Invisible Man in promoting awareness about cerebral palsy as a potent reminder of the interlinked construction of such margins.

Genealogies and Inflections

Disability scholarship allows us to glean certain repeated features from the general social treatment of the disabled (Stiker 1997; Braddock and Parish 2001). These repeated features will become pertinent for discussing the literary and aesthetic representation of disability, since I will be trying to show that the literary domain invokes some of these attitudes but dissolves them into the tapestry of representation. What follows next is not an attempt at a full survey of the history of disability discourse in the West, but only a review of some salient features that will become pertinent to my later literary discussion. Disability studies scholars already familiar with this history may wish to skip to the next section, where I outline the main theoretical emphases of this study. In this brief review section, I shall at various points correlate the social treatment of disability to specific texts and generic conventions in preparing the way for outlining what I mean by the concept of *aesthetic nervousness*.

Classical antiquity shared with the biblical period the fact that various forms of disability were interpreted as signs of the operation of a spiritual or metaphysical realm. Various texts in the Old Testament insisted, for example, that lepers could not be admitted to the world of normals. In the Old Testament, legal uncleanness attached to people with disabilities, who, even though permitted to participate in cultic observances, could never become priests who made sacrifices (Stiker 1997, 24). The Greeks, on the other hand, saw disability and disease as punishment from the gods, while for the ancient Egyptians, disability and disease were no longer instances of punishment for sin but the signs of a metaphysical drama (Stiker 1997, 39–46). From the ethnographic essays on disability in Ingstad and Whyte's *Culture and Disability* (1995), one can also get the impression that various tribal peoples share a similar perspective with regard to disability to that of antiquity. Whyte (1995, 273–274) describes these as generally following a therapeutic itinerary governed by an impulse toward the placation of causal forces. In all these instances, the divine and metaphysical orders are seen to be proximate to the human lifeworld. Disability is then interpreted in various ways as a function and sign of that proximity.

"The body," Mary Douglas (2004, 142) tells us in *Purity and Danger*, "is a complex structure. The functions of its different parts and their relation afford a source of symbols for other complex structures." This observation is forcefully illustrated in the medieval period. In the early Middle Ages, writers such as Isidore of Seville (560–636) were able to proffer a taxonomy of monstrosity in which the disabled take their place beside monsters. His twelve-part taxonomic grid starts off as follows: (1) hypertrophy of the body, (2) atrophy of the body, (3) excrescence of bodily parts, (4) superfluity of bodily parts, (5) deprivation of bodily parts, and then through various gradations on to the mixture of animal and human parts and to monsters proper. Isidore of Seville's taxonomy of the monstrous proceeds from the view that the most useful model for such a taxonomy was the human body itself. Indeed, the symbolic force of the body throughout the Middle Ages is particularly strong because of the influence of Neoplatonism, which allegorized the body as the "little cosmos" within which was contained the cosmos itself (Williams 1996, 107–108). Isidore of Seville's taxonomy is ultimately also a normative grid; the degrees of embodied impairment-as-monstrosity are inherently part of a moral map of the corporeal body itself and the ways in which society might relate to it. Though his taxonomy seems extreme to modern eyes, the assumed ethical implications of impairment are also discernible in literary texts of different periods and cultures. In chapter 2, I shall outline a typology that takes account of such ethical implications as they relate to distinctions within the aesthetic domain in its attempts to "make sense" of the disabled body. As I shall show, the ways in which disability is represented in literary writing makes for a range of differentiated aesthetic dispositions that simultaneously reflect both an ethical *and* a literary dimension to such representations.

By the later Middle Ages, disability is defined by interlocking subsystems of social attitudes and treatment. On the one hand, charity is the dominant response to disability. Disability is seen as a sign of the variety of God's creation, the specific impairments being read off as challenges to man's sense of pride and self-sufficiency. Thus the nondisabled were encouraged by the church to respond with charity toward people with disabilities. Because disability was closely aligned to disease and disease was often interpreted as a form of plague and punishment for past sins, along with the encouragement to charity there also persisted an idea of disability as a sign of divine disfavor. The two attitudes—charity and fear—were by no means mutually exclusive.

In places such as France, lepers formed distinctive urban communities almost akin to monasteries (Stiker 1997, 68). Fourteenth-century England, on the other hand, saw a complex attitude of city authorities toward the management and containment of disease and disability. This was in spite of the persistent link made between the medical and religious grounds for social intervention. Furthermore, the fate of persons with disability was inextricably tied to that of the poor. With the progressive collapse of the medieval social structure and the decline of the monasteries and their eventual abolition in 1536, charity for the poor gradually moved from its traditional voluntary framework to become a special tax levied at the parish level. Starting in the 1500s, the Poor Laws that came out regularly for two centuries ensured that the link between the sick poor and people with disability—and the attempted alleviation of the causal connections between the condition of the disabled and poverty—increasingly became the focus of legislation and municipal activity. The 1571 census of the city of Norwich, for example, counted about a third of the sick poor as being either sick, sickly, or very sick. They were described as "weak, diseased, bed-ridden, lame, crooked, or suffering from stone, gout, dumbness, deafness, broken legs, diseases of the mouth, broken ribs, thigfola [fistula?], or were one-legged or one-handed" (Pelling 1998, 85). As was the case in France, lazarhouses for people suffering from leprosy and other communicable diseases were established outside the city walls. It was, however, traditional for lepers and lunatics as well as epileptics and sometimes the sick poor to share an asylum, thus making their later institutional prominence in the eighteenth and nineteenth centuries such as on Robben Island in South Africa in a sense unremarkable.

Health practices were quite multifarious in the later Middle Ages, with overlapping and sometimes contradictory elements. Thus, on the one hand, lazarhouses were used for the treatment of conditions that negatively affected the working capacity of the patient and also of the poor, in the case of infectious diseases. On the other hand, diseases seen as "intractable," such as those associated with people with severe mobility impairments or lunatics, were sometimes ignored. Intractable conditions "aroused a response from passers-by without involving the same risks of quarantine, confinement, and cure, even though such disabilities would not necessarily inhibit authorities from using the whip" (Pelling 1998, 96). It is clear that the boundary between disease and institutionalization was very thin indeed and that social attitudes extended from a sense of tolerant charity to one of moral panic.[2] At the same time, the late medieval period also saw a challenge to notions of aesthetic beauty. This is most marked in the paintings of Brueghel, who placed disabled characters in several of his most prominent paintings. As Mitchell and Snyder (2000, 4–5) show, Brueghel's masterworks "rely upon the representational power of deformity and disability to expose the bodily life repressed within classicism," seizing upon "disability's power to disrupt and variegate the visual encounter with unblemished bodies." We shall return to Mitchell and Snyder and their notion of the distortion and variegation of the visual encounter more fully in the next section.

Even as there appeared to be a variegated response to physical disabilities, madness, on the other hand, was consistently viewed throughout the Middle Ages and even into the Renaissance period as a form of divine punishment. Examples abound from the work of didactic writers such Aelfric, Abbot Leofstan of Bury St. Edmunds, John Mirk, and others to show how clearly the link was made between madness, divine retribution, and demoniacal possession (Harper 2003, 29–74). As Harper shows, this link was itself reflected in the Middle English romance and in the writings of people such as Chaucer, whose Miller and Summoner both tell stories that play upon such beliefs. Madness was also linked to witchcraft, with the bloody excesses of the witch and heresy hunts eventually breeding official and public skepticism about the links between madness and demoniacal possession. By 1563, Johannes Weyer was to write a medical thesis that wove an ingenious religious-cum-medical argument to show how mistaken the view was about the link between madness and demoniacal possession. He was followed by other writers who collectively cast scorn on the popularly held beliefs that had dominated the witch hunts (Porter 2002, 25–33). What is pertinent in these accounts, however, is the persistence of what we noted earlier with regard to the Greeks, Egyptians, and others in antiquity, namely, the idea that disability (in this case madness) reflected the proximity between the divine or metaphysical world and the human lifeworld.

By the eighteenth and nineteenth centuries, however, a marked shift came when, with the emergence of a scientific medical discourse, the disabled were subjected to taxonomies of scientific measurement and ordering. The idea of the education or reeducation of disabled people grows out of the Enlightenment. But coinciding with this is the consolidation of carceral complexes such as the prison and the hospital, the hospital for lunatics and other persons with disability having grown out of charity houses since the Middle Ages. Increasingly, concerns were also raised in the period about the primary role of sexuality in generating disease and disability. The 1889 *Report of the Royal Commission on the Blind, the Deaf, and the Dumb et Cetera* worried that disabled offspring might result from sexual intercourse between people with physical disabilities, leading to "one more of the minor streams which ultimately swell the great torrent of pauperism" (xii). In that period, an explicit link was established between diseases such as syphilis and blindness, to the degree that an immediate correlation was made between blindness and sexual behavior. Blindness was taken as a sign of presumed sexually questionable behavior and moral deficiency. This correlation finds a peculiar focus in the literature of the Victorian period (see Holmes 2002). In opera, on the other hand, the relation between disability and presumed sexual behavior is used as a shorthand for tragic failings. In their fascinating study of the relationship between opera and disease, Hutcheon and Hutcheon (1996, 22) write that "the history of syphilis in Europe from 1495 on has been a history of Christian interpretations of this disease based on the earlier plague model: as a divine scourge, but this time specifically against the sexually sinful" (22). They go on to show in their discussion of Wagner's *Parsifal* how Amfortas's shameful wound, tactfully transferred from the character's genital area to his chest by Wagner in a revision of his sources, prevents him from carrying out his social and moral tasks as leader of the Grail realm. But Amfortas receives his disabling wound as he sinks into the arms of the beautiful Kundry, "consistently represented in nineteenth-century cultural vocabulary of the syphilitic prostitute" (Hutcheon and Hutcheon 1996, 22, 62). She dies at the end of the opera as recompense, but not before the connection between sexually transmitted disease and the tragic and disabling effect it has on the hero has been suggestively established.

Even though many wars had historically been fought in the West and had led to the proliferation of disabilities, it may be argued that part of the sense of outrage we share today—and how that fed into specific legal instruments and institutions for addressing the needs of people with disabilities—derived mainly from World War I and World War II. The literary writing of direct participants in the wars bore witness to the degree to which war proliferated impairment and disability in the name of unsustainable ideals. In Britain, noted World War I soldier-poets such as Siegfried Sassoon and Wilfred Owen depicted the mental and physical disorders that were caused by the war (see Sassoon's "They" and Owen's "Disabled" as interesting examples). The two poets met in Craiglockhart War Hospital, where Owen was undergoing treatment along with a hundred and fifty other British officers for mental conditions related to trench warfare. Sassoon had been sent there on suspicion of mental illness for criticizing the war in a London newspaper.

The two World Wars not only led to the consolidation of psychoanalysis, with terms such as post–traumatic stress disorder being properly understood in relation to shell-shocked soldiers, but also generated the main parameters of disability rehabilitation and compensation as they are known today. In the United States, as medical treatment for people with disabilities borne from the wars merged with vocational education and training, a fundamental ideal of rehabilitation began to gather momentum through the activism of figures such as Howard Rusk, Mary Switzer, Henry Kessler, and others (O'Brien 2001, 31–45). And as prostheses for soldiers developed, so also did the more widespread notions of replacement, compensation, and rehabilitation evolve and become part of the institutional apparatuses that were put in place to take care of all people with disabilities. Today's special-education programs are direct descendants of the medical discourse of rehabilitation from the two World Wars.

Attitudes to disabilities in the West also evolved in response to interactions with other races. The colonial encounter and the series of migrations that it triggered in its wake served to displace the discourse of disability onto a discourse of otherness that was correlated to racial difference. Even as colonialism provided extra-European "social laboratories" for the development of discourses to do with bourgeois civility, female sexuality, and the nature of criminality and policing, it also led to the intermeshing of such external colonial realities into the rhythms of the West's own social evolution. Part of this intermeshing involved the increasing mixture between Europeans and outsiders both in the colonies and in Europe itself, with sharp lines regularly being suggested about what constituted the inside and outside of society.[3] Disease provided a particularly supple set of metaphors to modulate some of the social anxieties that emerged in the colonial period around interracial encounters, both in Europe and in the United States, with the discourse on leprosy in the period being particularly productive. Whereas the disease had disappeared from Europe and had declined as a salient theological concept by the end of the Renaissance, during the period of nineteenth-century imperialism the disease was discovered as quite common in parts of the world that the Western nations were annexing and colonizing. And with the germ theory of disease having emerged as one of the more important scientific advances, a new anxiety about race relations began to take hold. Vaughan (1991, 77) writes of "the projection on to Africa of a powerful Christian disease symbolism and the attempt to engineer socially a 'leper identity' in the particular circumstances of colonialism" by the British. In the United States, on the other hand, the germ theory heightened fears that contact with "inferior" races might threaten the safety and future of the "superior" race; new immigration laws were drafted to take account of this perceived new threat (Gussow 1989, 19–20). In certain quarters, an increasingly paranoid connection was made between foreign migrants, the transferability of diseases, and the dangers that these posed to the United States:

At the present day Louisiana is threatened with an influx of Chinese and Malays, with filth, rice [sic] and leprous diseases. An inferior and barbarous race transferred from the burning heats of Africa has already been the occasion of the shedding of the blood of more than one million of the white inhabitants of the United States, and in the shock of arms and the subsequent confusion and chaos attending the settlement of the question of African slavery, the liberties of the country have been well nigh destroyed, and it is but just that patriots should contemplate with dread the overflow of their country by the unprincipled, vicious and leprous hordes of Asia. The contact of a superior with an inferior race must lead eventually to two results: the annihilation of one or the other, or the amalgamation of the two. The mixture of the blood of a noble race with that of one of inferior mental and moral constitution may depress the former to the level of the latter, but can never endow the brain and heart of the African and the Asiatic with the intelligence, independence, love of liberty, invention and moral worth of the Anglo-Saxon race.

(Joseph Jones, "The Leprosy Question in Louisiana," cited in Gussow 1989, 56–57)

Note the moral panic intricately interwoven into the references to then contemporary American history. Tellingly, the foreigners are already marked out as morally dangerous in the phrase "unprincipled, vicious and leprous hordes of Asia," so that the entire discussion of the effect of race mixture is not just one inflected by the terror of miscegenation but essentially by the idea of threatened moral negation. What is evident from these and other similar remarks is that the West's continuing contact with the rest of the world through the colonial adventure and the attendant flows of people across borders serves to problematize and disrupt any straightforward trajectory of attitudes toward disability that might be adduced in looking solely at developments in the West itself. I shall pay some more attention to the colonial encounter and the status of the intersection between disease, criminality, and disability in chapter 7, on the history of Robben Island.

If, as Ingstad and Whyte's 1995 collection of ethnographic essays on disability persuasively demonstrates, in many non-Western cultures disability is tied to normative injunctions and to powerful enactments of metaphysical beliefs, then it has to be conceded that the constant migration of people from other parts of the world to the West also implies a transfer of such beliefs and interpretations. Whyte's concluding essay in the collection is particularly useful in arguing the dialogical relationship between non-Western and Western attitudes to the disabled. Even though she does not state this explicitly, it is possible to glean a synchronic model from her account, in which to simultaneously read off attitudes to disability in the West and elsewhere. Thus we might speak of multiple discourses of disability operating in the West today, one that proposes itself as entirely scientific and rational and another that is still tied to different therapeutic itineraries that involve the placation of causal forces. The two discourses are not necessarily contradictory but must be seen as part of a continuum of responses around disease and disability today.

Even though in the modern world the notion of the proximity of the divine and metaphysical orders to the human lifeworld is no longer predominant, such beliefs have still flared up from time to time in a variety of contexts. The idea of the proximity of the two realms has only been re-sidualized as opposed to being entirely superseded. The relation between residuality and emergence is not to be seen as a cycle but rather as a dia-lectical mutation in which a variety of "old" and "new" ideas are some-times reconstellated to produce new perspectives and realities (Williams 1977). Such a reconstellation regarding disability is what led to the at-tempt to exterminate people with disabilities along with Jews during the Third Reich.[4] Even though there had always been people with disability in Germany, historically treated in similar ways to others elsewhere in Europe, the intense nationalist redefinition that took place during the Third Reich shifted the salience of disability as a socially meaningful sign. Disability ceased being a mere cipher of the proximity of the meta-physical realm to the human lifeworld and rather became the signal of danger to the purity of the nation as such. Joined to the presumed in-alienable racial otherness of Jews, disability came to bear the burden of a moral deficit that was thought to threaten the national character as such and thus, along with Jews, had to be violently extirpated.

Certain present-day responses to disability even among people presum-ably sharing an enlightened mode of thinking still hark back to unexam-ined sentiments of a bygone era. Thus it is not at all uncommon for some still to think that impairments are a sign of some special metaphysical disorder, or that people with disability carry their impairments because of mistakes in their past life. A classic instance of such a disposition is seen in the remarks made by Glen Hoddle, who was quoted as saying that peo-ple with disabilities are born that way for karmic restitution. His remarks led directly to his sacking as manager of the English soccer team, but it was the furor that broke out in the wake of his comments that is of signifi-cance. Coming from a Christian who also believes in reincarnation, Hod-dle's remarks divided opinion sharply. Whereas disability groups and poli-ticians were incensed at his remarks, commentators from various parts of the world including from well outside the United Kingdom jumped to his defense.[5] But it is the range of disablist images that were used to describe him in the media that was telling about largely unacknowledged social attitudes toward persons with disabilities. As was quietly pointed out in a letter in *The Guardian*:

> Glenn Hoddle is described as nuts, an imbecile or village idiot. Your leader tells us that Hoddle has a disabled intellect. You should avoid

attacking the use of discriminatory language with disablist imagery that further marginalises people. Perhaps you should learn to involve the experts, disabled people, in disability issues.[6]

In other words, the choice of language in the media to condemn Hoddle suggested that attitudes toward people with disabilities were unexamined at best and utterly atavistic at worst.

There are three key elements I want to highlight from this brief historical account of the social treatment of disability. First is the implicit assumption that disability is an "excessive" sign that invites interpretation, either of a metaphysical or other sort. As will be clear from the work of the various writers we will be looking at in this study, the category of the "metaphysical" is dissolved into that of an aesthetic problematic, sometimes figured in the form of an interpretative difficulty or impasse, at other times as something that is concealed from view but that has serious ramifications for how interpersonal relationships among the characters are conducted. Following from this first point is the issue of subliminal fear and moral panic. Several disability scholars have already noted the degree to which the disabled body sharply recalls to the nondisabled the provisional and temporary nature of able-bodiedness and indeed of the social frameworks that undergird the suppositions of bodily normality. I will suggest, however, that in literature this subliminal unease manifests itself within the structures of the literary discourse itself, generating a series of crises in the protocols of representation. Finally, I want to highlight the degree to which the social treatment of disability has historically been multifaceted and sometimes even contradictory. Again, these contradictions take on a particular salience when we come to the literary-aesthetic domain, because what we find is that literature refracts social attitudes and sometimes renders them even more complicated than they are in reality. As already noted, the reality of people with disability is overlaid with the suppositions and implicit social attitudes of a nondisabled world, making their "reality" as much a product of excessive interpretation as of mundane fact (if mundanity can ever be ascribed to the condition of disability). Literature does not merely reflect any already socially interpreted reality, but adds another tier of interpretation that is comprehensible within the terms set by the literary-aesthetic domain. In the next chapter, I will address a typology of the figuring of disability in literature to provide a provisional map of the interconnections between these three observations. But first, we require a definition of key terms.

What Is Aesthetic Nervousness?

Let me begin formulaically: Aesthetic nervousness is seen when the dominant protocols of representation within the literary text are short-circuited in relation to disability. The primary level in which it may be discerned is in the interaction between a disabled and nondisabled character, where a variety of tensions may be identified. However, in most texts aesthetic nervousness is hardly ever limited to this primary level, but is augmented by tensions refracted across other levels of the text such as the disposition of symbols and motifs, the overall narrative or dramatic perspective, the constitution and reversals of plot structure, and so on. The final dimension of aesthetic nervousness is that between the reader and the text. The reader's status within a given text is a function of the several interacting elements such as the identification with the vicissitudes of the life of a particular character, or the alignment between the reader and the shifting positions of the narrator, or the necessary reformulations of the reader's perspective enjoined by the modulations of various plot elements and so on. As I shall show throughout this study, in works where disability plays a prominent role, the reader's perspective is also affected by the short-circuiting of the dominant protocols governing the text—a short-circuit triggered by the representation of disability. For the reader, aesthetic nervousness overlaps social attitudes to disability that themselves often remain unexamined in their prejudices and biases. The reader in this account is predominantly a nondisabled reader, but the insights about aesthetic nervousness are also pertinent to readers with disabilities, since it is the construction of a universe of apparent corporeal normativity both within the literary text and outside it whose basis requires examination and challenge that is generally at issue in this study. The various dimensions of aesthetic nervousness will be dealt with both individually and as parts of larger textual configurations in the works of Samuel Beckett, Toni Morrison, Wole Soyinka, and J. M. Coetzee. The final chapter, on the history of disability on Robben Island in South Africa, will be used to refocus attention from the literary-aesthetic domain to that of the historical intersection between disability, colonialism, and apartheid. This will help us see what extensions might be possible for the concept of aesthetic nervousness beyond the literary-aesthetic field.

There are two main sources for the notion of aesthetic nervousness that I want to elaborate here. One is Rosemarie Garland Thomson's highly suggestive concept of the normate, which we have already touched on briefly, and the other is drawn from Lennard Davis's and Mitchell and Snyder's reformulations of literary history from a disability studies perspective. As Thomson (1997) argues in a stimulating extension of some of Erving Goffman's (1959) insights about stigma, first-time social encounters between the nondisabled and people with disabilities are often short-circuited by the ways in which impairments are interpreted. She puts the matter in this way:

> In a first encounter with another person, a tremendous amount of information must be organized and interpreted simultaneously: each participant probes the explicit for the implicit, determines what is significant for particular purposes, and prepares a response that is guided by many cues, both subtle and obvious. When one person has a visible disability, however, it almost always dominates and skews the normate's process of sorting out perceptions and forming a reaction. The interaction is usually strained because the nondisabled person may feel fear, pity, fascination, repulsion, or merely surprise, none of which is expressible according to social protocol. Besides the discomforting dissonance between experienced and expressed reaction, a nondisabled person often does not know how to act toward a disabled person: how or whether to offer assistance; whether to acknowledge the disability; what words, gestures, or expectations to use or avoid. Perhaps most destructive to the potential for continuing relations is the normate's frequent assumption that a disability cancels out other qualities, reducing the complex person to a single attribute.
>
> (Thomson 1997, 12)

To this we should quickly recall Mitchell and Snyder's remark concerning the degree to which Brueghel's paintings succeeded in disrupting and variegating the visual encounter between bodies in painting. Clearly, disruption and variegation are also features of real-world encounters between the nondisabled and persons with disabilities. Thomson proposes the notion of the "normate" to explicate the cluster of attitudes that govern the nondisabled's perception of themselves and their relations to the various "others" of corporeal normativity. As she persuasively shows, there are complex processes by which forms of corporeal diversity acquire cultural meanings that in their turn undergird a perceived hierarchy of bodily traits determining the distribution of privilege, status, and power. In other words, corporeal difference is part of a structure of power, and its meanings are governed by the unmarked regularities of the normate. However, as the paragraph quoted above shows, there are various elements of this complex relationship that do not disclose themselves as elements of power as such, but rather as forms of anxiety, dissonance, and disorder. The common impulse toward categorization in interpersonal encounters is itself part of an ideal of order that is assumed as implicit in the universe, making the probing of the explicit for the implicit part of the quest for an order that is thought to lie elsewhere. It is this, as we noted in the previous section, that persistently leads to the idea that the disabled body is somehow a cipher of metaphysical or divine significance. Yet the impairment is often taken to be the physical manifestation of the exact opposite of order, thus forcing a revaluation of that impulse, and indeed, of what it means to be human in a world governed by a radical contingency. The causes of impairment can never be fully anticipated or indeed prepared for. Every/body is subject to chance and contingent events. The recognition of this radical contingency produces features of a primal scene of extreme anxiety whose roots lie in barely acknowledged vertiginous fears of loss of control over the body itself (Grosz 1996; Wasserman 2001; Lacan 1948, 1949).[7] The corporeal body, to echo the sonnet "Death Be Not Proud" by John Donne, is victim to "Fate, chance, kings, and desperate men" and subject to "poison, warre, and sicknesse" as well. The dissonance and anxiety that cannot be properly articulated via available social protocols then define the affective and emotional economy of the recognition of contingency. In other words, the sudden recognition of contingency is not solely a philosophical one—in fact, it hardly ever is at the moment of the social encounter itself—but is also and perhaps primarily an emotional and affective one. The usefulness of the social model of disability is precisely the fact that it now forces the subliminal cultural assumptions about the disabled out into the open for examination, thus holding out the possibility that the nondisabled may ultimately be brought to recognize the sources of the constructedness of the normate and the prejudices that flow from it.

Since the world is structured with a particular notion of unmarked normativity in mind, people with disabilities themselves also have to confront some of these ideas about contingency in trying to articulate their own deeply felt sense of being (Murphy 1990, 96–115). At a practical and material level, there are also the problems of adjustment to a largely indifferent world. As Wood and Bradley (1978, 149) put it: "On a material plane the disabled individual is . . . less able to adapt to the demands of his environment: he has reduced power to insulate himself from the assaults of an essentially hostile milieu. However, the disadvantage he experiences is likely to differ in relation to the nature of the society in which he finds himself." Contradictory emotions arise precisely because the disabled are continually located within multiple and contradictory frames of significance within which they, on the one hand, are materially disadvantaged, and, on the other, have to cope with the culturally regulated gaze of the normate. My use of the word "frames" in this context is not idle. Going back to the Scope poster, it is useful to think of such frames in the light of physical coordinates, as if thinking of a picture frame. The frames within which the disabled are continually placed by the normate are ones in which a variety of concepts of wholeness, beauty, and economic competitiveness structure persons with disability and place them at the center of a peculiar conjuncture of conceptions.

Thomson's notion of the relations between the normate and the disabled derives ultimately from a symbolic interactionism model. To put it simply, a symbolic interactionism model of interpretation operates on the assumption that "people do not respond to the world directly, but instead place social meanings on it, organize it, and respond to it on the basis of these meanings" (Albrecht 2002, 27). The idea of symbolic interactionism is pertinent to the discussion of literary texts that will follow because not only do the characters organize their perceptions of one another on the basis of given symbolic assumptions, but as fictional characters they are themselves also woven out of a network of symbols and interact through a symbolic relay of signs. Furthermore, as I shall show incrementally in different chapters and in a more situated form in the chapter on J. M. Coetzee (chapter 6), symbolic interactionism also implies the presence of an implied interlocutor with whom the character or indeed real-life person enters into a series of dialogical relationships, thus helping to shape a horizon of expectations against which versions of the self are re-hearsed. Following Thomson's lead, the first aspect of aesthetic nervous-ness that I want to specify is that it is triggered by the implicit disruption of the frames within which the disabled are located as subjects of sym-bolic notions of wholeness and normativity. Disability returns the aes-thetic domain to an active ethical core that serves to disrupt the surface of representation. Read from a perspective of disability studies, this active ethical core becomes manifest because the disability representation is seen as having a direct effect on social views of people with disability in a way that representations of other literary details, tropes, and motifs do not offer. In other words, the representation of disability has an effica-ciousness that ultimately transcends the literary domain and refuses to be assimilated to it. This does not mean that disability in literature can be read solely via an instrumentalist dimension of interpretation; any inter-vention that might be adduced for it is not inserted into an inert and sta-ble disability "reality" that lies out there. For, as we have noted, disability in the real world already incites interpretation in and of itself. Neverthe-less, an instrumentalist dimension cannot be easily suspended either. To put the matter somewhat formulaically: the representation of disability oscillates uneasily between the aesthetic and the ethical domains, in such a way as to force a reading of the aesthetic fields in which the disabled are represented as always having an ethical dimension that cannot be easily subsumed under the aesthetic structure. Ultimately, aesthetic nervous-ness has to be seen as coextensive with the nervousness regarding the disabled in the real world. The embarrassment, fear, and confusion that attend the disabled in their everyday reality is translated in literature and the aesthetic field into a series of structural devices that betray themselves when the disability representation is seen predominantly from the per-spective of the disabled rather than from the normative position of the nondisabled.

In his essay entitled "Who Put the *The* in The Novel?" Lennard Davis (2002) explores the links that have largely been taken for granted in liter-ary history between the novel form, an *English* nation, and the various destabilizations of the social status of character that help to define the es-sential structure of the novel in the eighteenth and nineteenth centuries. The realist novels of the two centuries were based on the construction of the "average" citizen. This average citizen was nonheroic and middle class. But the average citizen was also linked to the concept of "virtue."

As Davis notes, "Virtue implied that there was a specific and knowable moral path and stance that a character could and should take. In other words, a normative set of behaviours was demanded of characters in novels" (94). Entangled with these dual notions of the average citizen and of virtue were implicit ideas of wholeness, with no major protagonist in the entire period marked by a physical disability. Undergirding the novel's rise then is a binary opposition between normal/abnormal, with this binary generating a series of plots. Essentially, the key element of such plots is the initial destabilization of the character's social circumstances, followed by their efforts to rectify their loss and return, perhaps chastened, to their former position. Crucially, however, as the nineteenth century progresses the negative or immoral gets somatized and represented as a disability (95–98). One of the conclusions Davis draws from his discussion is that plot functions in the eighteenth and nineteenth centuries "by temporarily deforming or disabling the fantasy of nation, social class, and gender behaviors that are constructed norms" (97).

In taking forward Davis's argument, there are a number of qualifications I want to register. Distinctive in his account is the link he persuasively establishes between nation, the average citizen, virtue, and specific forms of novelistic emplotment. That cannot be questioned. However, it is not entirely accurate that the binary of normal/abnormal starts with the eighteenth- and nineteenth-century novels or indeed that they inaugurate the plots of the deformation of social status. On the contrary, as can be shown from an examination of folktales from all over the world, the plot of physical and/or social deformation is actually one of the commonest starting points of most story plots (see Propp 1958; Zipes 1979), so much so that it is almost as if the deformation of physical and/or social status becomes the universal starting point for the generation of narrative emplotment as such. As Davis points out, in agreement with established scholarship on the novel, the crucial term that is introduced in the eighteenth and nineteenth century is "realism," the notion that somehow the novelistic form refracts a verisimilar world outside of its framework. But realism is itself a cultural construction, since for the Greeks their myths were also a form of realism. What needs to be taken from Davis's account is the effect that the collocation of the social imaginary of the nation and the production of a specific form of bodily and sexual realism had on the way the novel was taken to represent reality. In each instance, the assumed representation of reality depended upon unacknowledged views of social order deriving not just from an understanding of class relations but from an implicit hierarchization of corporeal differences. Even though Davis is not the only one to have noted the peculiar place of the disabled in the eighteenth- and nineteenth-century novel (see Holmes 2000, for example), it is in clarifying the status of the disabled body as *structurally constitutive* to the maintenance of the novel's realism that he makes a distinctive contribution to literary history.

However, in trying to extend the significance of the constitutive function of deformation from the novel to other literary forms, we also have to note that "deformation" can no longer be limited solely to that of social or class position, as Davis suggests in his discussion. From the novels of the early twentieth century onward, the deformations emerge from the intersection of a variety of vectors including gender, ethnicity, sexuality, urban identity, and particularly disability, these providing a variety of *constitutive points for the process of emplotment*. Indeed, Davis himself notes in another context the reiteration of disability in the works of Conrad. A similar view can be expressed of the work of Joyce (*Ulysses, Finnegan's Wake*), Virginia Woolf (*Mrs. Dalloway*), Thomas Mann (*The Magic Mountain*), and T. S. Eliot's "The Waste Land," among others. I choose the phrase "constitutive points" as opposed to "starting points" to signal the fact that the social deformation does not always show itself at the beginning of the plot. In much of the work we will look at, from Beckett and Soyinka through Morrison and Coetzee, there are various articulations of a sense of social deformation. However, the deformation is not always necessarily revealed as inaugural or indeed placed at the starting point of the action or narrative as such. It is often revealed progressively or in fragments in the minds of the characters, or even as flashbacks that serve to reorder the salience of events within the plot. The varied disclosures of social deformation are also ultimately linked to the status of disability as a trigger or mechanism for such plot review and disclosure. In that sense, the range of literary texts we shall be exploring is not undergirded exclusively by the binary opposition of normal/abnormal, but by the *dialectical interplay* between unacknowledged social assumptions and the reminders of contingency as reflected in the body of the person with disability.

The notion of dialectical interplay is crucial to my model of interpretation, because one of the points I will repeat throughout the study is that a dialectical interplay can be shown to affect all levels of the literary text, from the perspectival modulations of the narrator (whether first or third person) and the characters to the temporal sequencing and ordering of leitmotifs and symbolic discourses that come together to structure the plotlines. Even though, as Davis rightly notes, the plots of social deformation dominated the eighteenth- and nineteenth-century novel, this view cannot be limited solely to novelistic discourse. Following the point I made a moment ago about the near universality of such plots, I want to suggest that we consider the plot of social deformation as it is tied to some form of physical or mental deformation to be relevant for the discussion of *all* literary texts. This is a potentially controversial point, but given the ubiquity of the role of the disabled in texts from a range of cultures and periods it is difficult to shake off the view that disability is a marker of the aesthetic field as such. Disability teases us out of thought, to echo Keats, not because it resists representation, but because in being represented it automatically restores an ethical core to the literary-aesthetic domain while also invoking the boundary between the real and the metaphysical or otherworldly. Along with the category of the sublime, it inaugurates and constitutes the aesthetic field as such. And like the sublime, disability elicits language and narrativity even while resisting or frustrating complete comprehension and representation and placing itself on the boundary between the real and the metaphysical. When I state that disability "inaugurates" the aesthetic domain, it is not to privilege the "firstness" or "primariness" of first-time encounters between the disabled and nondisabled characters, even though this has been implied in my reliance on Thomson. Rather, I intend the term "inaugurate" in the sense of the setting of the contours of the interlocking vectors of representation, particularly in narrative and drama, which are the two literary forms that will feature mainly in this study. My position overlaps with Davis's but extends his insights to accommodate a more variegated methodology for understanding the status of disability in literary writing.

The analogy between the inaugural status of the sublime and of disability serves to open up a number of ways in which the structurally constitutive function of disability to literary form might be explored. In the *Critique of Judgment*, Kant follows his discussion of the beautiful and its relation to purposelessness or autonomy with the discussion of the sublime and its inherent link to the principle of disorder. For Kant, "*Beauty* is an object's form of *purposiveness* insofar as it is perceived in the object *without the presentation of purpose*" (1987, 31), the idea here being that only the lack of a determinate or instrumental end allows the subjective feeling of beauty to occur. The sublime, on the other hand, is an aspect of under-standing in confrontation with something ineffable that appears to resist delimitation or organization. It exposes the struggle between Imagination and Reason: "[What happens is that] our imagination strives to progress toward infinity, while our reason demands absolute totality as a real idea, and so [the imagination,] our power of estimating the magnitude of things in the world of sense, is inadequate to that idea. Yet this inadequacy itself is the arousal in us of the feeling that we have within us a supersensible power" (108; translator's brackets). Even while generative of representa-tion, the sublime transcends the imaginative capacity to represent it. As Crockett (2001, 75) notes in glossing the nature of this struggle, "the sub-lime is contra-purposive, because it conflicts with one's purposeful ability to represent it." The implicit dichotomy in the *Critique of Judgment* be-tween the sublime and the beautiful has been explored in different direc-tions by scholars in the intervening three hundred and fifty years since its formulation, but what has generally been agreed upon is the idea of the re-sistance of the sublime to complete representation, even if this resistance is then incorporated into a motivation for representation as such.[8] What the representation of disability suggests, which both overlaps and distin-guishes itself from the sublime as a conceptual category, is that even while also producing a contradictory semiotics of inarticulacy and articulation, it is quite directly and specifically tied to forms of social hierarchization. For disability, the semiotics of articulation/inarticulation that may be per-ceived within the literary domain reflect difficulties regarding its salience for the nondisabled world. This, as can be gleaned from the Whyte and Ingstad collection already referred to, cuts across cultures. Thus even if the ambivalent status of disability for literary representation is likened to that of the sublime, it must always be remembered that, unlike the effects of the sublime on literary discourse, disability's ambivalence manifests itself within the real world in socially mediated forms of closure. We might then say that disability is an analogue of the sublime in literary-aesthetic repre-sentation (ineffability/articulation) yet engenders attempts at social hier-archization and closure within the real world.

Disability might also be productively thought of as being on a continu-um with the sublime in terms of its oscillation between a pure abstraction and a set of material circumstances and conditions. Considered in this way, we can think of the sublime as occupying one end of the spectrum (being a pure abstraction despite generating certain psychological effects

of judgment and the impulse to represent it in material forms) and disability occupying the other end and being defined by a different kind of
oscillation between the abstract and the material. For unlike the sublime,
disability oscillates between a pure process of abstraction (via a series of
discursive framings, metaphysical transpositions, and socially constituted
modalities of [non]response, and so forth) and a set of material conditions
(such as impairment, accessibility and mobility difficulties, and economic
considerations). It is not to be discounted also that many impairments
also involve living with different levels of pain, such that the categories of
pain and disability not infrequently imply each other. It is disability's rapid oscillation between a pure process of abstraction and a set of material
conditions that ensures that the ethical core of its representation is never
allowed to be completely assimilated to the literary-aesthetic domain as
such. Disability serves then to close the gap between representation and
ethics, making visible the aesthetic field's relationship to the social situation of persons with disability in the real world. This does not necessarily
mean that we must always read the literary representation in a directly
instrumental way. As noted earlier, the intervention of the literary representation is an intervention into a world that already situates disability
within insistent framings and interpretations. The literary domain rather
helps us to understand the complex *processes* of such framings and the
ethical implications that derive from such processes.

Finally, it is to Mitchell and Snyder's book *Narrative Prosthesis* (2003)
that I wish to turn in elaborating what I mean by aesthetic nervousness.
Mitchell and Snyder follow David Wills (1995) in trying to define literary
discourse as essentially performing certain prosthetic functions. Among
these prosthetic functions are the obvious ones of using the disabled as a
signal of moral disorder such that the nondisabled may glean an ethical
value from their encounter with persons with disabilities. Since Mitchell
and Snyder are also keen to situate narrative prosthesis as having significance for the lived experience of disability, they also assign an inherently
pragmatic orientation to what they describe as textual prosthesis: "Whereas an actual prosthesis is always somewhat discomforting, a textual prosthesis alleviates discomfort by removing the unsightly from view. . . . [T]he
erasure of disability via a "quick fix" of an impaired physicality or intellect
removes an audience's need for concern or continuing vigilance" (8). They
make these particular remarks in the context of films and narratives in

which persons with disabilities somehow manage to overcome their difficulties and live a happy life within the realm of art. In such instances, the representation of disability serves a pragmatic/cathartic function for the audience and the reader. More significantly, however, they also note that even while disability recurs in various works as a potent force to challenge cultural ideas about the normal and the whole, it also *"operates as the textual obstacle that causes the literary operation of open-endedness to close down or stumble"* (50).

This last observation brings their discussion of narrative prosthesis very close to my own notion of aesthetic nervousness, except that they proceed to expound upon this blocking function in what can only be nonaesthetic terms. This is how they put it:

> This "closing down" of an otherwise permeable and dynamic narrative form demonstrates the historical conundrum of disability. [Various disabled characters from literature] provide powerful counterpoints to their respective cultures' normalizing Truths about the construction of deviance in particular, and the fixity of knowledge systems in general. Yet each of these characterizations also evidences that the artifice of disability binds disabled characters to a programmatic (even deterministic) identity.   (Mitchell and Snyder 2003, 50)

Thus Mitchell and Snyder's idea of the shutting down or stumbling of the literary operation is extrinsic to the literary field itself and is to be determined by setting the literary representations of disability against sociocultural understandings. While agreeing with them that the ultimate test of the salience of a disability representation are the various social and cultural contexts within which they might be thought to have an effect, I want to focus my attention on the devices of aesthetic collapse that occur *within* the literary frameworks themselves. Also, I would like to disagree with them on their view of the programmatic identity assigned to the disabled, because, as I will try to show by reading the disabled character within the wider discursive structure of relations among different levels of the text, we find that even if programmatic roles were originally assigned, these roles can shift quite suddenly, thus leading to the "stumbling" they speak of. I choose to elaborate the textual "stumbling" in terms of aesthetic nervousness.

When it comes to their specific style of reading, Mitchell and Snyder are inspired by Wills to elaborate the following provisional typology:

> Our notion of narrative prosthesis evolves out of this specific recognition: a narrative issues to resolve or correct—to "prostheticize" in David Wills's sense of the term—a deviance marked as improper to a social context. A simple schematic of narrative structure might run thus: first, a deviance or marked difference is exposed to the reader; second, a narrative consolidates the need for its own existence by calling for an explanation of the deviation's origins and formative consequences; third, the deviance is brought from the periphery of concerns to the center of the story to come; and fourth, the remainder of the story rehabilitates or fixes the deviance in some manner. The fourth step of the repair of the deviance may involve an obliteration of the difference through a "cure," the rescue of the despised object from social censure, the extermination of the deviant as a purification of the social body, or the revaluation of an alternative mode of being. . . . Narratives turn signs of cultural deviance into textually marked bodies.
>
> (53–54)

Again, their method is defined by an assumption of narrative pragmatism or instrumentalism; that is to say, the literary text aims solely to resolve or correct a deviance that is thought to be improper to a social context. Unlike them, I will be trying to show that this prostheticizing function is bound to fail, not because of the difficulties in erasing the effects of disability in the real world, but because the aesthetic domain itself is short-circuited upon the encounter with disability. As mentioned earlier, disability joins the sublime as marking the constitutive points of aesthetic representation. Aesthetic nervousness is what ensues and can be discerned in the suspension, collapse, or general short-circuiting of the hitherto dominant protocols of representation that may have governed the text. To my mind, in this paragraph Mitchell and Snyder are attempting to define processes of representation that may occur separately (i.e., across individual and distinguishable texts) as well as serialized within a particular text. One of my central points is precisely the fact that even when the disabled character appears to be represented programmatically, the restless dialectic of representation may unmoor her from the programmatic location and place her elsewhere as the dominant aesthetic protocols governing the representation are short-circuited.

To establish the central parameters of aesthetic nervousness, then, a number of things have to be kept in mind. First is that in literature, the disabled are fictional characters created out of language. This point is not made in order to sidestep the responsibility to acknowledge language's social efficaciousness. Rather, I want to stress that as linguistic creations, the disabled in literature may trade a series of features with the nondisabled, thus transferring some of their significations to the nondisabled and vice versa. Furthermore, I want to suggest that when the various references to disability and to disability representation are seen within the broad range of an individual writer's work, it helps to foreground hitherto unacknowledged dimensions of their writing and, in certain cases, this can even lead to a complete revaluation of critical emphasis. Consider in this regard Shakespeare's *Richard III*, for instance, which is of course very widely discussed in disability studies. However, in Shakespeare disability also acts as a metaphor to mark anomalous social states such as those involving half-brothers and bastards. Indeed, there is a studied pattern in Shakespeare where bastards are considered to be internally deformed and villainous, their bastardy being directly correlated to a presumed moral deficit. And so we have the elemental and almost homicidal competition between half-brothers that reappears in conflicts between Robert Falconbridge and his bastard brother Philip in *King John*, between Don John and Don Pedro in *Much Ado About Nothing*, between Edmund and Edgar in *King Lear*, and between Richard III and Edward in *Richard III*. This last play is of course grounded on the resonance of jealousy and brotherhood, as well as on the Machiavellianism of a deformed protagonist. There the disability is placed at the foreground of the action from the beginning and brings together various threads that serve to focalize the question of whether Richard's deformity is an insignia of or indeed the cause of his villainy.[9] Thus to understand Richard III properly, we would have to attend equally to his disability and his bastardy in the wider scheme of Shakespeare's work. Once this is done, we find that our interpretation of the character has to be more complicated than just recognizing his villainy, which of course is the dominant invitation proffered by the play. The choice of Beckett, Soyinka, Morrison, and Coetzee is partly meant to serve this function of establishing the interrelations between disability and other vectors of representation among the wide oeuvre of each writer. However, comparisons and contrasts within the work of individual writers or indeed between them will not be made chronologically or with the suggestion of evolution and change in the representation of disability. Rather, I shall be focusing on thematic clusterings and on making links between apparently unrelated characters and scenes across the various texts to show how the parameters of aesthetic nervousness operate within individual texts as well as across various representations. Also, the writers will be used as nodal points from which to make connections to the work of other writers. Thus each chapter, though focusing predominantly on the individual writer in question, will also provide a gateway for connecting these writers to various others that have had something to say about disability. Each chapter is conceived of as comparative both in terms of the relations among the works of the main writers in the study and between these and the many other representations of disability that will be touched upon over the course of the discussions.

I want to emphasize my view that to properly establish the contours of aesthetic nervousness, we have to understand disability's resonance on a multiplicity of levels simultaneously; disability acts as a threshold or focal point from which various vectors of the text may be examined. Thus, as we shall see with respect to Toni Morrison, though her physically disabled female characters seem to be strong and empowered, there is often a contradiction between the levels of narratorial perspective, symbolic implication, and the determinants of the interactions among the characters themselves that ends up unsettling the unquestioned sense of strength that we might get from just focusing on what the disabled women in her texts do or do not do. With Beckett, on the other hand, we find that as he proliferates devices by which to undermine the stability of ontological categories, he ends up also undermining the means by which the many disabilities that he frequently represents in his texts may be interpreted. As can be seen from the vast scholarship on Beckett, it is very rare that his impaired characters are read as disabled, even though their disabilities are blatant and should be impossible to ignore. Rather, the characters are routinely assimilated by critics to philosophical categories and read off as such. This is due to the peculiarly self-undermining structures of his works, both the novels and the plays. Beckett is also unusual among the writers in this study in that he seems to fulfill a central feature of what Sandblom (1997) describes as the inextricable link between disease and creativity. Pertinent to the discussion of Beckett's work is that he himself suffered endless illnesses ranging from an arrhythmic heartbeat and night sweats to cysts and abscesses on his fingers, the palm of his left hand, the top of his palate, his scrotum and, most painfully later in life, his left lung. Often these cysts and abscesses had to be lanced or operated upon, leading to great and regular discomfort. It is not for nothing then that the deteriorating and impaired body held a special fascination for him. He used the disabled, maimed, and decaying body as a multiple referent for a variety of ideas that seem to have been at least partially triggered by encounters with others and his own personal experience of pain and temporary disability. This is something that has passed largely unremarked in the critical writings on Beckett, and I propose to center on it to discuss the peculiar status he assigns to disability and pain in works such as *Endgame* and *Molloy*, both of which should to all intents and purposes be "painfull" but are not.

In a way, Wole Soyinka's work is quite different from that of the other three in the study. His writing focuses more securely on a set of ritual dispositions drawn from a traditional Yoruba and African cultural sensibility. This sensibility is then combined with an intense political consciousness, such that each of his plays may be read as partial allegories of the Nigerian and African postcolonial condition. The combination of the ritualistic with the political is something for which Soyinka has become notably famous. What I shall show with regard to his work are the ways in which disability acts as a marker of both ritual and the political, but in ways that interrupt the two domains and force us to rethink the conceptual movement between the two. The final chapter, on Robben Island, will be used to bring to conclusion a particular vector of interpretation that will have been suggested in the chapter on Beckett, given further elaboration in the discussions of Morrison and Soyinka, and picked up and intensified in the one on Coetzee. I shall discuss this in various guises, but they will all come together under the conceptual rubric of the *structure of skeptical interlocution*. In essence, the idea derives from Bakhtin's proposition of the inherent dialogism of speech acts, that anticipation of an interlocutor even when the context of communication does not seem to explicitly denominate one. The choice of the plays of Beckett and Soyinka allows a certain salience to the idea of the (skeptical) interlocutor, since as dramatic texts they incorporate dialogue as an explicit feature of dialogism. But what I have in mind in relation to the structure of skeptical interlocution is a little bit more complicated than can be captured solely in dramatic texts. Rather, I mean to suggest that there is always an anticipation of doubt within the perceptual and imagined horizon of the disabled character in literature, and that this doubt is incorporated into their representation. This is so whether the character is represented in the first person, as we see in Beckett's Molloy, or in the third person, as we see in Coetzee's *Life and Times of Michael K.* The chapter on Coetzee will be used to focus on the difference between speech and the elective silence of autistic characters and on the ways in which these raise peculiar problems for the status of the skeptical interlocutor in literary writing. Autism features in that chapter not just as a dimension of disability but as a theoretical paradigm for raising questions about narrativity as such. However, it is when we come to the chapter on Robben Island that the structure of skeptical interlocution will be allowed to take life (literally and metaphorically, as will be demonstrated). The structure of interlocution with regard to the history of Robben Island will help to shed light on how aesthetic nervousness might be extended from discussions of the literary-aesthetic domain to an analysis of historical personages and real-life events.

I should like to address a point of potential confusion that may have arisen in this introduction. So far I have proceeded as though the literary representation of disabled persons and the aesthetic nervousness that attends such representation can be taken as an analogue to the real-life responses toward people with disabilities by society at large. This fusion of levels is only partially intended. For, as I noted earlier, there is no doubt that literary representation of disability somewhat subtends real-life treatment of disabled people in a variety of ways. However, I also want to note that the aesthetic nervousness of the literary-aesthetic domain cannot by any means be said to be equivalent to the responses to disabled persons in reality. To say that the literary model provides an analogue to reality does not mean that it is the same as that reality. The epistemological effect of representation is quite different from the emotional effects of misunderstanding and stereotyping in the real world. Thus the first may be used to illuminate aspects of the second but must not be taken to have exhausted or replaced it. Our commitment must ultimately be to changing the world and not merely reading and commenting on it.

It is important also to state at the outset that central to the ways in which I propose to establish the parameters of aesthetic nervousness is the device of close reading. This seems to me necessary in order to be able to do full justice to the subtle cues by which the literary text "stumbles" (to return to Mitchell and Snyder) and by which the literary representation reveals the parameters of aesthetic nervousness. Apart from Morrison, none of the writers in this study has previously been read from the perspective of disability studies. Part of my task will involve the rather boring process of taxonomizing the disability representations we find in the works in question. This will be done to provide a map of the varied uses to which the writers put the disabled in order to allow us to discern patterns that are elaborated upon or repeated across the works. It is a happy coincidence that all four writers are Nobel Prize winners and thus likely to be widely taken up in literary curricula. My choice of them was not informed by this fact, however (in fact, Coetzee was part of my study long before his Nobel Prize). I settle on them because of my years of teaching and thinking about their work in different contexts and the fact that they enable us to see a full range of discourses regarding disability and other details of literary representation. I wish to see students and other readers being able to pay close attention to all the subtle details of literary representation well beyond the focus on disability, even if that is their starting point. The focus on disability is thus meant to achieve two related effects: One is to make more prominent the active ethical core that is necessarily related to disability and that hopefully helps to restore a fully ethical reading to literature. The other is that from using disability to open up the possibility of close reading, I hope to encourage us to lift our eyes from the reading of literature to attend more closely to the implications of the social universe around us.

2

A TYPOLOGY
OF DISABILITY
REPRESENTATION

I N A LITTLE-KNOWN WORK PUBLISHED IN 1971 TITLED *The Limping Hero: Grotesques in Literature*, Peter L. Hays attempts the highly ambitious project of accounting for all representations of limping heroes in Western literature from classical times to the early twentieth century. His argument is at once simple and complex. Focusing exclusively on male characters, and drawing out implications from the Bible, the Torah, Homer, and other sacred and classical texts, Hays maintains that limping heroes may all be taken as emblematic variants of infertility. From this premise, it is a short step to suggesting that such limping figures be seen as residual signifiers of ritual and that the limping hero is often linked not just to natural infertility but also to emotional and spiritual sterility. Hays amasses a phenomenal range of examples to prosecute his argument. The examples range from Greek gods and heroes such as Hephaestus, Achilles, and Oedipus to figures in nineteenth- and twentieth-century novels by Melville, John Barth, James Joyce, Somerset Maugham, and many others. An appendix at the end of the book, titled "The Hospital," provides an extensive and fascinating list of such limping heroes in world literature. There are 308 entries on the list. This formidable enterprise by no means exhausts the range of limping characters in Western literature, but it at least sets out certain parameters about what can be achieved and the pitfalls to be avoided.

Even though Hays does not acknowledge this himself, it is clear that what he is attempting invites comparison with the broad literary overviews exemplified by the work of earlier critical synthesists such as Northrop Frye and Erich Auerbach.[1] The ambition in all these works is the same: to provide a model by which a vast range of literary texts might be read as illustrating recurrent tropes across history. In the cases of Frye and Auerbach, an attempt is made to historicize the emergence and transformation of certain tropes, but even this effort is subsumed under the task of establishing broad parameters for understanding such a literary history through detailed close readings of textual examples. Hays has not got the same historicizing impulse as the earlier two, but like them he is also intent on defining a universal literary history. Exclusively tropological readings of literary works were of course not uncommon in the heyday of New Criticism, where the literary text was taken to be autonomous and self-sufficient and the task of the critic was solely to unearth the processes by which paradox, contradiction, and irony served to give salience to particular literary details. The question of the ethical disposition of the literary texts under scrutiny by the New Critics was rarely raised as an independent question, except in so far as it could be connected to notions of poetic sincerity, itself to be seen as a set of literary devices. The readings were thus intrinsic and focused mainly on definitions of the literary-aesthetic field as a demarcation of the beautiful and the sublime.[2]

Hays writes out of that tradition, but he opens himself to special criticism in implicitly drawing an analogy between images of disability and the literary tropes of Nature, Quest, and Rebirth cycles without questioning the basis of that analogy. His argument is unsatisfactory for staging a complete and unexamined linkage between emasculation and impotence on the one hand, and physical disability (limping) on the other, thus suggesting that physical disability is the mark of a constitutive lack. Even though his examples center exclusively on masculine figures, the implications he draws out from them pertain to physical disability in general. This is a highly dubious proposition and allows the moral panic that has historically obtained in social encounters between disabled and nondisabled people and that often gets refracted within literary discourse to become normalized and unquestioned. In other words, *The Limping Hero* ends up being the rationalization of a questionable response to physical impairment, namely, that impairment is the sign of a moral or other deficit.

Hays's ambitious but ultimately deeply problematic project serves to outline one mode of scholarly response to disability that will not be taken up here. Instead, I will argue that the signs of aesthetic short-circuiting we find in literary texts subtend attitudes to disability that are widespread in the world today. And yet there is one thing that can be rescued from Hays's book, and indeed from the work of the New Critics, which inarguably was the inspiration behind his effort. Though abjuring the ambitious attempt to provide an ironclad and singular tropological description that would account for all manifestations of disability in world literature, I do take the view that in establishing the parameters of representations of disability, it is important to attempt a close reading of literary texts in their totality, and not just in the precise place assigned to the disabled characters. This is because, as I suggested in chapter 1 and hope to show throughout this study, the place of disabled characters in the literary domain is assigned within a structure of literary relations. The point is that the structure of such literary relations enjoins us to isolate the disabled character for examination only as a preliminary step toward reinserting them into the intervolving thresholds of signification that are established in the relationship to other characters and to the images, social settings, and broader spatiotemporal concepts that are manifest with-in the text. In other words, disability is to be read as a fulcrum or pivot out of which various discursive details emerge, gain salience, and ultimately undergo transformation within the literary-aesthetic field. This idea of disability-as-pivot will be most fully explored in the chapter on Toni Morrison.

A close reading of disability in literature reveals that the place assigned to characters with disability is not necessarily singular. It may be predominantly constituted in one direction and yet either undergo shifts in the course of the narrative or indeed alter altogether to carry contradictory meanings. Comparison between texts throws up even greater complications. For example, Jose Arcadio Buendia's madness in Marquez's *One Hundred Years of Solitude* is quite different from, say, Benjy's cognitive impairment in Faulkner's *The Sound and the Fury*, even though they both share the capacity for superior if inchoate insight about their social surroundings. What is more, Jose Arcadio Buendia's character is shaped within the context of magical realism, where the relations between realistic and fantastical details are nothing if not unsettled. It is in the totality of literary relationships established in the individual texts that their disability acquires distinctiveness, and a discussion of the two texts would have to pay close attention to such a totality. Additionally, it would be very difficult to sustain a sharp distinction in representations of physical and cognitive disabilities. As can quickly be seen, in literary writing physical impairments are often correlated to cognitive and mental conditions, even when the text might be focusing on one aspect as a preliminary to foregrounding a second or indeed third dimension of disability. As will be seen in chapter 3, in Samuel Beckett's *Molloy*, even though the eponymous character describes himself as having a variety of physical impairments, it is the flux of intricate and peculiar cognitive dispositions emerging from the first-person stream-of-consciousness mode of narration that defines the character for us. Furthermore, generic conventions serve to situate the disabled characters differently from genre to genre. In comedies, for instance, disability takes on a pantomime character and is meant to generate laughter. Thus we have the perennially effective potential for comedy inherent in works in which blindness and deafness are used to establish dramatic ironies. A well-known example is to be found in Hergé's *Tintin* series, where the scientist Cuthbert Calculus is given to hilarious malapropisms due to his hearing difficulties.[3] In Beckett's work, on the other hand, the comedic disposition of his disabled characters is used to deflect attention from the pain and anguish that are involved in carrying physical impairments. Attending to the generic conventions out of which the disabled character is created then helps to highlight the nature of the contradictions that surround the representation of disability. Much of this study will be driven by an impulse of close reading, not so much to establish the autonomy of the text as to convey the subtle relations that secure the place of disabled characters within the literary-aesthetic domain. What I argue to be aesthetic nervousness may also be misread as a codification of a particular form of aesthetic ordering, rather than the collapse and discomposition of the putative textual order around the figure of disability as such. It is only an attentive close reading that would allow us to identify the precise nature of aesthetic nervousness that is focalized through and around the disabled character.

A Provisional Typology of Disability Representations

It is important to bear in mind that attitudes to people with disabilities at any historical conjuncture are often multifarious, even in contexts that appear more enlightened and progressive. It is literature more than anything else that helps refract these multivalent attitudes toward disability. The opposition between reflection and refraction is a crucial one. The literary-aesthetic domain does indeed remind us of reality, but in such a way as to interrupt our memory or recognition of it in order to place different emphases on what might be taken for granted. Because disability in the real world already incites interpretation, literary representations of disability are not merely reflecting disability; they are refractions of that reality, with varying emphases of both an aesthetic and ethical kind. As with chapter 1, this chapter will also be a survey and overview, but this time designed to outline a thematic typology of the numerous representations of disability, both physical and otherwise, that obtain in literature. The categories are by no means mutually exclusive; often it is possible to find aspects of more than one category focused through a particular disabled character or different categories running sequentially as the character is involved in various interactions with others. As a rule, the more central a disabled character is, the more likely they are to be used as illustrations of multiple categories. As will quickly become evident, however, it is not entirely possible to mechanically apply the categories outlined here to any of the highly complex texts we will be encountering in this study. The preliminary typology being drawn up here acts only as a productive heuristic map that I will refer back to sporadically over the course of the book.[4] The provisional typology enables us to keep in view a way of correlating different texts and ultimately making generalizations about how such literary representations relate to social attitudes. This is a subject that will be returned to more fully in the concluding chapter.

The first and perhaps most obvious literary representation of disability is that in which it acts as some form of ethical background to the actions of other characters, or as a means of testing or enhancing their moral standing. Martha Stoddard Holmes (2002, 228) refers to this kind of representation as "critical null sets, convenient containers for the essential human emotions required by the nondisabled characters around them." This particular form of disability representation is so ubiquitous as to be almost universal. In medieval literature, for example, the figure of the

Loathely Lady, usually a hunchback with some repulsive facial features, was placed in the path of the chivalrous knight on one of his quests. Typically, the Loathely Lady extracted a promise of marriage in exchange for information with which the knight was to get himself out of a serious life-and-death conundrum, after which, bound by the codes of chivalric honor, he reluctantly fulfilled his promise. In most variants of the story, after sharing a bed with the knight the Loathely Lady transformed into a comely lass, thus signifying both the perceived enigma inherent in the boon of knowledge proffered by the Lady and the problematic nature of female sexuality that women represent to men. Indeed, the boon might be read as a metaphor for femininity itself, for the question to which the hapless knight had to find an answer was nothing other than "What do women really want?" The answer that was whispered by the Loathely Lady was "sovereignty," something that could be interpreted both contextually, in terms of the Loathely Lady's ability to exercise her choice of marriage partner, and ontologically, as women's essential desire not to be dominated by the patriarchal codes of the masculine world. It was never self-evident from the many variants of the story which of these two interpretations was correct, so that the difference between the Lady's repugnant exterior and the obvious beauty that this exterior concealed came to represent an ethical conundrum as such.[5] Though the Loathely Lady does not make a direct appearance in later Western literature, we find vestiges of the figure in various folk tales, with a good recent literary example in the figure of Circe in Toni Morrison's *Song of Solomon*. Let us designate this class of representations *disability as null set and/or moral test*.

From the late fifteenth century through to the eighteenth and nineteenth centuries, disability representations were used to raise a different set of problems, sometimes going well beyond concerns with social hierarchies and relationships to embrace the confluence of imperialism and the production of various Others. Rereading Shakespeare's *The Tempest* via a Wallersteinian world-system's approach, Paul Brown (1994) has suggested that the play was as much concerned with Ireland as a semiperipheral object of British attentions as it was with Britain's more distant imperial holdings in general. Thus Caliban, at once savage, wild man, and hunchback, could be read as a figure of the othered Irish. We find further salience for this unusual reading in nineteenth-century depictions of the Irish in British newspapers such as *Punch* and other London weeklies, in which the stereotypical Irish figure of Paddy was routinely depicted with

simian features and a stooped back.[6] The intersection of disability, imperialism, and the projection of otherness is also evident in other texts of
the period. Gayatri Spivak shows in a well-known article in postcolonial
studies how much the project of "soul making" in Jane Eyre depends fundamentally on a contrast being established between Jane and Bertha Mason, the madwoman in the attic. Interestingly, Spivak subsumes Bertha
Mason's insanity into her status as colonial other, but it is evident that
giving equal emphasis to the two vectors of Bertha's identity allows us to
see how crucial her madness is within the binary opposition established
between her and Jane. In tracking back the source of Bertha's madness to
a "colonial" encounter between her and Rochester in the West Indies of
Wide Sargasso Sea, Jean Rhys provides a corrective to readings that might
hastily ignore the progress of Bertha's distemper and subsequent madness,
only the latter of which is represented in Charlotte Brontë's novel.[7]

As Holmes (2002) also shows from a discussion of Victorian literature,
twin sets (one disabled, the other not) were often used to outline differential trajectories of sexuality and its fulfillment in marriage. In such
writing, female disabled characters were proffered in such a way as to deflect acute anxieties about the disabled person's reproductive capacities as
well as of the exercise of women's sexuality in general. With a few excep-
tions, in the period disabled women become the focal point for playing
out intense social anxieties about disease, sexuality, and disability. Contrastively, in the children's genre of the masculine adventure narrative
disability acts as a cipher of otherness-cum-moral test, with equal emphasis placed on the two parts of the equation. In Robert Louis Stevenson's
Treasure Island, for example, disabled characters are used as a means of
outlining the complex moral choices open to the protagonist as he tra-
verses a strange geographical landscape away from home. Jim Hawkins is
drawn into an adventure in which nearly every sailor he encounters
has a defining impairment. The pirate who comes to stay at the Admiral
Benbow and whose map is the initial starting point for the treasure quest
has a horrible gash along his right cheek. Pew is a blind man, Black Dog
is said to have a talonlike hand missing two fingers, and there is finally
the stereotypical one-legged and now legendary Long John Silver himself.
Being seafarers, these characters are all definitively anti-homely and other
as well as carrying a variety of impairments. Jim is cast into an alien world
populated by men whose disabilities are markers of a sharp otherness and
moral deficit. It is for him a rite of passage, a process of self-discovery not

just of strength of character, but also of how much their moral deficit echoes within him. This masculine adventure narrative, of a piece with others in the nineteenth century by J.M. Ballantyre, H. Rider Haggard, and Rudyard Kipling, among others, placed the male protagonist in an extrametropolitan setting in which the difference he encountered was supposed to trigger a process of self-discovery that ultimately affirmed his superior status. This second class of representation will be designated *disability as the interface with otherness (race, class, sexuality, and social identity)*.

Children's genres also provide a useful way into understanding the subtle variations in the use of disabled characters within more complex forms of literary representation. In Disney's 2003 oceanographic *Finding Nemo*, we see a quite remarkable and contradictory use of disability. Dory, who suffers from short-term amnesia, is clearly a superior guide to the paranoid and petulant Marlin, father of the lost Nemo for whom he is out searching the ocean. It is Dory who gets Marlin through many close dangers, as much by her superior wit as by her sheer ability not to be defeated by the sense of imminent danger. Hers is a moment-by-moment existence that does not bother either with the immediate past or the imminent future. And yet something peculiar happens at a critical turning point in the film. Marlin and Dory have made it through a forest of stinging jellyfish and onto the EAC (East Australian Current), which should take them to Sydney harbor, where it is believed Nemo was taken by the divers who had captured him earlier in the film. Both Marlin and Dory wake up from their misadventure in the jellyfish forest on the backs of turtles that are part of a large shoal on the EAC. When Marlin wakes up, he believes Dory is badly hurt, but as always, he is completely mistaken. She is already awake and excitedly playing hide-and-seek with the little turtles on the journey. They see him and pounce on him, pleading with him to tell them the story of his adventures. Marlin is reluctant at first but then proceeds with his story, which we are familiar with, having already seen it unfolding up to that point. The story he tells is picked up by the little turtles and in a series of relays is passed on as a form of oral mythmaking to swordfish, crabs, and dolphins (who talk while diving in and out of the surface of the ocean), and then on to birds, who in their turn pass the story on to the seagulls way out in Sydney harbor. Marlin's story has thus become the currency of legend; he is a myth in his own time. The production of what is clearly meant to be the "memory" of the film in the form of an oral epic narrative, however, shows one apparently innocent but quite significant absence. At no point either in his account or in the long and complicated process of its dissemination and redaction across the seas is mention made of Dory's role in their adventures. Ever. In other words, the mythmaking is a memory that itself suffers from some form of amnesia. But because the amnesia affects the remembered status of Dory—the only disabled character in the film that suffers from amnesia—it is almost as if to suggest that the process of mythmaking mimes her own forgetfulness on her behalf. Thus even though her disability makes her central to the process by which the main protagonist is aided in his quest, it is precisely that which discursively allows her to be effaced out of the memory of the action. We see in this particular use of disability a bifurcation of effects. On the one hand, Dory is clearly the instrument for clarifying motivational impulses for Marlin and for helping him to overcome the effects of the extreme paranoia of the sea he developed following the death of his wife at the start of the film. And yet, on the other hand, in the wider narrative discourse by which the medium establishes either proximity or distance with the perspective of different characters, there is a subtle design to memorialize the nondisabled character's actions while peripheralizing that of the character with a disability. And it is not insignificant either that the nondisabled is male and the disabled is female, so that the enactment of memorial effacement has gender implications as well. By means of this effacement, Dory is rendered simultaneously central *and* peripheral, an insider *and* an outsider to the subtler meanings of the film. Surface reading will of course affirm her extremely important role, yet a closer examination reveals that all does not cohere properly around the surface interpretation.[8]

A similar duality between content and overall narrative design is evident in Bapsi Sidhwa's *Cracking India*. There the centrality of the disabled child narrator is undermined by the fact that her precociousness is a feature only of the relationship between herself and the reader but not in the relations between herself and other characters within the novel. There is thus a contradiction that borders on implausibility, because she behaves like an adult to us but is an ordinary child within the narrative itself. In the case of *Cracking India*, the problem seems to be that Lenny is being proffered as an analogy for Pakistan, a young and mutilated country emerging from the partition of India that is nonetheless ancient in pedigree. The disability is thus a device of analogy and does not allow for the

mimetic complexity that inheres in the experience of people with disabilities themselves. In this respect, the representation of such disabled
figures is still distinct from the representation of nondisabled people, who
in many demonstrable cases often reflect upon their sexuality, education,
emotional predilections, and other aspects of their experience in their relationships with others. As can be seen, in these instances the disability
is being used as a means of establishing multiple and often contradictory
values. There is often a disjuncture between the content and the narrative structure, and the level at which this disjuncture manifests itself is
around the disabled character. Noting the fact that it is impossible to entirely separate form from content, for heuristic purposes we shall designate this category *disability as articulation of disjuncture between thematic
and narrative vectors.*

On a continuum with the categories we have seen thus far is one in
which it is disability itself that carries the burden of moral deficit and evil
directly. This does not prevent disability from also acting as the means by
which to test the other characters with whom the disabled character in-
teracts, but in this mode of representation they are taken as metaphorical
encapsulations of the moral problematic as such, either in the form of a
moral deficit or indeed of evil. When Macbeth is informed in V.v about
the death of his wife, his much quoted "Tomorrow and tomorrow and tomorrow" speech contains an unanticipated reference to disability. He
says, among other things, that life "is a tale / Told by an idiot, full of
sound and fury / Signifying nothing." Why a tale told by an idiot? The
point is not so much to suggest that he is faced with a life that resists interpretation, but that Life as he sees it is generically deformed and monstrous. It is for that that the idiot is referenced; it is at one and the same
time a marker of deformity *and* unintelligibility. But the thing to note is
that this reference is made only at the turning point of the action for the
protagonist, when he is bereft of all support and has to recognize what
paltry resources of self he has to fall back on. In a way, the choice of metaphor reflects more upon the protagonist himself as a self-fashioned monster than it does upon his environment. However, the reference to the
idiot is supposed to encapsulate a deep insight about deformity *and* evil,
whether these are taken as intrinsic to Macbeth's character or as reflections of the moral decay he has engendered in the play.

As we noted in chapter 1, in Shakespeare disability also acts as a metaphor to mark anomalous social states such as those involving half-

brothers and bastardy. *Richard III* is an exemplary play grounded on the resonance of jealousy and brotherhood as well as on the Machiavellianism of a deformed protagonist. There the disability is placed at the foreground of the action from the beginning and brings together various threads that serve to focalize the question of whether Richard's deformity is an insignia of his villainy or the primary cause of it. Richard himself interprets his impairment as making him almost elementally different to all others: "I can add colours to the chameleon / Change shapes with Proteus for advantages / And set the murderous Machiavel to school" (*3 Henry VI*, 3.2.191–193).[9] Contrastively, in *Julius Caesar* Cassius points out that because Julius Caesar is deaf in one ear and suffers from epilepsy he is not fit to rule; this serves as part of the justification for his assassination. Then in *The Tempest*, Caliban is the focus for disability-as-otherness and moral-conundrum. Whereas Ariel is a genial and androgynous shape-shifter whose freedom, as promised, is delivered, Caliban, on the other hand, is described as a "savage and *deformed* slave." The question remains open whether Caliban is congenitally evil, having been born that way by Sycorax, or becomes warped because of his loss of the island and his mistreatment at the hands of Prospero. We shall designate this category of representation *disability as moral deficit/evil*.

Sometimes, in texts in which disability is a marker of a moral conundrum the impairment is concealed until a particular ethical impasse is arrived at within the text. Here, its use as signifier of moral disorder or deficit is more in terms of a sudden epiphany for the nondisabled character than a slow process of unfoldment about the disabled character's problematic sense of his or her own identity, as is the case in *Richard III*. This is to be distinguished from instances where an impairment is mentioned as a mere detail of characterization that serves either to provide a mark of distinctiveness about the disabled character or as a means of differentiation for the nondisabled ones, but which nonetheless promptly recedes from the text.[10] A good example of the epiphanic use of disability is provided in Ralph Ellison's *Invisible Man*. Brother Jack, who conscripts Invisible Man into the Brotherhood, is described from the beginning as a "short insignificant-looking bushy-eyebrowed man with a quiet smile on his face" (287). The only peculiarity about him is his gait, which is described as a "rapid, rolling, bouncy, heel-and-toey step" (288). He is on the whole a genial person, and there is nothing to raise suspicion about him. After conscripting the narrator, Brother Jack becomes his defender when other members of the Brotherhood criticize what they see as the backwardness of his early speechmaking. As Invisible Man becomes more prominent in the Brotherhood, certain hitherto concealed ideological differences begin to emerge between him and other members of the organization. Matters of overall strategy come to a head after the politicized funeral of a former member of the Brotherhood in Harlem. Whereas Jack and the Brotherhood think that the people are only the seat of mindless passions that need to be "scientifically" channeled for a proper revolution to take place, Invisible Man insists that they be accorded the respect due a highly self-conscious people, who, through their experiences of racism and injustice, have a much deeper insight about what is best for them than the Brotherhood imagines. At the special meeting that has been called, tempers rise, there is thumping of the table, voices are raised at cross-purposes, and then, suddenly:

"Now see here," he [Brother Jack] began, leaping to his feet to lean across the table, and I spun my chair half around on its hind legs as he came between me and the light, gripping the edge of the table, spluttering and lapsing into a foreign language, choking and coughing and shaking his head as I balanced on my toes now, set to propel myself forward; seeing him above me and the others behind him as suddenly something seemed to erupt out of his face. You're seeing things, I thought, hearing it strike sharply against the table and roll as his arm shot out and snatched an object the size of a large marble and dropped it, plop! into his glass, and I could see the water shooting up in a ragged, light-breaking pattern to spring in swift droplets across the oiled table top. . . . I stared at the glass, seeing how the light shone through, throwing a transparent, precisely fluted shadow against the dark grain of the table, and there on the bottom of the glass lay an eye. A glass eye. A buttermilk white eye distorted by the light rays. An eye staring fixedly at me as from the dark waters of a well. . . .

I stared into his face, feeling a sense of outrage. His left eye had collapsed, a line of raw redness showing where the lid refused to close, and his gaze had lost its command. I looked from his face to the glass, thinking, he's disemboweled himself just in order to confound me. . . .

(473–474)

The uncanniness of this sudden "disembowelment," as the narrator puts it, should not detract from the fact that until this point there has not been the slightest hint that Brother Jack had a glass eye. Even going back to carefully trace references to his eyes from the very beginning of his introduction into the text does not yield any sign of his impairment. There are many references to him wiping his eyes or his face with his hands, or staring intently at his interlocutors, but none of these descriptions betray the fact that there is anything wrong with his eyes. It is only now, at the point when a serious ethical distinction is being drawn between his ideas about class struggle and the narrator's personal experiences among the people, that his disability is suddenly, and without prior preparation, foisted upon us. The *unheimlich* nature of this moment is registered in the mind of the narrator in the simultaneous speeding up and slowing down of the perception of the event: "ragged, light breaking patterns in swift droplets"; the repetition of the word eye attached to various metaphors from buttermilk and white prism distorted by light to the eerie eye staring from out of a well. Also, the offending eye seems to "erupt" out of Brother Jack's face, as if invested with personal agency. By these means, the suddenness and unanticipated emergence of the impairment with the multifarious metaphors that are attached to it become the means to accentuate the unusualness of the entire event. The disclosure of the impairment acts much like a discursive punctuation mark, providing a vehicle for the intensification of ethical contradictions made sharply evident at that point in the text.

Similarly, in Harper Lee's *To Kill a Mockingbird* (1960), the disability of Tom Robinson, who has been falsely accused of raping a white girl, is concealed from us until the high point of the court scene. Told from the perspective of the child narrator Louise Scout Finch, the story progresses strictly as a pattern of discoveries open to her. Yet the disclosure of Tom Robinson's disability is a multifaceted epiphany both for her and for the reader. The accused man is mentioned many times in the novel ahead of the trial scene, and each time we are given a little bit of information to add to the evolving picture of a hardworking and God-fearing black man who is innocent of the crime of which he has been accused. Yet a residual sense of doubt still remains for the child narrator because of the insistence with which the rest of the community outside the inner circle of Scout, her brother Jem, and her lawyer father Atticus are convinced of Tom's guilt.

As in *Invisible Man*, there is a buildup of tension in the immediate lead-up to the disclosure. The tension is almost unbearable and becomes palpable at the trial itself. Witnesses for the accused are called and questioned, and Tom is the last to be called in a long and absolutely riveting courtroom drama. He stands up slowly, and a revelation takes place:

> Tom Robinson's powerful shoulders rippled under his thin shirt. He rose to his feet and stood with his right hand on the back of the chair. He looked oddly off balance, but it was not from the way he was standing. His left arm was fully twelve inches shorter than his right, and hung dead at his side. It ended in a small shriveled hand, and from as far away as the balcony I could see that it was no use to him.   (188)

> Thomas Robinson reached around, ran his fingers under his left arm and lifted it. He guided his arm to the Bible and his rubber-like left hand sought contact with the black binding. As he raised his right hand, the useless one slipped off the Bible and hit the clerk's table. He was trying again when Judge Taylor growled, "That'll do, Tom." Tom took the oath and stepped into the witness chair.   (192)

Unlike what we saw with Brother Jack, here the sudden disclosure of the disability is meant not to raise doubts about the moral stature of the disabled character but to dispel them. When the jury, in spite of all the evidence that has been presented, returns a unanimous verdict of guilty, we sense with Louise Finch and her brother Jem that a major rupture has taken place in their view of the world. Tom Robinson's withered arm joins the list of other disabilities we find in the novel—those of Calpurnia, Boo Radley, and Mr. Dolphus Raymond—all of which define the need for a cautious withholding of judgment in how different characters are evaluated. For it is not only Tom who is a victim of prejudice. Prejudice is the product of a tribal desire to demarcate between inside and outside, between what is acceptable behavior and what is not, and it cuts across understandings of race, class, and gender among the people of Maycomb. We may usefully name this category of disability representation *disability as epiphany*.[11] We shall have more to say on this in chapter 4, when we come to look at Toni Morrison's *Sula*, *Beloved*, and *Paradise*.

The next major category of disability representation I want to high-light is that in which the disabled character is taken as a signifier of sacred or ritual processes. Examples abound in Greek literature and include fig-ures such as Oedipus, Philoctetes (limping), and Ajax (madness). In the cases of both Oedipus and Philoctetes, their disability is taken to be sa-lient only after they have committed a transgression that is considered to be polluting. In Oedipus's case, it is the much commented upon patricide and incest, whereas with Philoctetes, his pollution comes from inadver-tently stepping on the sacrificial snake and by that profaning the holy sacrifice the Greeks were performing on their way to the Trojan War. In both cases, their transgressions are considered as marking them with rit-ual danger, so that they have to be driven out to avoid the total destruc-tion of the rest of the community. At the same time, there is also a desire by the wider society to acquire or at least gain access to a boon that these disabled characters possess and which is seen as critical for the well-being of the society. What is to be noted in these two cases is the temporality of the schema that defines the shift from innocence to ritual transgres-sion and contagion and on to sacredness. Thus, in the case of Oedipus, it is only in *Oedipus at Colonnus*, a play that places him many years after his banishment, that we find the Thebans and the Athenians appealing for his blessing. In *Philoctetes*, on the other hand, the eponymous hero is first condemned to exile on the island of Lemnos and only later sought out by Odysseus and the Greek army to try to gain possession of the magic bow that had been bequeathed to him by Herakles. The entire encounter be-tween Neoptolemus, tasked with tricking him out of the bow, and the an-guished and homesick Philoctetes, is that between conscience and pain, between the call of duty and the bearing witness to the melancholy of the indescribable loss of homeland.

In other traditions, such as those of the Yoruba, Eshu, the limping trickster god of the crossroads, is not seen to carry any such contagion. His ritual role is quite different. As the trickster god, he often represents a trial of human perception, confounding what seems self-evident in or-der to establish the requirement of humility in the face of the ultimate in-explicableness of the human lifeworld. Robert Farris Thompson (1983) suggests that the spirit of improvisation central to African American mu-sic is a legacy of the improvisational performance qualities of the god that the slaves brought with them from Africa. On the other hand, Henry

Louis Gates Jr. (1988) asserts that a direct line may be traced between the signifying monkey of African American folklore and the Yoruba Eshu. Eshu's limp is thus the paradigm of access to multiple realities of both the real world and that of the gods. He represents a disabled character/god who provides superior insights into the phenomenal world and in this may be likened to similar characters from Greek myths such as Hephaestus, Tiresias, and Cassandra. Seen alongside the proliferation of Eshu-Elegbara cults in the New World, it is clear that the limping god of the Yoruba is interpreted as having a transhistorical and modern significance that goes beyond any ritual position assigned him in the traditional Yoruba pantheon from which he came. This class of disability representation may be termed *disability as signifier of ritual insight*. I shall illustrate this class more fully in the chapter on Wole Soyinka's drama.

The blind hermaphrode Tiresias is well known in Western culture from his roles in Sophocles' *Oedipus Rex* and Euripides' *The Bacchae* and perhaps needs no introduction. What is not often noted is the degree to which other disabled characters such as Cassandra and Io, both afflicted by madness through the Olympian gods' capriciousness, share with Tiresias the role of uncommon insight but also become conduits for the articulation of the sense of tragic ethos that saturates the worlds in which they find themselves. Cassandra, a prophetess cursed by Apollo to carry the gift of prophecy yet never to be believed, foretells her own death to people who stand utterly in doubt about what she prophesizes to them. That is the poignant picture we get in Aeschylus's *Agamemnon*. When Cassandra tells the Argive chorus of old men about the murder of Agamemnon, which is taking place as they speak, she also serves notice of her peculiar ability to capture and express in her very person the tragic ethos of the unfolding action. A similar observation may be made about Io, who, transformed into a cow by Hera because of Zeus's amorous interest in her, acts as a counterpoint to Prometheus in Aeschylus's *Prometheus Bound*. Even though Io lacks the prophetic insight of Cassandra, her wails as the gadfly stings her represent the saturation point of the tragic ethos. For unlike Prometheus, the trajectory of whose defiant response to Zeus's punishment makes him decidedly epic rather than tragic, Io is bereft of any such grandeur and yet bears a burden of tragic knowledge that must nonetheless remain inarticulable. Further contrasts provided by Aeschylus in the play between Prometheus and Io deepen this meaning. Whereas

Prometheus is immobile throughout the play (he is supposed to be bound to a rock, after all) and thus defines a locus of stability in that dramatic representation, Io has traversed many regions and climes before she enters the play. Her wanderings have been in search of relief from the gadfly's painful stings. Yet her wailing must not be taken solely as wails of pain; they also embody a clouded knowledge of her condition that is frustrated from being properly articulated because of the attentions of the gadfly. Prometheus's geographical stability, which is nevertheless coupled to an overarching prophetic reach, is then in sharp contrast to Io's geographical range, which is undermined by the contraction and fragmentation of her consciousness. Io cannot express the full extent of her anguish and indeed knowledge of what has been made visible to her through her wanderings. She is condemned to a series of penetrating and desperate questions (making up fully sixteen of the first fifty lines assigned to her) that progressively prompt Prometheus to divulge a prophecy about the coming apocalyptic end of Zeus's reign and the contribution that her own descendants will make to this.[12] In other words, her anguish issues forth in endless questionings only part of which can be answered by Prometheus, who even then assimilates his answer to a prophecy that serves to further emphasize his epic status. Read in terms of the apparently inarticulable burden of the tragic ethos, what we might term the Cassandra-Io complex of disability is to be found replicated in female figures as different as Shakespeare's Ophelia, Brecht's Kattrin, Marquez's Rebeca (in One Hundred Years of Solitude), Allende's Clara (in House of Spirits), Yvonne Vera's Mazvita (in Without a Name), and Baby Suggs and Consolata, both of whom we shall see more of in the chapter on Toni Morrison. This is not to say that the category applies only to female characters. Yet it seems to me that it is female figures that exemplify it best, not because they are women but because the dialectical coupling of tragic insight with loss of articulation seems to be a structural feature generated through the prism of gender as opposed to prisms of race and class. Rarely does a routing through race and class reveal such poetic and charged figures as we have enumerated, yet gender always seems to provide the template by which the peculiar ontological difficulty is brought into view, especially when it is coupled with some form of violence or violation of the disabled female character. In all such instances, the recognition of the tragic ethos by the disabled female character coincides precisely with their inability to speak of the terrible tragic knowledge to which they bear witness. All that is left is a series of fragmented enactments of the self, posing an enigma for the characters around them as well as for the reader and spectator. This form of disability representation is a counterpoint to the more common one in which disabled characters are shown as bearers of superior insight. I want to term this class *disability as inarticulable and enigmatic tragic insight* and will have more to say about it in relation to Krotoa, the first Khoikhoi Christian convert, whose fragmented and tragic life will be part of the subject of the chapter on Robben Island.

Closely connected to the representation of disability as enigmatic tragic insight but in a much more elusive register are cases where the disability is considered the site of a major hermeneutical impasse. The lack of closure implied in this kind of representation may also have ethical implications, yet it is the problem of interpretation that remains paramount. Thus, in Nabokov's short story "Signs and Symbols" the young suicidal patient's strange mental symptoms—shown in the impulse to interpret the natural elements as harboring something directly pertinent to his being—are labeled by a scholar as "referential mania," thus providing a key both to the patient's illness and to the process of inference that is installed at the heart of the story. Yet the referential mania is exactly what it is, a manic urge to interpret, provoked by the disability, which nevertheless does not lead to any enlightenment. In such cases, it is the process of open-ended interpretation that is made salient, as opposed to any disclosure of meaning as such. Another good example of this process is provided in Michael Ondaatje's *The English Patient*. The context in which we find Count Almasy in Ondaatje's novel, set in the deserts of Egypt during World War II, is such as to proliferate hermeneutical difficulties for both characters and readers. The English patient's acute burns ensure that he remains a "skinless" and identityless being throughout the narrative. And precisely because of this he is the center of much interpretative interest. Each of the three other characters trapped in the bombed-out villa try to read meanings both into and out of him. Matters are complicated by the fact that he himself has what appears to be an encyclopedic cartographic knowledge of the desert. He says of himself that he is "a man who can recognize an unnamed town by its skeletal shape on a map." He has information "like a sea" inside of him and inhales history from books as if becoming at one with them (18). The height of the hermeneutical delirium

implied by the English patient is made manifest in the relationship between him and Caravaggio, who seeks to extract information from him
about his true identity:

> All day they have shared ampoules of morphine. To unthread the story
> out of him, Caravaggio travels within the code of signals. When the
> burned man slows down, or when Caravaggio feels he is not catching
> everything—the love affair, the death of Madox—he picks up the sy-
> ringe from the kidney-shaped enamel tin, breaks the glass tip off an
> ampoule with the pressure of a knuckle and loads it. He is blunt about
> all this now with Hana, having ripped the sleeve off his left arm com-
> pletely. Almásy wears just a grey singlet, so his black arm lies bare un-
> der the sheet.
>
> Each swallow of morphine by the body opens a further door, or he
> leaps back to the cave paintings or to a buried plane or lingers once
> more with the woman beside him under a fan, her cheek against his
> stomach.
>
> Caravaggio picks up the Herodotus. He turns a page, comes over a
> dune to discover Gilf Kebir, Uweinat, Gebel Kissu. When Almásy
> speaks he stays alongside him reordering the events. Only desire makes
> the story errant, flickering like a compass needle. And this is the world
> of nomads in any case, an apocryphal story. A mind travelling east and
> west in the disguise of sandstorm.
>
> (248–249)

Doors, passageways, caves and sandstorms, nomadism and wandering.
These terms define a desert of labile and interchangeable data that is
both mental and physical, thus raising a serious hermeneutical crisis for
Caravaggio. He is obliged to travel "within the code of signals" unfurled
by the patient's account. What this calls for is an intensification of
Caravaggio's capacity for interpretation, something that does not necessarily yield him the truth he so desperately seeks. For the truth does not
reside within the interiority of the English patient's message; rather, it
lies upon its labile surface, like a mocking enigma. This category of disability representation will be designated *disability as hermeneutical impasse*
and will be further elaborated in relation to the work of Samuel Beckett
in chapter 3.[13]

The final category that we should bear in mind is the one in which the disabled characters are completely normalized and exist within the full range of human emotions, contradictions, hopes, fears, and vague ideas, just like any other character. The life writing of disabled people themselves has ensured an increasing number of such accounts, but such complex accountings are not solely from the pens of persons with disabilities. One difficulty with ascertaining the range of texts in this category is that if a writer does not declare him or herself to carry an impairment, it becomes almost impossible to detect signs of their disability from their writing.[14] In terms of the nature of aesthetic nervousness in this set of disability representation, the key distinction to be drawn would have to be that between texts of a biographical or autobiographical kind and those that are plainly fictional. I have already referred to Murphy's *The Body Silent* (1990) in chapter 1. Murphy's autobiography is significant in that being a professional anthropologist, he pays close attention to the process by which his body progressively succumbs to the debilitating disease while also noting the changing reactions of people around him. The book then becomes a simultaneous documentary of his own subjective attitudes to his disability and the responses of the world around him. And in Michael Bérubé's (1996, xii–xv) touching account of parenting Jamie, a child with Down syndrome, he writes of the unbearable cognitive dissonance that inheres in the situation. For, on the one hand, he contemplates what it must be to see his son through the eyes of others, yet, on the other, his engagement with the events of Jamie's everyday life ensures that the child can only be seen by his parents as a unique individual. In both of these instances, the accounts are being written with a full sense of the complexity of responses that attend disability; it is not a stereotype or condition that can be easily assimilated to an essentialized category. Thus, even though there is often some degree of nervousness and anxiety about the implications of living with a disability, there is none of the aesthetic nervousness that we find in the literary accounts. And recall that one of the definitions of aesthetic nervousness is the collapse of the dominant protocols that govern the representation. Since in the (auto)biographies of persons with disability the representation is conducted consistently from the point of view of the persons with disabilities and their caregivers, the opportunities for a "collapse" of the dominant protocols are curtailed. The textual dominant is that which is pertinent to the exploration of the full complexity of living with disability. In the literary texts that fall under the rubric of representation of disability as normality, disability is used as a pointed critique of social hypocrisy and indeed of social institutions as such. This may be seen either in the depiction of the crisis of the individual, such as in Flaubert's *Madame Bovary*, D.H. Lawrence's *Lady Chatterley's Lover*, John Steinbeck's *Of Mice and Men*, and W. Somerset Maugham's *Of Human Bondage*, or in terms of a critique of the entire carceral economy of medicalization, such as is found in Thomas Mann's *The Magic Mountain* or Ken Kesey's *One Flew Over the Cuckoo's Nest*. Signs of aesthetic nervousness may be discovered in such texts, yet the important dimension is the focus on acute social critique that provides the central emphasis to the writing. This final set will be termed *disability as normality*.

Let us recapitulate our categories:

1. Disability as null set and/or moral test
2. Disability as the interface with otherness (race, class, and social identity)
3. Disability as articulation of disjuncture between thematic and narrative vectors
4. Disability as bearer of moral deficit/evil
5. Disability as epiphany
6. Disability as signifier of ritual insight
7. Disability as inarticulable and enigmatic tragic insight
8. Disability as hermeneutical impasse
9. Disability as normality

These nine sets must be taken as a provisional mapping of the field only. There is no doubt that combinations of different categories will produce different emphases and therefore varying potential sets. As we will see in the course of this study, certain categories of disability representation are more dominant in the work of some writers than in others. Thus, in a purely preliminary way that will be further elaborated in specific chapters, it is possible to suggest that Beckett's work displays a leaning toward a combination of categories 7 and 8 (disability as enigmatic insight and disability as hermeneutical impasse), while categories 5, 7, and 9 (disability as epiphany, disability as enigmatic insight, and disability as normality) seem more pertinent to a discussion of Toni Morrison. On the other hand, Wole Soyinka's plays clearly invite exploration via categories 4, 6, and 8 (disability as moral deficit/evil, disability as ritual, and disability as hermeneutical impasse), with the inflection being heavily on ritual. We shall find in our discussion of autism and J. M. Coetzee, however, that his writing exemplifies a combination of 1, 2, and 8 (disability as null set/moral test, disability as interface of otherness, and disability as hermeneutical impasse). The chapter on Robben Island will be used mainly to illustrate sets 2 and 7, but this time from the perspective not of literary characters but historical figures whose identities were defined in confrontation with colonialism and then apartheid. I shall have moved by the end of the study from the close reading of textual details and literary genres to an exploration of the social and political conditions that undergirded concerns about disability within a specific historical context. The ideal of the provisional conceptual map outlined in this chapter and of *Aesthetic Nervousness* as a whole is thus a program for future reading and interpretation of both the literary and sociopolitical domain. This study is offered in that spirit.

3

SAMUEL BECKETT

Disability as Hermeneutical Impasse

I N THIS CHAPTER, I POSE A SIMPLE BUT QUITE PROVOCATIVE question, namely: what happens to our interpretation when we examine the status of disability within a representational system in which *the discomfort of disability is* not *accounted for*? "Discomfort," as I use it here, is a euphemism for a broad range of perturbations that afflict the character with disability, from embarrassment to physical discomfiture to pain, both mental and physical. As we shall see, pain is particularly relevant to a discussion of disability in Beckett because it is the one element that we do not find properly accounted for in his writing. In his work, categories such as emotion and memory, the temporality of past and present, and the vicissitudes of language are placed within a structure of persistent doubt, to the point of making them all elusive and absurd. The one thing that allows us to properly evaluate the significance of this structure of absurdity, however, is pain and its relation to disability. On this point we find a certain stubborn lacuna in Beckett's texts, a lacuna that is not due to an absolute absence of pain as such, since his characters sometimes talk about it, but one that is linked to the ways pain is shown to be only a shadowy part of their consciousness. However, once we take the status of pain to be equivalent to that of impairment and disability in the texts, it serves to short-circuit the process by which the absurdity is maintained. The not-accounted-for pain of the apparently impaired characters creates a blank space that undoes the dominant discursive modality governing the Beckettian representation. Thus to read Beckett closely in terms of the status of pain within the totality of discursive relations among the elements in his work is to critically review the process by which he might be read as a writer of disability.

The reception of the 2004 London production of Endgame at the Albery Theatre in London suggests the tone for how Beckett is generally perceived.[1] The production, directed by Mathew Warchus with Michael Gambon as Hamm and Lee Evans as Clov, was hailed by critics as "outstanding and astutely judged" (Kate Basset) and as an "apocalyptic vaudeville act" (Michael Billington). Lavish praise was heaped on the actors, with Alistair Macauley writing in the Financial Times that their very dissimilarity enlarged the play and that their keen attention to each other gave it a moment-by-moment immediacy. Susannah Clapp saw Gambon as presiding over the empty stage "like a deposed monarch, or a tramp guarding his favourite park bench"; he was described by her as sometimes looking like the blinded Gloucester—with darkened eyes and bloodied handkerchief—and at other times like an Eastern potentate. Evans, on the other hand, is praised by Billington for accentuating Clov's gift for "mislaying ladders and telescopes, as if he is at the endless mercy of material objects."[2] Even though Hamm's blindness and immobility and Clov's difficulty in walking were frequently referred to, the general tenor of the reviews tended to focus on either the production's literariness and indebtedness to earlier dramatic traditions (such as Shakespeare and/or the Absurdists), to art and painting, and to the tradition of the comedy circuit, Lee Evans himself being a noted British comedian. At no point was it noted that Evans's Clov was cast as a person with cognitive disability or that the way Gambon's Hamm declaimed his lines served to fundamentally shift the emphasis away from his impairments. In this the reviews of the play were repeating the overall manner in which Beckett has been understood by literary critics.

The almost subliminal move away from accounting for the reality and discomfort of the impaired body as such by reviewers of the London production is a staple of commentary on Beckett in general. Despite the abundance of figures with physical and mental impairments and mobility difficulties in works as varied as *Waiting for Godot, Molloy, Murphy, Play,* and *Happy Days,* among others, what is quite odd in studies of Beckett to date is the degree to which physical disability is assimilated to a variety of philosophical categories in such a way as to obliterate the specificity of the body and to render it a marker of something else. Thus discussions of maimed and disabled characters in Beckett are often conducted around two broad rubrics: existential phenomenology and deconstructive anti-humanism.[3] Even the very insightful analyses of Pierre Chabert, Jonathan Kalb, Lois Oppenheim, and other directors and critics who have paid attention to the status of Beckett's stage bodies tend to see these within various modalities of theater performance. A good example of this tendency is in Katherine M. Gray's essay on the various "emergences" of Beckett's stage bodies, in which, through a reading of Judith Butler's work, she persuasively shows that the stage bodies are troubled out of their "presumed conventional unity into a radicalized multiplicity" (1996, 1) and thus cannot be assumed to possess normal referentiality. In her discussion, however, there is no room to consider the Beckettian disabled bodies in their specific phenomenological materiality. For even the word "materiality" in her account is aimed at pointing out the transgressions that bodily fluids and gases perform by breaking the apparently closed surface of the body in performance: "As the material body sweats, salivates, drools, spits, coughs, belches, weeps, sneezes, hiccoughs, tears, urinates, bleeds, suppurates, or has gastric distress, it shows the factic/performative body to be a porous performer's body" (8). Thus what is ruptured is the representation of the body in its factual and performative dimensions, each of which normally tends to locate the stage body within a predictable dimension of discourse. We need to ask a number of simple questions with regard to Gray's observations: What about pain? Of the body-in-pain? Why, despite the many obvious referents to the body's deterioration in Beckett do critics fail to talk about the phenomenology of the body's pain? I shall speculate later on the reason for this persistent assimilation of disability to philosophical categories, tracing it directly to the problematic status of pain in Beckett's work and how, despite the many descriptions of physical impairment, pain itself is treated quite differently from all other categories in his work. Because of the strong process of the undermining of certainties in Beckett, the vector of pain is easily mistaken as being analogous or equivalent to other philosophical categories, thus allowing it to be missed out as a potential source for understanding the peculiar function of short-circuiting that pain performs in his writing.

Whatever inventory of disabled, maimed, and constrained figures in Beckett we are able to draw up serves in the end to obscure rather than clarify the complexity of Beckett's attitudes to disability.[4] For all the inventory serves to do is to bring together an array of different images of corporeality, each of which would, properly speaking, have to be contextualized and related to their inspirations within the author's aesthetic and philosophical concerns as well as to his life experiences. However, what an inventory also makes quickly evident is the persistence with which images of impairment and constraint feature in his work. Disability has almost the character of an aesthetic repetition compulsion in Beckett, a return to the impaired human body as a means of framing a series of concerns of a creative and philosophical kind. Without attempting to make too strong a link between the details of his own life and that of the characters in his writing, it is interesting to note that Beckett regularly encountered various disabled figures at close quarters in his lifetime. As background research to the writing of the Mercyseat scenes in *Murphy*, he closely questioned his friend Geoffrey Thompson, who in February 1935 had started working as a senior house physician at the Royal Hospital in Beckenham in Kent, a place for the treatment of mental illness. And from August to December 1945, Beckett worked as a "Quartermaster/Interpreter" for the Normandy Hospital at St.-Lô. Furthermore, Beckett's aunt, Cissie Sinclair, is acknowledged to have been the model for Hamm. Beckett used to wheel her around in her wheelchair when she was crippled with arthritis; she frequently used to ask him to "straighten up the statue." She also had a telescope with which she used to spy out the ships in Dublin Bay (Knowlson 1996, 367; Haynes and Knowlson 2003, 52). Furthermore, *Endgame* was completed shortly after the death of his brother Frank, after a period of cancer that left Beckett devastated. Knowlson (1996, 367) describes *Endgame*'s "flintlike comedy" as being "sparked out of darkness and pain." As noted in chapter 1, however, perhaps what is even more pertinent to the discussion of Beckett and disability is that he himself suffered endless illnesses including arrhythmia, night sweats, and cysts. These caused him regular bodily discomfort (Knowlson 1996). It seems then that the deteriorating body had a special attraction for Beckett because his own body reminded him of its pain and mortality in a forceful way. He was thus able to use the disabled, maimed, and decaying body as a multiple referent for a variety of ideas that seem to have been at least partially triggered by encounters with others and by his own personal experience of pain and temporary disability.[5]

There are thus three propositions I would like to pursue in this chapter: first, to suggest that pain has an elusive and problematic status in Beckett, but that it provides a way of short-circuiting the play of absurdity in his work; second, to show the degree to which the configuration of disability representation in his work is largely underpinned by the category of "disability as hermeneutical impasse," which I introduced in chapter 2; and third, following on from these first two points, to define the nature of aesthetic nervousness we find in his work with reference to the representations of physical and mental impairment and the absenting of pain. While referring to a wide range of texts from his oeuvre, I will focus primarily on *Molloy* and *Endgame* for the discussion in this chapter.

Molloy and the Plenitude of Immediacy

Molloy suffers from a variety of ailments, the most significant of which is the stiffness in his leg, which makes him dependent on crutches for mobility. But that is by no means the whole problem. Apart from his stiff short leg (he is not sure which it is, left or right), he is completely toothless (24), has weak eyesight, a weak bladder, and very bad body odor (50, 81); he is also asthmatic, bristles with boils, and suffers from arthritis (79, 81, 90). He describes himself as having a "hideous appearance." It is not clear whether his various ailments are simply due to old age or have a different genesis. Additionally, there are several other characters with impairments and illnesses that appear in his narrative. Lousse's dog, which he accidentally runs over on his bicycle, is described as "old, blind, deaf, crippled with rheumatism and perpetually incontinent" (33). The description of the dog uncannily echoes what Molloy says about his own mother: she is as "deaf as a post," a "deaf blind impotent mad old woman," and "quite incontinent, both of faeces and water" (19, 17). The old woman to whom he periodically makes love is described as suffering from both rheumatism and lumbago, and dies suddenly while taking a hot bath in her room (56–57). Yet despite all the references to *physical* impairments and illnesses, the novel is defined for us not so much by the references to these as by the nature of the eponymous protagonist's perspectives and recollections. Molloy describes everything so as to insist upon verificatory impasses regarding the reality of the categories in his own mind and how these interact with the natural and social environment around him.

Molloy might be said to be immersed within an elusive plenitude of immediacy. That is to say, he feels impelled to describe in great detail everything that is happening to him, both from within his own mind and from his external environment, and yet everything he describes remains uncertain. The key to an understanding of this elusive plenitude of immediacy is provided by what he says about the relationship between his sense of identity and the namelessness of things: "And even my sense of identity was wrapped in a namelessness often hard to penetrate, as we have just seen I think. And so on for all the other things which made merry with my senses. Yes, even then, when already all was fading, waves and particles, there could be no things but nameless things, no names but thingless names" (31). This is not to say that things are not named or have no names; on the contrary. They are named, but even as they are named they are placed within a horizon of doubt so as to always raise suspicion about the veracity of their specific identities in space and time. All the things described by Molloy emerge in a series of tactile, visual, and auditory evocations that give them a powerful and almost sensuous quality. At the same time, being relayed in a language that is designed to raise doubt about their identities repeatedly undermines the sensuous quality assigned to each object or thought. This then leads to a sense of the continual dissolution of all the details that he gives to us, whether these emerge from the external environment or as objects from his own memory. Every object within Molloy's purview, whether an object external to himself or, as is often the case, a figment of his own memory and imagination, is submitted to this rigorous process of unnaming.

There are several effects of this elusive plenitude. First and foremost is the question of fundamental epistemological doubt, since all essentialisms about phenomenal identity are abolished except for one, which is the non-negotiable status of the quest for his mother, a person he describes as absolutely hating. Indeed, it is the desire to go and see his mother that provides a justificatory framework for his peregrinations in the first place, even though the mother-quest is abandoned somewhere along the line as a rationale for the narrative. In that sense, Molloy abolishes all essentialisms except one: the quest for his mother. The quest acts for him like a hypothetical imperative. This hypothetical imperative is itself sometimes felt to recede, leaving him "stranded" (86–87). Much can be made of this particular maternal hypothetical imperative, except that the objective he has for getting to his mother is neither love nor tenderness but the practical necessity of once again extracting money from her. All that is, remains "nameless."

The second effect of Molloy's commitment to fully describing everything that happens to him is to fit the external world to his own felt experience rather than privileging what appears on the surface of normality. In the novel, normality appears to be ultimately tyrannical, and is signaled especially by the scheme of surveillance that hovers disturbingly on the edge of Molloy's consciousness.[6] This scheme is represented directly in the text by the police sergeant who arrests him and takes him to the station for what is a minor traffic infringement on his bicycle. At the same time, and quite disturbingly, the periphery of his perception, the outer limit of normality, is the source of latent violence. He tells us on being interrogated by the police that he had always "gone in fear all my life, in fear of blows. Insults, abuse, these I can easily bear, but I could never get used to blows" (22). The threat of violence is repeated elsewhere, when the mob that gathers after he runs over the old dog displays every intention of lynching him. His accidental killing of the dog is itself part of this overall trope. Finally, the subterranean violence underpinning the text bursts into the open when Molloy violently kills the charcoal burner encountered in the forest toward the end of his circular quest. Thus we see that normality is edged round by violence and threats of violence, making it even more important for him, as a weak old man with various impairments, to attempt a direct translation of the immediate into forms of sensual and intellectual comprehension that would enable him to navigate what is really a world gone awry. Indeed, the episodic and almost picaresque nature of Molloy's account serves to underscore this awry dimension of the world around him. For at all times, the sense we get is that there is no knowing what will happen next. Things seem to happen all of a sudden, some pleasant (like being taken into Lousse's house and cared for) and some potentially violent, the key thing being that he has no control over his environment except for the residues he filters through his own mind.

Third and finally, Molloy's account raises for us the issue of the skeptical interlocutor integrated into the very system of one's own thought.

Throughout his reflections there is a hint of the presence of an implied interlocutor or addressee. As we shall see in other chapters, but particularly in the ones on Coetzee and on Robben Island, the skeptical interlocutor provides an important horizon against which the disabled character defines him or herself. Molloy's narrative, however, is essentially a dramatic monologue (emphasis here on dramatic), but one in which there is the endemic anticipation of doubt about what is being expressed. Thus he integrates a skeptical interlocutor into the body of his own thought. And yet this skeptical interlocutor need not be conceived of as someone different from himself. Often, the interlocutor appears to be different parts of Molloy engaged in an attenuated and dubious dialogue. As he himself notes: "For in me there have always been two fools, among others, one asking nothing better than to stay where he is and the other imagining that life might be slightly less horrible a little further on" (48). His constant questioning of the categories of his experience are a means toward verifying his identity:

But in there you have to be careful, ask yourself questions, as for example whether you still are, and if no when it stopped, and if yes how long it will go on, anything at all to keep you from losing the thread of the dream. For my part I willingly asked myself questions, one after the other, just for the sake of looking at them. No, not willingly, wisely, so that I might believe I was still there. And yet it means nothing to me to be still there. I called that thinking.

(49)

The implied interlocutor that perforce incites the narration is also to be seen again in the Moran section of the novel, where, quite distinctly from what we see in Molloy's account, the implied interlocutor is the spy chief to whom Moran is obliged to address his report. And yet, in the case of Moran the extreme and unexamined confidence in his various subject positions as father, employer, and indeed spy delays his recognition of his interlocutor as a skeptical one. At the beginning of his section, he assumes that he shares a horizon of assumptions with the spy chief, managing to read between the lines of what Gaber tells him to discern what the spy chief really means by the message Moran has been sent. He is also flattered that he is the one chosen to pursue this particular task. For much of Moran's narrative he is supremely confident in his own views and interpretations of events, always anticipating the perspectives of others and situating himself in a privileged position vis-à-vis his addressees. It is only toward the end of his narration/report, when he has suffered from the inexplicable impairment in his legs and can barely walk, been abandoned by his long-suffering son, and discovers after a long and labored return journey home that his property has fallen into decrepitude, that his tone changes and he allows a note of uncertainty to enter his voice.

We can already see in this notion of the skeptical interlocutor the seeds of the later and much more explicitly worked out dialogical contexts of works such as *Waiting for Godot, Endgame, Krapp's Last Tape,* and *Play.*[7] As we shall soon see with specific reference to *Endgame,* the category of the skeptical interlocutor has multiple articulations along an axis of dialectical oppositions that include those of Invalid/Caregiver, Parent/Child, Master/Slave, and Prospero/Caliban-Ariel.

We are bound to ask, however, whether these features of Molloy's account do not make of him an instrument of excessive ambiguation rather than a representation of disability, whether physical or otherwise. The main reason why this question arises is due to the absence of a crucial element from his structure of interlocution, namely pain. In fact, this is an absence we will also note in *Endgame,* where, despite all the characters living in various states of extreme physical disability and discomfort, physical pain is referred to only tangentially in the play. Molloy does refer passingly to the pain in his legs, except that unlike everything else that percolates through his consciousness, pain is the only category that is not subjected to the structure of skeptical interlocution we noted a moment ago. Even though he is clearly in pain, it does not enter into the structure of doubt within which every category he invokes is tested as to its truth value. Everything that comes into his purview is subjected to the same structure of skeptical verification, be it the name of his mother, the quality of the moon, his notions of time, or even his manner of narrating his experiences. The only thing that is never subjected to this structure of interrogation is physical pain. We are thus led to suspect that his disability is a philosophical abstraction of the frailty of the aging body, rather than referring to the phenomenologically impaired body as such.

Merleau-Ponty suggests that the body is not an instrument or a means but rather the conduit by which the deepest affective movements are tied to the external world. He describes the relationship between the individual's body and the external world in this way:

> We find that perceived things, unlike geometrical objects, are not bounded entities whose laws of construction we possess a priori, but that they are open, inexhaustible systems which we recognize through a certain style of development, although we are never able, in principle, to explore them entirely, and even though they never give us more than profiles and perspectival views of themselves. Finally, we find that the perceived world, in its turn, is not a pure object of thought without fissures or lacunae; it is, rather, like a universal style shared by all perceptual beings. While the world no doubt co-ordinates these perceptual beings, we can never presume that its work is finished.
>
> (1964, 5–6; italics added)

One implication of these remarks is that the external world, like the mind of man, is riddled with lacunae, thus mirroring in its way the gaps in our own knowledge. At any rate, this is how the external world is bound to appear within man's limited perception. But with Molloy we have to confront a problem. Since the entire narrative is governed by a scrupulous stream-of-consciousness narrative method, it is impossible to differentiate between what occurs in Molloy's own mind and what is actually in reality outside of it. And so the lacunae that proliferate seem to have as much to do with the intensities of Molloy's own perceptions as they do with any breaks on the outside. These perceptions, however, do not accommodate pain as a vector of the understanding, thus implying that his "body" is really a no-body: it seems to be pure mind as opposed to body. What Merleau-Ponty's suggestion does not take account of and which Molloy forces us to confront is the degree to which different mind/body dispositions, especially coming together as representational matrices, go to intensify rather than reflect the perceived lacunae of the objective world.[8] Thus in Molloy's case his mind may not be reflecting his environment but intensifying and maybe even distorting it. And, dialectically, that intensification and distortion, percolating as it does through his mind, serves to almost dematerialize his body, making of it a transparent template from which pain is abolished. For if pain were admitted into account, the mind/body dichotomy within the interpretation would have to be resolved in favor of body and away from mind. It is this that allows critics to write about Molloy without remembering his physical impairments.

It is clear that despite the fact of Molloy's many impairments noted earlier, the main way in which we remember him is by way of his internal discourse, the stream-of-consciousness that helps define his sense of self. The attenuation of his physical disabilities as the primary vectors through which Molloy might be interpreted is generated by the text itself. The mixture of close sensory descriptions of his surroundings with specific details of his experience, the overall structure of skeptical self-questioning, and the concomitantly rapid fragmentation of temporal markers make the novel a good example of the representation of disability as a hermeneutical impasse. For at every level that we slice the text we are confronted with a problem of the structure for interpretation. Everything seems labile and elusive, even Molloy's impairments themselves. As we have noted, the only category that falls outside the circle of hermeneutical delirium is pain. Unlike the many other categories that are refracted through Molloy's consciousness, pain stands outside the structure of skeptical interlocution that defines his narrative. To come to a fuller evaluation of the status of pain in *Molloy* and in Beckett's work more generally, however, we have to take a lengthy digression through *Endgame*, the subject of our next section.

Endgame and the Play of Contingency

Whereas *Molloy* allows us to forget or ignore the specificity of the character's disabled body for much of the time, focalizing the disability through the mental as opposed to the physical domain, in *Endgame* such a luxury is not available. The physical manifestation of disability is perpetually on stage, and its specificity is only assuaged by the elusive play of language that we are made alert to as if pursuing the threads of an inexhaustible enigma. Significantly, *Endgame* also displays several of the categories of disability representation we saw in chapter 2. Supervening all the possible disability sets we might interpret *Endgame* by is that of disability as hermeneutical impasse, which emerges quite strongly because of the random manner in which the action of the play unfolds.

As is readily to be noticed on encountering the play, the various categories with which the characters attempt to make sense of their existence always seem to be constitutively dependent upon an ineluctable structure of negation. This structure is central to the unfolding of the action at all levels and can be explored in relation to what I want to describe as the *process of rapid oscillation* between positive assertion and its opposite, that is, problematical negation. This is most strongly to be seen at the level of the dialogue between the characters, in the fact that they seem to be constantly talking at cross-purposes even when they echo each other at different points in the play. The pauses in the dialogue between the characters also tend to obliterate the transition between different thematic referents in their conversation, leading to a series of fragmented conversational tableaux. That is to say, the characters' language does not mean anything other than what is defined contingently by them at any particular time. Thus even an apparently simple matter such as the existence or otherwise of nature is strictly redefined within the purview of their own immediate exchange:

> HAMM. Nature has forgotten us.
> CLOV. There is no more nature.
> HAMM. No more nature? You exaggerate.
> CLOV. In the vicinity.
> HAMM. But we breathe, we change! We lose our hair, our teeth! Our
>   bloom! Our ideals!
> CLOV. Then she hasn't forgotten us.   (97)

Clov's attempt at recontextualization—"In the vicinity"—is what we expect from our knowledge of the background of desolation that lies on the outside of the play. It also smuggles in a small measure of doubt about whether the question can be answered in totality, since the only knowledge he has of nature depends on the immediate vicinity. Yet Hamm goes a step further in suggesting that nature resides within a process of change, both natural (our hair) and ethical (our ideals), thus immediately shifting the meaning of "nature" to a much more subtle level that reflects directly upon the characters' own ontology of progressive decay (hair) yet incorporates an epistemological dimension as well (ideals). Thus language is not taken as unproblematically naming a referent that lies out there in the real world, but rather as scrupulously contingent upon the specific discursive contexts of the dialogue. Hamm's "nature" is then a corrective to Clov's "nature," even though they are both using the same word, and, on the surface, seem to be referring to the same concept.

A degree of nonidentity between language and contextual referent is furthermore seen in the extent to which the text encourages an allegorical or indeed metaphysical identification with various elements of the action, not so much to assert these identifications as to efface them, while at the same time retaining their allegorical residue. Thus, following the hint provided by the title of the play, it could be interpreted as implying the winding down of the characters' lives, when everything is coming to an end. It has been variously interpreted also as an allegory of a post-Holocaust world, the inside of a man's skull, the moves on a chessboard, and a quasi-biblical account of the quest for salvation. One critic has noted that Clov's "It is finished" early in the play has direct echoes of the bible, but that the play is really the reversal of the biblical creation myth. Hamm has also been likened to Prospero and Clov to Caliban or Ariel, suggesting that their relationship is at once paternalistic and exploitative in the manner of Shakespeare's play.[9]

However, despite the allegorical allusiveness of various references in *Endgame*, it is utterly impossible to impose any specific allegorical interpretation on it. Because the play is so obtuse, the effect of the coupling of allegorical allusiveness to the impossibility of allegorical interpretation serves to entice us into interpretation while abrogating our capacity to conduct interpretation as such. We are led toward always reading and interpreting an excess or supplement to what has been displayed before us, while recognizing simultaneously that our capacity for actually gaining any certainty about the status of that supplement is constantly being undermined by the gaps that exist between assertions in the dialogue and their contextual referents. We are not allowed to dwell wholly upon an allegorical interpretation, even though the text seems to encourage this at every turn. Rather we veer from one potential meaning to another, possibly contradictory, potential meaning. The hope of a meaning is kept alive so long as it is thwarted: that is the residue of the allegorical implication. The fragmentary nature of the language and the fact that it is teasingly allegorical means that there is an encouragement to try constantly to assemble and reassemble the pieces of the action in pursuit of meaning.

This is not insignificant, as it then serves to mirror the problems with the bodily schema of the impaired characters within the action itself.

The play has many references to corpses and decay, while also representing characters in various attempts to forestall this imminent decay. This is particularly so with the character of Hamm, who regularly asks Clov for his painkillers. But to capture the peculiar struggle between decay and the efforts against it, both at the level of the characters' own interaction and as part of the governing ethos of the play, it might perhaps be useful to imagine the stage set as smelling of antiseptic, as in a hospital. This would be to take seriously Hamm's remark that "We stink already. The whole place stinks of corpses" (114). Even though this might go directly counter to Beckett's own intentions (there is no evidence in any extant production of an invocation of hospital conditions), this would help to counter the critical anaesthetizations that seek to assimilate the impaired and ailing body in Endgame to an abstract philosophical category. By suggesting a different dimension to the action, the smell of antiseptic would forcefully locate the audience and the reader in a place they most likely would not like either to be at or be reminded of, thus situating them in a conceptual domain that directly subtends the condition of immobility and discomfort displayed on stage.

As many commentators have noted, Hamm's disability complements Clov's in a variety of ways. He is wheelchair bound,[10] while Clov cannot sit; Hamm is completely blind, while Clov is partially so. But this apparent inextricable interdependency is also consolidated at other levels: Clov needs Hamm for sustenance (the combination to the larder), while acting in practical terms as Hamm's prosthesis. Hamm's insistence on knowing what lies outside their desolate room is satisfied by Clov's spying out the landscape with the telescope, another prosthesis of vision that, significantly, also renders Clov himself dependent to a degree upon a notion of bodily extension. Another counterpoint is that set up between movement and stillness. Whereas Hamm is perforce stationary unless he can get Clov to move him around the stage, Clov is constantly moving about doing things: opening the curtain, adjusting the painting that hangs up close to the window, moving the ladder backward and forward, and reporting movement in the kitchen. The movement in the kitchen is itself metonymically displaced onto the mouse that Clov designs to kill, as if to suggest that that movement has to be stilled. Then there is his repeated threat to leave Hamm, to *move away* to some place else, as it were. Nothing happens on stage, and yet this nothingness is marked by the almost frantic movement of one of the characters. In this way, as Pierre Chabert (1982) argues, Beckett sets up a constitutive contrast between immobility and movement. Hamm's immobility serves to accentuate Clov's labored movements and to intensify his every gesture, while Clov's movements serve to further highlight the immobility and sometimes even statuesque posture of the other characters. When Clov himself stops moving, it is almost as if he is winding down to the position of immobility of the other characters. The dialectical relationship between mobility and immobility in a play constituted exclusively by characters that carry impairments serves to further accentuate the existential constraint of disability. Every move within this dialectic is constitutively dependent on its opposite, thus suggesting that impairment/disability/immobility and nondisability/mobility are part of a single continuum.[11]

And yet the contrast between Clov's movement on- and off-stage and the immobility that is enjoined for Hamm, Nagg, and Nell is not so much a demarcation of the opposition between mobility and immobility as between different temporalities. For at one level, the counterbalance of movement/nonmovement is that between different *rates of action and decay*. The differentiated temporalities of movement/immobility are predominantly suggested in the contrast between the current condition of the characters and the stories they tell about their past to assuage their impotence. These stories often serve to demarcate a different world of action to that which we see depicted on stage. More importantly, in the stories of their past, Hamm, Nagg, and Nell were not disabled, but appeared to have had active and interactive lives. Contrastively, nothing seems to happen in the now of the dramatic action. All that is left for the characters is the recollection of past events. Central to Hamm's characterization, in particular, is his capacity to adopt various narratological positions to invoke the past in order to counteract his sense of present inadequacy. Discussing this feature of *Endgame*, Jonathan Boulter (1998, 41) notes that acts of narrative in the play function as the momentary liberation from constraint, especially for Hamm. As he points out, "Narrative operates hermeneutically in the sense that it offers the possibility of inscribing an alternative temporality, an alternative way (or time) of being." Boulter focuses on what he calls an "act of historiography" on the part of the characters that allows them to interpret and rewrite the past. We have to add, however, that the rewriting of the past is not just an act of interpretative predisposition. Rather, involved in the interpretation of the past are struggles about agency. This agency does not mirror the present but displaces it onto an earlier phase of temporality, which earlier phase is more active and carries greater vitality than the one enacted on stage.

The past that the characters have recourse to appears to suffer a certain degree of sterility. This is mainly because there can be no easy agreement about what it means, either in the case of Hamm, for himself, or in the case of Nagg and Nell, in terms of how they view their commonly shared past. The past becomes animated only in the process of recollection. In the case of Nagg and Nell, the stories of the tailor and of their shared experience on Lake Como are mutually interdependent for the meanings that might be implicitly unearthed for establishing their agential dispositions out of that past:

NAGG. What does that mean? [*Pause.*] That means nothing. [*Pause.*]
   Will I tell you the story of the tailor?
NELL. No [*Pause.*] What for?
NAGG. To cheer you up.
NELL. It's not funny.
NAGG. It always made you laugh. [*Pause.*] The first time I thought
   you'd die.
NELL. It was on Lake Como. [*Pause.*] One April afternoon. [*Pause.*]
   Can you believe it?
NAGG. What?
NELL. That we once went out rowing on Lake Como. [*Pause.*] One
   April afternoon.
NAGG. We had got engaged the day before.
NELL. Engaged!
NAGG. You were in such fits that we capsized. By rights we should
   have been drowned.
NELL. It was because I felt so happy.
NAGG. It was not, it was not, it was my story and nothing else. Happy! Don't you laugh at it still? Every time I tell it. Happy!
NELL. It was deep, deep. And you could see down to the bottom. So
   white, so clean.
NAGG. Let me tell it again. [*Raconteur's voice.*]

(101–102)

Their disagreement about what it was that made Nell laugh is fundamental to how they interpret that event. But why did she laugh so uncontrollably at the time? She says it was due to happiness, but he insists it was his story of the tailor that did it. From her impassive response to the tailor story when he has finished retelling it to her for what must be the umpteenth time, we suspect that the story is not incredibly funny after all. But what if her impassive response now in the time of the dramatic action is meant to be read back onto the past and to suggest that it is a replica of her response then? More significantly, are we not encouraged to use this contradiction (between laughter/impassiveness) to question the entirety of their lives together through the basic institution of marriage, one of the key ideals of which is "conjugal harmony"? The laughter now becomes the central point of ambiguity: did she really laugh then because the story was funny? Or because she was happy? If it was because it was funny, was she not happy? And if it was because she was happy, was it not funny? And why does she not laugh now? Is it because she does not find the story funny anymore or because she is no longer happy? Focusing still on the status of laughter—whether she laughed because the story was funny or because she was happy—also allows us to fold the laughter/impassiveness back into their current condition of immobility. Might her impassiveness now not be related to the fact that their condition of inertia makes it impossible for her to laugh? In which case, is Nagg's story recalling the past not really an attempt to recapitulate a different form of temporality to revivify their current condition, even if for one fleeting moment? Thus we find that the stories that they tell have to be related to their current conditions of immobility as well as contrasted to their previous situation.

Also at stake between Nagg and Nell is something well beyond laughter, for their disagreement also implies a contested interpretation of causality and of the relationship between the past and the present. For if from Nell's uncontrollable laughter there followed the capsizing of the boat, it is important to know what caused them (both the laughter and the consequent capsizing). Nagg's insistence that it was his story that made her laugh uncontrollably is nothing less than claiming, in the ultimate instance, that it was he who caused the capsizing of the boat. That he was the god of the lake, and not she. But to assert such a privileged claim is not merely about the interpretation of the past; it also serves as an attempt to neutralize the effects of futility within the dramatized present. The contrast between movement and mobility in both the Lake Como and the tailor accounts and their own current condition of incarceration inside the dustbins is significant in that respect. As we have noted, it is the process of recalling the past into the present that revivifies the present and enables contesting claims to be made about both past and present. Thus, the process of recalling the past is at the same time a process of animating what is potentially sterile and inert, that is, dead and only enlivened in memory. On this reading, the story of the tailor is also open to contradictory interpretations. Is it merely the story of an incompetent tailor and an equally gullible customer filled with sexual innuendoes, or is it, as Nagg implies at the end, a parable about God's own fallibility in creating an imperfect world? Again, what appears sterile is subject to multiple interpretations; the failure of triggering an expected response (laughter) then marks the necessity for interpretation. Is it a funny or sad tale? Is it tragic (if viewed from a theological standpoint) or merely sexual (if viewed from the various references to different parts of the trousers)? Or is it, in the final analysis, just an instance of a bad joke, and in that case revealing the overaggrandized sense of the ego of its teller? Or is it all of these at once?

In the case of Hamm and Clov, their relationship contrasts sharply with Nagg and Nell's, for whereas Clov is highly mobile and Hamm is not, it is Hamm who controls the narrativization of the·past and constantly attempts to return to it in accounting for both past and present. Unlike the case of Nagg and Nell, Clov does not seem to have any clearly shared past from which to challenge Hamm. In their case, mobility and immobility are themselves obverse displacements of the impulse to narrate (countering the immobility of the present) and the fixedness of the position of listener or addressee (canceling out the capacity for action and mobility in the present). The sterility of Hamm's past derives from a different source from that of Nagg and Nell's. In his case, the sterility comes from the fact that he is alone in having access to that past but does not interrogate himself in retelling it. Unlike what we saw with regard to Molloy's narrative of his past, Hamm's is what might be termed a monological accounting, only partially open to skepticism in the process of the telling. Apart from one instance where Clov refers to some passing kindness that Hamm had shown him in the past, Hamm is almost utterly alone in that past and is the only one who has access to it. It is perhaps this aloneness in the past that makes him so insistent on constituting the other characters as his captive listeners, almost as if to relieve the loneliness of that past by the dialogical contexts of the present.

As a character, Hamm thrives on imagining himself as having the power of dispensing life and death, something that is obviously undermined by his impairments. In all his relationships he attempts to replicate this impossible ideal: keeping the combination to the larder, rationing biscuits for Nagg and Nell, telling the story of the supplicating man begging him for bread for his son. The supplicating man within his story is discursively replicated on stage by the three-legged dog:

> CLOV. Wait! [*He squats down and tries to get the dog to stand on its three legs, fails, lets it go. The dog falls on its side.*]
> HAMM. [*Impatiently.*] Well?
> CLOV. He's standing.
> HAMM. [*Groping for the dog.*] Where? Where is he?
> CLOV. There. [*He takes* HAMM's *hand and guides it towards the dog's head.*]
> HAMM. [*His hand on the dog's head.*] Is he gazing at me?
> CLOV. Yes.
> HAMM. [*Proudly.*] As if he were asking me to take him for a walk?
> CLOV. If you like.
> HAMM. [*As before.*] Or as if he were begging me for a bone. [*He withdraws his hand.*] Leave him like that, standing there imploring me.
> [CLOV *straightens up. The dog falls on its side.*]   (112)

Note that in the final analysis, Hamm's questions about the dog taper off from straightforward questions to a statement disguised as a question— "Or as if he were begging me for a bone"—suggesting his attempt to annul doubt as to the supplicatory pose of the dog even while entertaining a degree of uncertainty about this (after all, he cannot actually see the dog). Significantly, since Clov lies to Hamm when asked whether the dog is standing, Hamm's surge of self-aggrandizement is immediately placed on chimerical foundations. He is the victim of an illusion of grandeur, pitiable in that he takes it completely seriously. Boulter is right to focus his analysis of the efficacy of the acts of narration predominantly on Hamm, for it is clear that Hamm tries to occupy various narratorial and subject positions over the course of the action. He adopts several "voices" that can be labeled formulaically as Prophetic, Narratorial, Hectoring, and, at the very end, Acting, almost as if self-conscious of his role as an

Actor and Playwright on stage. The suggestion here is that Hamm is rapidly taking on and discarding various identities. It is this that his literary hyperconsciousness points to; the fact, as he puts it, that he is "warming up for his soliloquy" (130).

Of the many implied dialectical relationships suggested between Hamm and Clov that we may note, such as Master/Slave, Invalid/Caregiver, and so on, the most significant with respect to the different claims to agency inherent in the dialectic is that within the Prospero/Caliban-Ariel pairing. Clov himself retorts to Hamm, Caliban-like, about the efficacy of the language he has been taught by Hamm to speak:

> HAMM. Yesterday! What does that mean? Yesterday!
> CLOV. [Violently.] That means that bloody awful day, long ago, before this bloody awful day. I use the words you taught me. If they don't mean anything any more, teach me others. Or let me be silent.
>
> (113)

Hamm-as-Prospero is directly referenced when he states cryptically, after Nagg's lament on fatherhood, "Our revels now are ended," and, groping blindly for the dog, initiates a new trajectory for the dialogue with a plaintive complaint: "The dog's gone" (120). The echo from *The Tempest* is to IV.i.148, but the significance of this echo lies not so much in what it allows us to see about the Master/Slave relationship between Hamm-Prospero and Clov-Caliban/Ariel as in the desire to control the narrativization of the past. In the many bad-tempered exchanges between Prospero and Caliban, on the one hand, and Prospero and Ariel, on the other, what is repeated without fail is Prospero's absolute claim to an interpretation of the past. Like Prospero, Hamm's impulse to narrate is similarly a will to power. In Hamm's case, even though the will to power remains intact throughout the play, the nature of his dependency on Clov makes it such that he is always undermined in his desire for power and authority. The dependency is no idle one; it gains the force of Necessity (Fate, almost) in that he is ontologically validated at various levels by the presence of Clov. This validation is even true of his role as Narrator:

> CLOV. What is there to keep me here?
> HAMM. The dialogue.   (120–121)

But "the dialogue" ends up being a metonymic displacement of the interdependent relationship between the speaker and his addressee/interlocutor, establishing, as we saw in the case of Molloy, a skeptical interlocutor that incites narration. Hamm reluctantly implies the question of the necessary interlocutor as part of his own efforts at stemming the tide of self-effacement. In a rare soliloquy when he is briefly alone on stage, he says: "Then babble, babble, words, like the solitary child who turns himself into children, two, three, so as to be together, and whisper together, in the dark" (126). As we saw earlier, the structure of interlocution in *Endgame* is assimilated to certain dialectical oppositions. It could be said, however, that supervening all these oppositions and providing them their ontological ground is that of Speaker and Interlocutor. The Speaker/Interlocutor dialectical binary is different from all other ones within the series that define the complex relationship between Hamm and Clov because it is also foundationally the engine of dramatic action as such. When in the sixth century b.c. Thespis decided to alter the structure of the dithyramb by introducing a speaker to interact with the singers, the structure of interlocution was born for Greek drama and for all subsequent dramatic forms. What Beckett does with what is constitutive to drama is to elevate this aspect of dramatic structure into the status of an ontological necessity. The force of that elevation lies in the fact that its effacement is always being threatened by Clov's constantly reiterated but frequently deferred decision to leave. His departure would coincide not just with the threatened death of Hamm, but, concomitantly, with the death of the essence of dramatic action as such. For Hamm, the situation is desperate, because Clov is his primary and only caregiver. Being disabled, he requires Clov to keep him alive, literally. His persistent reversions to a narratorial mode, then, can be read as his attempt to maintain the necessary interest of Clov, both so as to allow him to renarrativize his agential positions in the past and also to keep Clov fixed in the function of Caregiver/Interlocutor, both of which are mutually defining and central to the relationship between the two characters.

So far, we have been exploring *Endgame* at what, following Gerard Genette (1982), we might describe as an "intradiegetic" level, that is, at the level of events inside of the drama itself. However, it is also possible to view the action on stage as balanced carefully between contrasting, if not contradictory, diegetic domains, both internal and external. We have already noted the degree to which the play encourages an allegorical reading while scrupulously undermining it. The relationship between past and present is also part of these intervolved diegetic domains. The inter-volved diegeses depend for their effect on a layering of contrastive fore-grounds and backgrounds. At the most immediate level is the foreground of the sparse stage against an external background of what has been in-terpreted by Adorno and others as one of post-Holocaust desolation. This nexus of foreground and background leads to the problematization of the status of the represented disabilities on stage, the genesis of the charac-ters' impairments never being clarified satisfactorily for us. Even Nagg and Nell's accident on their tandem bike is not directly related to their present condition as occupants of the bins. (How did they get from their accident to this particular condition, one wonders?) Nor do we get any clear sense of how Hamm became blind and wheelchair bound. From what he darkly prophesizes to Clov—"One day you'll say to yourself, I'm tired, I'll sit down, and you'll go and sit down. . . . But you won't get up"—it is almost as if to suggest that, from his own experience, such impairments descend upon one without warning. The connection between past events and the characters' present condition of impairment is left at the level of an infer-ence rather than stated directly. At the same time, there is a split between the foreground of the action (the characters and their attempts to make sense of their lives) and the reported desolate background off-stage. Thus the environmental background, which we are of course only allowed to "see" through the reports of Clov, insinuates a grand cause for the various impairments we see before us. For how could it be otherwise in a post-Holocaust world? In this way, the foreground of disabilities is connected to a background of world-historical processes, thus enjoining us to read the impairments in their own materiality as well as in the degree of their representativeness as residual but no less tragic effects of a world-histori-cal event. In that sense, the diegesis on stage is part of a larger narrative. Through the device of splitting—that is, a foreground of impairments and maiming without clear causes suggestively but not explicitly tied to a background of post-Holocaust desolation that enacts the grand cause of *all* impairments and disabilities—Beckett helps to both raise the ethical dimension and to render it nonfoundational as a vector for interpretation. In *Endgame*, the grand cause suggested by a post-Holocaust world of deso-lation is itself impaired as a representational and causal template for the various disabilities on stage, since we can only speculate as to its relation-ship to the foreground of the action. Since the etiology of impairments displayed in the dramatized action is never given to us, and the relation-ship between foreground and background is only left as an inference, the effect is to fragment the background and force it to be a metaphorical ef-fect rather than a cause of what is displayed before us. In other words, it is almost as if it is the characters that produce and are accountable for the background of desolation, rather than vice versa. This is sharply different from what we see in, say, Brecht's *Mother Courage and Her Children*, where Kattrin's disability is directly interpreted as connected to the Thirty Years War, various aspects of which are dramatized on stage for us. Or indeed in Wole Soyinka's *Madmen and Specialists*, in which, as we shall see in chap-ter 5, the Biafran War is taken to be fully responsible for the wretched lives of the disabled mendicants on stage.

As we have already noted, the relationship between Hamm and Clov is a contradictory one. Hamm obviously cannot survive without Clov and yet he also seems to detest his dependence on him. His heartlessness to-ward Clov is partly an admission of his own frailty. At another level, the interdependency of these two is a sign of the radical contingency that governs the entire play. One significant feature of the relationship be-tween Hamm and Clov, and one which leads us further into the discus-sion of intra- and extradiegetic domains, is that on the whole Hamm ad-dresses Clov by way of a stream of imperatives. At one point, Clov complains about this, "Do this, do that, and I do it. I never refuse. Why?" (113) and, much later, "There is one thing I'll never understand. Why I always obey you. Can you explain that to me?" (129). Following the point we made earlier about the dialectic of interlocution, the stream of impera-tives might also be interpreted as Hamm's attempt to convert Clov into a specific function within the action. In other words, it is not just that Hamm is conscious of having a role to play as an Actor warming up for his soliloquy, but that he also wants to exercise the power to assign Clov a role to play. This attempt at assigning a dramatic function to his inter-locutor, which emerges directly out of the structure of imperatives, then suggests that one of Hamm's functions is to transcend that of Actor and to enter into that of Playwright or Director. Commentators have noted that the name Hamm recalls Hamlet, and, as we know, Shakespeare's character was a pristine Actor as well as Director-of-Action, at least in his instigation of the Mousetrap play to catch the conscience of Claudius. Hamm's impulses also accord with those of Prospero as a director of the actions of others, something that inspires Peter Greenaway's interpretation of the character's role in the film *Prospero's Books* (1991), where Prospero generates the entire action of the film along with all the character articulations through the force of his imagination. Hamm's role as both Player and Playwright helps explain his "directorial" exclamations regarding the placing of the three-legged dog as well as his many directorial intrusions on Nagg's stories. We also get a flavor of this dual function in his self-conscious corrections of his own voice during the story he tells of the supplicating man. If, however, we push the matter even further and take Hamm's directorial dimension as deriving directly from the structure of imperatives by which he addresses other people in the action, then it forces us to reinterpret his soliloquy at the end of the play. For at his final soliloquy, several actantial roles are activated that serve to suggest a shifting boundary between different diegetic levels.

At the most basic level, Hamm's final soliloquy is the delivery of the promise he has regularly made in the course of the play. It also highlights the self-conscious quality of many of the lines of dialogue he has initiated earlier, often prefixing these with the statement "Me to play." The curious thing about this final soliloquy is that it is itself filled with explicit commands directed at himself: "Discard; raise hat; and put on again; wipe; and put on again; now cry in darkness; speak no more; you . . . remain" (133). Each imperative is followed by a direct response to the command to perform a particular action. These are interspersed with the adoption of multiple subject positions: "It was the moment I was waiting for. [*Pause.*] You don't want to abandon him? You want him to bloom while you are withering? Be there to solace your last million last moments? [*Pause.*] He doesn't realize, all he knows is hunger, and cold, and death to crown it all. But you! You ought to know what the earth is like, nowadays. Oh, but I put him before his responsibilities [*Pause. Normal voice*]" (133). By this point, it is not clear whether Hamm is still addressing Clov, who has put on his coat preparatory to leaving but is still on stage watching him, or whether Hamm is even conscious of Clov's presence on stage, even though the early part of the soliloquy was a direct appeal, couched as a command, for Clov to cover him up with the sheet. In terms of the adoption of multiple voices, this part of Hamm's soliloquy echoes his story about the man who comes to beg for bread for his sick son. In his recounting of that story, Hamm goes through a spectrum of voices, attempting to replicate the man, himself in the past, as well as adopting a critical tone regarding his manner of telling the story. The same multiplicity occurs in his final soliloquy. The point to note, however, is that if in the final soliloquy he is giving instructions to himself as to how to act, his instructions directly subtend the stream of imperatives by which he has conventionally addressed Clov. In that way, his instructions to himself invoke the extradiegetic level of Director or Playwright. We might even venture to say that at this point Hamm is Beckett himself at one remove, ghosted, as it were, by the self-consciousness of his own creation. And yet, at another level, we cannot escape the impression that the self-referential directorial commands are no more than an extension of the imperatives by which Hamm has hitherto attempted to regulate relationships *within* the intradiegetic domain of the dramatic action itself. What we see then is that in his final soliloquy Hamm is at multidiegetic interstices of the text. This suggests a volatile proximity between inside and outside, detail and allegory, and performance and reality that has governed the play throughout. In this, his farewell, Hamm surreptitiously echoes Prospero again, because, like him, his parting is that of acknowledging the role of Playwright, something that has led Shakespearean scholars to suggest that *The Tempest* was Shakespeare's farewell to his dramatic craft. Thus, in bidding farewell, all the roles accorded Hamm are intensified and brought together within the single gesture, that gesture itself serving to collapse various boundaries that have been evident within the play and have governed the play thus far. If, as I have suggested here, Hamm's final soliloquy helps to collapse those boundaries and binary oppositions, it also produces a mode of transcendence for the disabled character. We are never allowed to forget his disability; the bloodstained handkerchief he uses to cover his face at the end will ensure this, since it takes us back to the opening sequences and the semireligious declaration of "It is finished" we noted earlier. Yet, the rapid oscillation the soliloquy defines among various vectors of performative identity then ensures that Hamm is not limitable to any single one of them, rather eluding them all to suggest the transcendent logic of an intensified consciousness.

The Body (Not) in Pain in Beckett

As we noted at the start of this chapter, critics have managed to anaesthetize the disabled body in Beckett by assimilating it much too rapidly to abstract philosophical categories. We must now address this problem, and the answer lies in something that seems worryingly absent in the body of Beckett's work itself. *This is the status of pain as a mode of intersubjective recognition and identity.* This is not to say that Beckett's characters do not mention or indeed feel pain. They often do. Clov states at one point that the pain in his legs is unbelievable and that it threatens to stop him from thinking (115). Hamm's persistent requests to have his painkillers can be interpreted as his attempt to forestall pain. In fact, Hamm asks for his painkillers six times over the course of the action, and in each instance Clov puts him off with a different excuse, until the sixth and final time, when he tells him the painkillers have run out. To which Hamm uncharacteristically loses control:

HAMM. Is it not time for my pain-killer?
CLOV. Yes.
HAMM. Ah! At last! Give them to me! Quick!
[*Pause.*]
CLOV. There's no more pain-killer.
[*Pause.*]
HAMM.[*Appalled.*] Good . . . ! [*Pause.*] No more pain-killer!
CLOV. No more pain-killer. You'll never get any more pain-killer.
[*Pause.*]
HAMM. But the little round box. It was full!
CLOV. Yes. But now it's empty.
[*Pause. CLOV starts to move about the room. He is looking for a place to put the alarm clock.*]
HAMM. [*Soft.*] What'll I do? [*Pause. In a scream.*] What'll I do?
(127)

The moment at which Clov discloses that there are no more painkillers is the point at which the relation of power between the two men begins to shift decisively, progressively deteriorating until Clov strikes Hamm on the head with the three-legged dog and proceeds to make good his oft-repeated threat to leave.

In *The Body in Pain* (1985), Elaine Scarry suggests that one of the complex things about pain is that it produces epistemological certainty for the pain sufferer but the possibility of doubt for the nonsufferer. The bearer of pain cannot *not* be in certainty about his or her own pain, whereas the one not in pain may entertain some doubt about the veracity or intensity of what the bearer of the pain claims to be feeling. This conundrum recalls Adriana's words to Luciana in *The Comedy of Errors*:

> A wretched soul bruised with adversity,
> We bid be quiet when we hear it cry;
> But were we burdened with like weight of pain,
> As much, or more, we should ourselves complain.

(II.i.34–37)

As Scarry shows, the contradiction between the epistemological certainty of the bearer of pain and the doubt of the beholder leads to all kinds of implications for understanding regimes of torture, war, and aesthetic representation. It also leads to the problem of analogical verification, since in contexts in which previously assumed social verities are in doubt the body itself is conscripted as an instrument for verifying the values of the system. Hence the historical emergence of various regimes of sacrifice used to affirm the efficacy of religious systems, the state, and, more problematically, the logic of necropolitics (Scarry 1985, 124–27).[12]

It is, however, to her remarks on the difficulty of epistemological verification of pain by the nonsufferer that we need to turn. For therein arises the implied question of witnessing. The pain sufferer feels his or her knowledge of the truth of pain somewhat validated by the recognition bestowed upon them by the witness to that pain. The shift from a nonsufferer of pain to that of a witness to pain is fundamentally one of empathetic repositioning. Empathy is to be seen not only in interpersonal relations; it is also evidenced in entire public apparatuses of witnessing, such as the proceedings of the Truth and Reconciliation Commission in South Africa. The witness is one who acknowledges, empathizes, and attempts to alleviate the physical suffering of another, be this through compassion, medicine, or through shared public rituals of acknowledgement, such as those of the TRC. In the particular case of the TRC, the alleviation of pain is tied to the pursuit of forms of restorative justice, something that is central to the process of identity formation in postapartheid South Africa. The point about witnessing to pain is that certainty is epistemologically recuperated for the beholder through the process of witnessing, thus reassuring the sufferer that their pain is not a figment of their imagination but is *real* in whatever problematic sense this is defined between the sufferer and the witness, or indeed culturally and politically. In other words, witnessing to pain helps to reframe its character by providing it with a different structure of interlocution within which it might be expressed *and* acknowledged.

In *Endgame*, and indeed in much of Beckett's work, what we find is that even though the characters do mention pain from time to time, pain is not part of the overall structure of interlocution within which it would gain coherence as a phenomenological fact linked directly to disability. Beckett's characters may be alienated from their bodies (Malone and his reflections on his useless limbs, for example), but they rarely reflect on pain as such. This is true of both Pozzo and Lucky in *Waiting for Godot*, as much as it is for people in the Magdalen Mental Mercyseat in *Murphy*, many of whom have to be watched carefully so that they don't attempt to commit suicide. *Waiting for Godot* gives pain a particularly shifting status between the first and second acts. In the first act, Vladimir often has to rush out to urinate, and his urinating pains are frequently referred to. Indeed he walks on stage with his legs spread wide apart to protect his painful penis from further soreness. However, something strange happens in the second act. Vladimir is desperate for certainty about what happened "yesterday." No one appears to be certain about anything that took place the day before except for him. Vladimir keeps trying to jog the memory of the other characters about the previous day's events. On his part, Estragon seems to have forgotten everything that transpired; the only thing that registers residually about the events of the previous day in his mind is the pain on his shin where he was violently kicked by Lucky. Fundamental to Estragon's characterization are his keen efforts to avoid pain. He has an almost paranoid fear of being beaten up at night. Significantly, it is Vladimir who reminds Estragon of his being kicked by Lucky, thus jogging his memory momentarily. The only memory that allows Estragon to connect residually to the "yesterday" of the first act is the pain that he remembers from being kicked by Lucky. Seeing that Estragon is alive to pain (at least his own), it is then strange that the only detail Vladimir does *not* recall in trying to moor his sense of yesterday for himself and Estragon is his urinating pains. It is almost as if in the second act there is an annulment of pain, the only thing that might have instituted a link between yesterday and today. By this annulment, then, yesterday ceases to exist because the characters are allowed to "forget" the only thing that would have provided epistemological certainty about that yesterday, namely pain. This is part of the process that helps to define the dramatic action as an allegory of existential meaninglessness and randomization of identity.

In *Endgame*, on the other hand, even though Hamm is obviously in pain, two factors serve to blur the reality of this in the play. The first, as we have seen, is that Clov does not seem to recognize it, rather behaving in an uncharacteristically sadistic manner in the way in which he announces that the painkillers are finished and in the speed with which he shifts from the issue of painkillers to moving about the room to find a place to put the alarm clock. In that way, Clov suggests that whatever pain the painkillers were meant to alleviate is not as significant as the immediacy of his concern to be relieved of the burden of carrying the alarm clock around the room. Clov does not pause to bear witness to Hamm's pain. In this, Clov is only replicating the lack of empathy that has been shown him by Hamm when it was his turn to complain about the bitter pain in his legs.

What is even more curious, however, is the speed with which Hamm himself moves away from worrying about pain on being told about the painkillers. He shifts from a primal scream of frustration and pain to asking Clov to look out the window with his telescope in the space of barely three lines, never again to refer either to the painkillers or indeed to his pain for the rest of the play. What happens here is that like every thematic referent that has appeared over the course of the play, pain itself has become a nondescript part of an array of constitutive digressions. There is no privilege given to it whatsoever. But if pain is allowed to become equivalent with the many things that have fleetingly emerged across the relationship between the two men, then might it not be said also that their impairments are themselves only part of the textual apparatus of constant negation and deferral and nothing more? To put it more bluntly, if discomfort and pain are not recognized as pertinent either to their disabled and constrained condition or to the structure of interlocution between them, then to what degree might it be said that their impairments are themselves merely a cipher of the condition of frailty as opposed to the referent of real suffering as such?

A similar problem is pertinent to the status of pain in *Molloy*. For in *Molloy*, even though the eponymous protagonist is clearly in pain, pain does not enter into the structure of doubt within which every category he invokes is tested as to its truth claim. In *Molloy* also we are led to suspect that Molloy's disability is a philosophical abstraction or cipher about the frailty of the aging body, rather than referring to the phenomenological body as such. Our doubts become more pronounced at the point where he describes riding his bicycle:

> This is how I went about it. I fastened my crutches to the cross-bar, one on either side, I propped the foot of my stiff leg (I forget which, now they're both stiff) on the projecting front axle, and I pedaled with the other. It was a chainless bicycle, with a free-wheel, if such a bicycle exists. . . . So I shall only add that every hundred yards or so I stopped to rest my legs, the good one as well as the bad, and not only my legs, not only my legs. I didn't properly speaking get down off the machine, I remained astride it, my feet on the ground, my arms on the handle bars, my head on my arms, and I waited until I felt better.
>
> (16)

Even here we see the structure of skeptical interlocution we noted earlier (no certainty about which leg it was he propped; not sure whether a chainless bicycle did indeed exist or not). But what is of interest is the patent impossibility of riding a bicycle (any bicycle) with crutches tied to the crossbar *and* with a stiff leg propped up anywhere on the bicycle (never mind the projecting front axle). For one thing, there would be serious problems with steering the bicycle, and, for another, it would be almost impossible to maintain one's balance with one foot off the pedal and propped up somewhere else (anywhere else) on the contraption.[13] We might take the benign view that this is just an instance of Molloy's mental confusion, or that Beckett did not properly visualize the scene before writing it, which is more what I am inclined to believe. Or that Molloy, despite the many descriptions of his impairments and disabilities, was not "disabled" at all. His physical disabilities are not determinant factors of his identity and can thus be set aside quickly once they are mentioned. Like Clov and Hamm, Molloy's impairments are ciphers of the frailty of the human condition and not to be read as markers of any real disability as such.

The absence of a structure of interlocution for addressing pain in Beckett is what allows his drama in particular to reside uneasily between tragedy and comedy. The dianoetic laughter that often attends plays such as *Endgame* is possible because the characters' suffering is not physical or even indeed emotional. They are not perceived to be in pain in any physical sense of the word. In the Albery Theatre production of *Endgame*, Clov was cast not only as one with difficulties in walking but also as a person with a cognitive disability. Throughout the play, his hands were held in a half-folded way, and he walked around the stage with his back partially bent and with facial gestures suggesting a cognitive disorder. This immediately puts a new inflection on his many moments of forgetfulness in the play. In my view, however, what was most interesting about Clov's portrayal was that when he first enters, and before he even opens his mouth for the first time, people in the audience break into long laughter. To them, it seems, this is vintage clowning. But looking at the play from a perspective of disability studies, it becomes very difficult not to feel some degree of uneasiness at the response to such a touching portrayal of cognitive disability. Perhaps it was my response that was the wrong one, I thought for a moment, since the entire production history of *Endgame* does not seem to have prepared for the response that I was bringing to bear on the performance. This was borne out by the many rave reviews about the performance that appeared in its immediate aftermath. Not one noted the implications of Clov's casting for thinking about cognitive impairments.

But how does a focus on pain help us to reinterpret Beckett? It is the "absenting" of pain in his writing, in part, that serves to place the many impaired bodies in his work on the boundary between comedy and tragedy. For because pain is not a central part of their characterization, the phenomenological specificity of their impairments gets blurred and thus easily assimilable to philosophical categories. Since pain is the one thing that is not submitted to the dominant aesthetic and structural dispositions of his texts, they mark both an external element, an element properly outside of the structure of representation, and a definitive and constitutive element of the inside of those structures. It is precisely because the pain does *not* feature properly either in the minds of the characters or in the relationships between them that it is possible to read the characters off as philosophical ciphers. In other words, the lacuna produced by the discursive absence of pain is what has allowed Beckett's characters to historically not be considered as disabled. It is this absence in itself that helps us to understand the peculiar aesthetic nervousness of Beckett's representation of disability. Disability in Beckett is represented predominantly via the mode of hermeneutical conundrum, not so much so as to raise doubt about what it might mean, but so that the entire apparatus of representation is riddled with gaps and aporia. The primary effect of evacuating the facticity of disability is that its significance then serves to permeate the entire representational nexus while being simultaneously absented from that nexus as a precise site for interpretation. Yet to read Beckett through a framework of disability is to have to forcibly intervene in the signifying chain that allows disability to be so easily assimilated to philosophical categories. Indeed, this would be the central task of a criticism informed by a consciousness of disability studies and its place in the critique of the overall schema of aesthetic representation. As Aldo Tagliaferri (1985, 249–250) puts it:

> In Beckett's work we can recognize the revelation of a void-filled gap, a putting off, a self-negation that cannot be reduced to a number of valences to be balanced, to a simple question of unfinishedness, but which imply a question, a proposal, an act of refusal as art now aims at denying rather than imitating, not an invitation to a free game of possibilities, but the obligation, the commitment to continue directed by the precise metacritical function of negation of all hypostatic values, the blanket that a thousand years of western tradition has woven to cover the untenable exposure of naked human subjectivity.

It is the central terms of Tagliaferri's account that we have to rely upon to gradually bring to the surface the nature of the aesthetic nervousness that attends the disabled characters in Beckett. For once we take these aporia and lacunae not as transpositions of a philosophical template but as generated by the ambivalent presentation of the disabled characters, we find that our reading of his work is much enriched, and, more significantly, can be used to illuminate a general problem for the aesthetic domain that we see manifested repeatedly in various representations of disability. Since the complicated and multifaceted structures of Beckett's texts resist any assumptions of mimesis, we are bound to ask whether we can ultimately claim him for disability studies. The elusive status of impairment in his work makes no straightforward answer available. And yet I take a cue from Tagliaferri's "commitment to continue" in attempting to open up ways by which pain and the impaired body in Beckett are accounted for as a crucial step toward understanding his complex and elusive literary universe.

4

TONI MORRISON

*Disability, Ambiguity, and
Perspectival Modulations*

ORRISON'S WORK TELESCOPES A VARIETY OF CORPOREAL
differences onto the foreground of representation: black, female, and disabled. Even in *Playing in the Dark* (1992), her
book of interlinked essays in which she excavates the repeated tendency
in white American writing of aligning internal crises to socially governed
relationships with race, it is interesting to note that at least half of the
texts to which she pays close attention have to do with disability.[1] There
is not a single one of her novels published thus far that does not have at
least one disabled figure. As Rosemarie Garland Thomson (1997, 115–
116) persuasively argues, this choice of variant marginalities is a way of establishing affinities between historically peripheral figures in order to reclaim difference as a mode of reconfiguring the established orders of value
and validation. The disabilities Morrison depicts are both wide ranging
and variable, embracing cognitive and mental disorders, physical impairments, and what Thomson calls marks of "formal particularity" (119).

And yet disability in Morrison occupies a complex position. Unlike
the category of race, which in commentary on her work has often been
interpreted as a sociological marker of the condition of black people in
America, it would be a mistake to take disability in her work in the same

sociological vein. In her writing disability takes on the role of a polyvalent fulcrum within a larger discursive configuration, allowing a variety of meanings to radiate out of the disability as well as leading to a number of shifts and transformations in the very texture of the writing itself. The shifts and transformations may themselves be seen in terms of perspectival modulations; that is, they encourage us to always be prepared to shift perspectives along with the characters or with the overall structure of the novels.

As I hope to show, disability in Morrison often lends a peculiar symbolic charge to her characterization of the category. This symbolic charge is not, however, designed to generate singular or straightforward significance for her characters. Rather, there are various shifts that take place in the meanings that might be assigned to each disabled character, serving to place them within a wide spectrum of the typology of disability representation we outlined in chapter 2. The overall allusiveness of her characters' impairments leads to each of them potentially bringing together a multiplicity of conflicting and opposed values such as good/evil, maternality/infanticide, erotic love/divine love. The way that these sets are specifically and variously brought together frustrates our capacity for establishing any clear hierarchies among the several meanings that accrue to each disabled character. This refusal of hierarchies is itself manifested in the texture and complexity of Morrison's writing. Throughout her writing career she has experimented with different forms of narrative technique and has been keen to multiply narrative perspectives rather than settling on single viewpoints. Thus in *The Bluest Eye* (1970), the story is told predominantly from the perspective of a third-person narrator, but is also serially qualified by sections explicitly attributed to Claudia, Pauline, and, much later, to Pecola herself when she goes mad. By *Song of Solomon* (1977), this pursuit of multiple perspectives has become much more subtle, with the third-person narrator oscillating between different degrees of proximity and distance from the characters. The narrator of *Song of Solomon* also scrambles the sequence of events such that the reader is encouraged to participate in the labor of reassembling the story that unfolds while struggling to keep all the various perspectives in view simultaneously. This requirement for keeping various and often contradictory perspectives in view has implications for certain characters in the novel more than others. Thus Milkman has to understand the lessons about his heritage that Pilate gives him, but to do this properly he also has to place these lessons against the stories that his father tells him and alongside the bitter interpretations of the vengeful Seven Days, whose mouthpiece in the novel is his very good friend Guitar. In this way, Milkman's initially reluctant but later laborious interpretative exertions on the quest for his heritage mirror our own exertions in trying to piece together the meanings of the novel. *Beloved* and *Paradise* provide another installment of these perspectival modulations, again moving subtly in and out of different characters' perspectives while exploring issues of slavery, community, fragmentation, and tragedy.

What I am describing as perspectival modulations, however, go beyond the mere oscillation of narratorial perspective. This is particularly pertinent to the discussion of the disabled characters upon whom the perspectival modulations in the writing are centrally focused. We find on the whole that not only do the often opposing meanings that accrue to each disabled character resist clear hierarchization, but that the various meanings themselves shift, dissolve, and blur into one another, making the narratives performative in terms of the ways in which they constantly transform the discursive entities that are first proffered to us. The modulations that arise out of the allusiveness of disability have implications for the way that we understand different levels of the texts, such as in the relationship between past and present, between foreground and background, and between the characters' subjective perceptions of reality and the objective descriptions of reality that allow us to place them within various "real," as opposed to their own self-imagined, contexts. I shall show how several of these levels become pertinent to an understanding of the blindness of Consolata in *Paradise*. Close analysis of the range of meanings of the disabilities also shows, however, that there is a limit to the performativity of the Morrison text. This is particularly evident when disability is coupled with the theme of motherhood. Motherhood in Morrison is an unstable category that is both mythical and coupled with notions of death. Once we take disability and motherhood together, we see the interaction of sets of significations in which the disability serves to short-circuit the range of meanings that are attributable to motherhood. We shall see the significance of this short-circuiting with regard to Eva Peace in *Sula* and also in the relay of meanings that take place *between* Sethe and Baby Suggs in *Beloved*, both of whom carry impairments. Ultimately, my argument will be that the rapid perspectival modulations that Morrison's narratives enjoin of the reader are both enabled and frustrated by a primary focus on disability, but that this is inescapable, given that disability enters her text both as an image and as a highly complex ethical force field. Each text to be discussed will incrementally lead to our understanding of the parameters of this ethical force field.

Consolata and the Structure of Surrogacy

In *Paradise*, Consolata is a figure of blindness and insight, both literally and metaphorically. Rescued from certain destitution by a Catholic nun at the age of nine, she is taken into a convent and spends thirty years of her life offering her "body and soul to God's Son and His Mother as completely as if she had taken the veil herself" (225). Her dedication to God and to Mary Magna, the nun by whom she is adopted, is unwavering and complete until she falls in love with Deacon, one of a set of twins who helped found the black community of Ruby, not far from the convent where she lives with Mary Magna. The effect of the love affair and its aftermath are emotionally and spiritually damaging, yet they give her a quality of spiritual insight she did not possess before. However, the precise progress of the love affair and the unanticipated process of its dissolution bear exploration. For it is the intricate intertwining of erotic love with sacred sentiment that fragments her consciousness and inaugurates her new and fraught spirituality.

Consolata meets Deacon entirely by accident on a trip with Mary Magna into town to pick up some medicines. By chance, there is a horse race on at the same time, part of the celebrations to commemorate the founding of Ruby. The third-person narrator makes the horse race a discursively configured point from which various trajectories of the narrative take off, such as the stories that establish the characters of Billie Dean, KD, Deacon, and Consolata. Thus the horse race is a pregnant focal point of variant significations for several characters. Since it is such a significant radiating point and one to which we are invited to return at various stages over the course of the novel, it becomes a form of textual memory. This textual memory is only partially shared by the characters themselves; it is mainly given back to us later in an interwoven pattern of innuendoes, partial reflections, and fragmentary echoes.[2] Because Consolata, and indeed Mary Magna, are peripheral to the life of Ruby, their encounter with this highly pregnant narrative moment is represented with a veneer of awe and wonder:

> Even before they reached the newly cut road it was clear something was happening. Something unbridled was going on under the scalding sun. They could hear loud cheering, and instead of thirty or so energetic people going quietly about the business of making a town, they saw horses galloping off into yards, down the road, and people screaming with laughter. Small girls with red and purple flowers in their hair were jumping up and down. A boy holding for dear life onto a horse's neck was lifted off and declared winner. Young men and boys swung their hats, chased horses and wiped their brimming eyes. As Consolata watched that reckless joy, *she heard a faint but insistent Sha sha sha. Sha sha sha.* Then a memory of just such skin and just such men, dancing with women in the streets to music beating like an infuriated heart, torsos still, hips making small circles above legs moving so rapidly it was fruitless to decipher how such ease was possible. These men here were not dancing, however; they were laughing, running, calling to each other and to women doubled over in glee. And although they were living here in a hamlet, not in a loud city full of glittering black people, Consolata knew she knew them.
>
> (226; italics added)

The perspective is clearly that of Consolata herself, even if told from the standpoint of the third-person narrator. Words such as "unbridled" and the subtle but implicit judgment in the phrase "instead of . . . making a town" suggest the viewpoint of a character attempting to adjust to the surprise of the scene unfolding before her. The scene of reckless laughter and abandon acts like an objective correlative for the unbridled love Consolata is shortly going to experience. It is not insignificant that the scene evokes in her the memory of another such scene, presumably from the first nine years of her life in South America. It is almost as if the unfolding event triggers a sense of abandon that comes to overlay the scene and influence her judgment of it. At any rate, immediately after this she sees Deacon riding one horse and leading another: "His hips were rocking in the saddle, back and forth, back and forth. Sha sha sha. Sha sha

sha. Consolata saw his profile, and the wing of a feathered thing, undead, fluttered in her stomach" (226). The reference to rocking hips, which has already been mentioned as invoking a memory of things past is now rein-scribed in her consciousness with sexual connotations, and, more signifi-cantly, *aligned to a specific figure that has been separated from the general background of the pregnant scene.* The unfurling of the birdlike sensation in the pit of her stomach hints at a form of possession and loss, and to a feel-ing much too strong for easy conscious conceptualization.[3] Thus Deacon, though being seen for the first time, is recreated in her mind as something already known from her past. She falls in love with him completely, with a love that "after thirty-nine celibate years took on an edible quality" (228). The casual reference to the edible quality of her love will be echoed later and will attain an incremental significance, when after near-ly two years of lovemaking in fields and unexplored places she is faced with the prospect of losing him to his sense of marital responsibility and duty as one of the respectable elders of Ruby.

After two years of clandestine meetings, it is no longer possible for him to fulfill his increasingly irregular Friday midday trysts with her. Another way must be found. Consolata is desperate, and in her desperation she commits the cardinal error of attempting to eat him up (at least, that is how he sees it):

"Listen," she whispers. "There is a small room in the cellar. No. Wait, just listen. I will fix it, make it beautiful. With candles. It's cool and dark in the summer, warm as coffee in the winter. We'll have a lamp to see each other with, but nobody can see us. We can shout as loud as we want and nobody can hear. Pears are down there and walls of wine. The bottles sleep on their sides, and each one has a name, like Veuve Clic-quot or Medoc, and a number: 1-9-1-5 or 1-9-2-6, like prisoners waiting to be freed. Do it," she urges him. "Please do it. Come to my house."

While he considers, her mind races ahead with plans. Plans to cram rosemary into the pillow slips; rinse linen sheets in hot water steeped in cinnamon. They will slake their thirst with the prisoner wine, she tells him. He laughs a low, satisfied laugh and she bites his lip which, in retrospect, was her big mistake.

. . .

The poison spread. Consolata had lost him. Completely. Forever. His wife might not know it, but Consolata remembered his face. Not when she bit his lip, but when she hummed over the blood she licked from it. He'd sucked air sharply. Said, "Don't ever do that again." But his eyes, first startled, then revolted, had said the rest of what she should have known right away. Clover, cinnamon, soft old linen—who would chance pears and a wall of prisoner wine with a woman bent on eating him like a meal?

(237, 239)

Here, in Consolata's attempted conversion of amorous love into a sacred sacrament, the text makes plain a device of discursive structuration around Consolata's character that has been used to define her persistently from the beginning. This is the device of surrogacy or layering, in which one defining category, be it a described attitude, gesture, or feature of perception, becomes the surrogate for another category that is either parallel to or behind it. However, that other concealed category, once admitted to the foreground, forces a reconfiguration of the entire field of representation around the character; our understanding of the character in question is immediately shifted, leading to a modulation of our perspective. There are three areas in which this structure of surrogacy takes shape, two of which we have noted in passing: the love of God/amorous love, horse-race celebrations/city dancers from childhood, and blindness/ insight. These three sets are discursively quite different, even if mutually defining of Consolata's characterization. Love of God/amorous love are inextricably linked because of the overlap in the two poles of the binary opposition through the key term "love." Coming from the breast of a dedicated but fragmented consciousness, the love of God may be expressed simultaneously in the form of love of man, which is what we see in Consolata's case. The horse-race celebrations/city dancers from childhood pair, on the other hand, are linked by being metonymic displacements of the idea of abandon along a temporal axis. In other words, both scenes invoke the idea and indeed a feeling of deep abandon and therefore become contiguously connected in her consciousness even though separated by a period of nearly thirty years. In the blindness/insight pair, the two items in the set are connected by being dialectical antinomies of each other: to go blind in most tragic literature is often linked to gaining special ethical or spiritual insight. This pair mirrors the category of disability as providing special ritual insight, which we noted in chapter 2, except that since it is not autonomous as a binary but is closely associated with others within the structure of surrogacy, it would be inadequate to fit it solely into that category of disability representation.

To fully understand the status of Consolata's later blindness and the uncanny spiritual insight that comes out of it, we are obliged to fully grasp the nature of the structure of surrogacy that defines the first two sets of concepts. Whereas the God/amorous love set is wholly abstract and the blindness/insight set is partially so (blindness is represented but insight has to be inferred), the horse-race celebrations/city dancers set is entirely concrete in terms of the material representation that it is accorded in the text. And yet it is the horse-race celebrations/city dancers set that triggers the inexorable process by which the other sets are going to be radically inverted in a restless movement within the discursive configuration centered on the character. We can then see that the structure of surrogacy also governs the relationship between different conceptual sets, the materially represented horse race set acting as a surrogate for the series of transpositions whose force is only made manifest when we place all three sets alongside one another and perceive the rapid discursive oscillations established among them.

It is evident from the text that Consolata's religious dedication stands in a peculiar relationship to her love and gratitude to Mary Magna for rescuing her and loving her as her own child. In fact, Mary Magna is called by that name late in the novel; when we first encounter her in an earlier chapter (which is set in a period temporally subsequent to the chapter in which the horse race-celebrations are found), she is on her deathbed and being tended by the already blind Consolata. In that earlier chapter, she is just called Mother. Concomitantly, in the earlier chapter Consolata is known simply as Connie, with no hint whatsoever of her deeply religious impulses. So uncompromising is Connie's dedication to tending Mother that all the other women who happen upon the convent at that time think it is a real mother-daughter relationship. Thus Consolata's love of God is also shown to be a conduit for expressing familial sentiments, the direct source and object of this being Mary Magna/Mother. The thing to note about the relationship between the familial and divine loves here is that the religious domain, though clearly at the foreground of the chapter devoted to Consolata, is placed in the background of the narrative for much of the novel, until we get to the horse race chapter.

Since we are introduced to her as Connie earlier on and she is referred to by that name until very late in the novel, it comes as something of a surprise that she had an identity completely different from what we had been led to assume from the earlier context we were given. In other words, what is really a religious structure of feeling around Consolata is not displayed as such for much of the novel, but is narratively withheld in order to provide a focus for an example of filial love and duty. Thus when we come to Consolata's chapter (each chapter is named after a different female character), we are forced by the narrative into the first of a series of perspectival modulations, shifting our earlier understandings of her as a slightly absentminded but loving surrogate daughter to one who has an immense sense of religious devotion and who is actually not related to the person she is shown caring for.

Contrastively, Consolata's love for Deacon is plainly the profanation of her love of God. When she attempts to "eat him up," as he sees it, it represents the sudden rupturing of the amorous love by the divine love that has been dormant in the background of her characterization until that point. The trajectory of the movement of these loves may be displayed as follows: familial love → love of the divine → amorous love → and back to divine love, except that what we have defined linearly does not fully encapsulate the complex intertwining of the various levels of love, especially toward the end of the Consolata chapter. What we see then is that the "/" between the binary pair love of God/amorous love defines a process of extremely restless movement between the two that is neither linear nor amenable to any easy hierarchical schematization. That is what the narrative discourse, seen not in its individual elements but in relation to the totality of elements working together, gives us to understand. The rupturing of amorous love by divine love has dramatic consequences, for not only does it generate acute confusion for Consolata, a confusion that is a mixture of regret, loss, and guilt, it also institutes the process by which the phenomenal world recedes from her and becomes internalized as a series of vague correlatives of emotion and spirituality within her own psyche.

In the immediate aftermath of her loss of Deacon, the narrator tells us that "the next few days were one long siege of sorrow" and that "romance stretched to breaking point broke, exposing a simple transfer" (240). The "simple transfer" that is exposed here is the transfer of divine love into an earthly domain, its articulation not as divine but as erotic. On returning to the fold, she is taken by Mary Magna for absolution in the chapel. As always, Mary Magna is full of understanding for whatever has happened to her surrogate daughter without her having to explain anything. It is when they step out of the chapel into the sunlight that the process that will lead to Consolata's blindness begins. In this context, Mary Magna's understanding without the need for words is both poignant and misplaced, since it depends on an uncertain grasp of what exactly Consolata has really been through:

> Consolata virtually crawled back to the chapel (wishing fervently that He could be there, glowing red in the dim light. . . . "*Dear Lord, I didn't want to eat him. I just wanted to go home.*"
>
> Mary Magna came into the chapel and, kneeling with her, put an arm around Consolata's shoulder, saying, "At last."
>
> "You don't know," said Consolata.
>
> "I don't need to, child."
>
> "But he, but he." Sha sha sha. Sha sha sha, she wanted to say, meaning, he and I are the same.
>
> "Sh sh sh. Sh sh sh." Said Mary Magna. Never speak of him again.
>
> She might not have agreed so quickly, but as Mary Magna led her out of the chapel into the schoolroom, a sunshot seared her right eye, announcing the beginning of her bat vision, and she began to see best in the dark. Consolata had been spoken to.
>
> (240–241; italics added)

It is not insignificant that she tells the Lord that she "just wanted to go home," thus suggesting a homology in her consciousness between the three levels of the familial, the amorous, and the divine, which we have already seen being worked out discursively in the chapter. Between the "Sha sha sha" of amorous love and the "Sh sh sh" of enjoined silence and contemplation lies the sudden abbreviation of her identity. This, however, is an abbreviation that implies not a severance of an already whole self, but the internalization of one self that has always been enamored of the phenomenal world into another self that refigures this phenomenal world into the internal world of spirit. On this reading, the affective transfer stretched over the horse-race celebrations/city dancers from childhood binary pair gains further significance. For what is invoked in her memory when she sees the horse-race celebrations is a self that has not been properly acknowledged, and which then becomes progressively foregrounded as her relationship with Deacon unfolds. With the loss of Deacon and the onset of her "bat vision," that self is then reassimilated into an internal chamber of the psyche that then offers the ground upon which a new form of spirituality is defined. In this way, as noted earlier, the horse-race celebrations scene is a trigger for a chain of restless significations, all of which transform, shift, and force us to modulate our perspective of the character of Consolata.

An additional way of interpreting her blindness is that Consolata becomes her own sacrament, and that in trying to eat up the object of amorous love she succeeds in internalizing a part of her own self. The blindness is not merely a punishment, as the narrator implies by her remark that she had been "spoken to." Consolata's progressive blindness is a signal of the position of liminality that she has implicitly occupied from the beginning. Her liminality derives from the fact that she straddles three worlds of sentiment simultaneously—familial, divine, amorous—with none of these allowed ascendancy over the others within her psyche. Crucially, her blindness allows her to understand the world better, for now the outside world has been fully integrated into her internal world in the necessary process of spiritual self-discovery. It is out of this liminality, which is at once profane and numinous, that her new spiritual tasks are defined. The first of these tasks is what Lone calls "stepping in." But what Lone defines for Consolata as her duty to use her new spiritual strength to restore the dead to life is only a staging post for a definition of a much larger and more difficult task: the saving of the living from a living death. It is to this task that she turns in the séance we find at the end of the chapter in an attempt to rescue the convent women from their pasts and liberate them into ownership of their own bodies. As the narrator tells us in announcing the séance: "Gradually they lost the days." The women undress and lie in relaxed postures on the cold uncompromising floor. They lie completely still in the mould that they have created on the bare floor, and then Consolata speaks to them, first about her mistake in almost eating up her love, and then, gradually, about an imagined place of spiritual freedom. Significantly, the place that she describes is saturated with sensual details and appeals to a full perspectival sensorium:

Then, in words clearer than her introductory speech (which none of them understood), she told them of a place where white sidewalks met the sea and fish the color of plums swam alongside children. She spoke of fruit that tasted the way sapphires look and boys using rubies for dice. Of scented cathedrals made of gold where gods and goddesses sat in the pews with the congregation. Of carnations tall as trees. Dwarfs with diamonds for teeth. Snakes aroused by poetry and bells. Then she told them of a woman named Piedade, who sang but never said a word.

(263–264)

This is the Paradise of the title. But to get there, the women have to claim their bodies for themselves and away from the traumatic histories that have marked these bodies. And so they begin the "loud dreaming." These dreams entail half-tales and never-dreamed-of things escaping from each individual and mixing with the others' dreams. And in the loud dreaming "monologue is no different from a shriek; accusations directed to the dead and long gone are undone by murmurs of love" (264). This process continues from January to May, until it is noticeable even by casual observers that "unlike some people in Ruby, the Convent women were no longer haunted. Or hunted either . . ." (266). In this way, the now blind Consolata "lends" her spiritual insight to these lost women. They benefit from her position as spiritual beacon that modulates spirituality for the discovery of their own hidden selves. Consolata has performed a role that transcends even that attributed to the Greek Tiresias: though blind, she gives others the capacity of claiming the full force of their lives, but lives that are understood as simultaneously encapsulating a beclouded past, a confused present, and a liberated future within each moment.

The contrast with Beckett's Molloy, whom we encountered in the previous chapter, is telling. In the case of Molloy, we are not told how he managed to arrive at his mental state of immersion within the plenitude of existence. However, being a first-person narration, we get a more intimate and direct sense of how he converts objects of the phenomenal world into a universe of his own interlocution. Molloy comes across as a much more self-involved character than Consolata, for unlike Molloy, who appears to be completely satisfied with the categories generated by the structures of doubt within his own mind, Consolata is bewildered by her internal states and desires to love the world in whatever way she can. She achieves this by providing an unquestioning haven for the many women who drift into the convent; later, in a powerful reclamation of her spiritual power of reconstituting identity, she helps the women reclaim their bodies by immersing themselves within the plenitude of the immediate, an immediate, however, that has been corrected by being opened up to the shaded saturations of the multiple and traumatic identities that have shaped their world.

Beyond Consolata, the convent itself is also defined by way of opposing elements. It had first been the mansion of a wealthy embezzler before being bought up by the religious order, and it is populated by features that define liminality and in-betweenness in its architecture and interior design. It is this mixing of the sacred and the profane that induces the chauvinistic men from Ruby to shudder in their contemplation of what they interpret to be the utter depravity of the convent women. For them, the perspectival modulation that is required for a proper understanding of the confusing objects that they see before them is short-circuited by their sense of threat and the desire to dominate and control the women. The modulation of perspective, which, as we have seen, is a dominant feature of the narrative itself, is not something that is reflected in the characterization of the Ruby men. For them, no provisional judgments are tolerated; they are desperate for manageable certainties. The contrast with Consolata is complete. It is a contrast that is manifest mainly in the nature of her disability, which allows her an insight that is not given to others, and most definitely not to the men of Ruby. They bear a moral deficit that shows itself in their terror of what they cannot understand. No such elaborate and rich discursive transformations are evident around any other character in the novel except for Consolata. Thus it is Consolata, a disabled character, that becomes the fulcrum around which the narrative distinguishes its rhetorical and ethical registers. Her blindness and the entire process by which she becomes blind is itself a focal point for structuring the perspectival modulations that are necessary for interpreting a novel as complex and richly textured as *Paradise*.

Eva Peace: Reorienting Motherhood and Caregiving

Of those with manifest physical disabilities in Toni Morrison's work, the character with the greatest vitality by far is *Sula*'s Eva Peace. Eva is the direct opposite of a character such as Polly Breedlove in *The Bluest Eye*. For Polly Breedlove, her bad foot is initially the grounds for pity, the reason why, on first seeing her, Cholly feels an overwhelming desire of protection. It is described as an "archless foot that flopped when she walked—not a limp that would eventually twist her spine, but a way of lifting the bad foot as though she were extracting it from little whirlpools that threatened to pull her under" (86). Polly always thinks about her foot. The disabled foot is a sign of the disjunctiveness of her imagined world, something that is given particular poignancy in the scene where she goes to the cinema and her tooth drops out of her mouth. She is so devastated by this that after that she settles for "just being ugly" (95–96).

No contrast could be sharper than that between Polly Breedlove and Eva Peace in the novels that, respectively, are first and second in Morrison's oeuvre. In contrast to Polly's childhood impairment, we see Eva's deliberate choice to put her leg on the train track in order to claim the insurance money that would free her from poverty and enable her to look after her children. (The business of her amputated leg is something the narrator is elusive about. We are never certain what exactly happened, but the narrator does not confirm or deny the generally held view in the community that Eva deliberately had her leg run over by a train.) For Polly's lack of vitality, we see Eva's epic claiming not just of her own body but also of the bodies of those closest to her. Eva performs a series of deity-like functions and acts like a goddess: naming people, being worshiped by people, and ultimately coolly deciding the manner of her son Plum's death.[4] Significantly however, she performs all these functions out of compassion rather than out of any desire for self-aggrandizement. This is what reinforces her status as a secular goddess figure within the narrative.

Also in contrast to Polly is Eva's sexuality. Polly's sexuality is hardly pertinent to how we might interpret her, save for her attempt to imagine herself as one of the film stars she so admires, something that ends in complete and unmitigated disaster, as we have noted. Eva's sexuality, on the other hand, is a choice she exercises and through which she defines the ethos of her entire household. The particular sexuality of the women in her household is called "manlove." Manloving women exist as sexually desiring subjects/agents rather than as mere objects of male desire. More significantly, they want to experience men without necessarily acquiescing to the patriarchal codes that often define male-female relationships. They also signal the model of a counterfamily, something that Morrison returns to elaborate again in Song of Solomon and Beloved and to which she gives a most forceful expression in Paradise. Whereas Eva's daughter

Hannah ripples with sex and lusts for other people's husbands without passing judgment on either them or their wives, Eva's manlove is expressed as the slow but steady erasure of men's desire for competition and individualism. Even though she sits in an improvised wheelchair made out of a wagon, people looking down at her get the impression they are looking *up* into her eyes, rather than down into them.

> One of her men friends had fashioned a kind of wheelchair for her: a rocking-chair top fitted into a large child's wagon. In this contraption she wheeled around the room, from bedside to dresser to the balcony that opened out the north side of her room or to the window that looked out on the back yard. The wagon was so low that children who spoke to her standing up were eye level with her, and adults, standing or sitting, had to look down at her. But they didn't know it. They all had the impression that they were looking up at her, up into the open spaces of her eyes, up into the soft black of her nostrils and up at the crest of her chin.
>
> (*Sula*, 31)

All these details help to reinforce the generally held critical view of Eva's power and agency, which is of course not to be easily dismissed. However, there is at least one area that this view somewhat ignores. This is in the contradictory relationship between disability and caregiving, and the degree to which the ambiguities that disabled caregivers feel about themselves affect the ways in which they enact caregiving for others, whether these be their own offspring or those closest to them. The matter is already fraught for nondisabled women with children with disabilities, but becomes accentuated when it is the mother, as primary caregiver, who is the one with a disability.[5]

The relationship between disability, motherhood, and caregiving becomes particularly salient in view of the fact that the normate world has a specific view of what it is to be a mother. This is further concentrated and reenacted in the practices of health-care professionals, most of whom come to their task with a specific idea about the role of maternal caregiving. Barbara Hillyer (1993) writes about her firsthand experience of this, having had to deal with professionals around her disabled daughter Jennifer for many years. Jennifer had a number of disabilities but no major medical problems. Yet the list of health-care professionals with whom she and her mother had to contend is truly formidable: psychologists, social workers, a physical therapist, nurses, a neurologist, a neuropsychologist, an orthopedist, a cardiologist, an ear-nose-and-throat specialist, an audiologist, a family doctor, an eye doctor, a dentist, an orthodontist, three surgeons, special-education teachers, school counselors, vocational trainers, psychometrists, sheltered workshop coordinators, several home caregivers, and nine or more attendants each day for seven years. These healthcare professionals participated in the daughter's life in an ongoing way. More critically, most of them were women, and they all had ideas about what her mother should do (176–177). Furthermore, as Hillyer points out, mother-blaming is ubiquitous in the professional literature about disability, with the commonest of negative judgments being that mothers are "overanxious, overprotective, out of touch with reality, guilt-ridden, arrested in denial, malicious, indifferent, emotionally divorced, lacking in empathy, rejecting, unconcerned, overinvolved, hysterical, and/or emotional" (90). The attitudes that inform the discourse of professionals already has an echo within the minds of the mothers themselves, as most cultures enforce a particular view of what it is to be a mother. The sense of responsibility that mothers of children with disabilities feel is conjoined to a feeling of impotence in not being able to alleviate the suffering of their loved ones. At the same time, there are also the vague but persistent worries about the implications for self-actualization. As is well known, families with severely disabled children often tend to suffer the economic effects of the high cost of care. Quite often, it is mothers or other female members of the family who are required to hold themselves back from actualizing their own aspirations in order to "be there" (whether financially, physically, or emotionally) for the children with disabilities. The effect on the self-image of the maternal primary caregiver is often damaging, leading to an oscillation between self-blame and resentment, on the one hand, and extreme feelings of self-sacrifice, on the other. Ambiguity thus becomes constitutive for the maternal primary caregiver of the child with a disability.

As mentioned previously, the issue is rendered more complicated when it is the mother who is the bearer of the disability and who has to try to both care for her children and protect them from the apparent effects of her own difficulties. A poignant sense of this is captured in the biographical narrative of Ellie O'Sullivan (1994). A social worker from the local council comes to O'Sullivan's home to ascertain her needs. The social worker and O'Sullivan go through the entire apartment, arriving finally in the bathroom. O'Sullivan desperately needs an expensive gadget that would allow her to enter and leave the bath on her own without calling on her husband for assistance. The critical moment of vulnerability for her and the fraught links between maternal caregiving and selfhood is best relayed in her own words, which we are obliged to quote at some length:

"And the bathroom?"
I feel hot, the room is too hot.
I must tell her about the bath.

If only Charlotte weren't here. If only she'd go downstairs. If only someone would ring for her, because I have to tell about the business of the bath.

I must tell the woman about how when Pete helps me out of the bath I am afraid. I am afraid that he will damage himself. It is an awkward movement bending to lift someone out of a bath and I am afraid I will be too heavy for him and that he will fall and I will fall with him. But I am also afraid when I struggle alone. My legs will not do what is necessary and I can no longer remember how they ever did. So I am afraid as I lever myself up on to the back of the bath.

And I have another fear—I remember the time sitting in the bath. I am ready to get out but I cannot. I call for Pete but he cannot hear me. I call and call until I am afraid that I shall never be heard. And this makes me so afraid that I stop calling. And I start to cry and I cannot stop. Pete comes and he is overwhelmed with remorse because he did not hear. And my daughter comes and sees her mother in the bath unable to get out, and she cries with shock and fear.

So I must tell this woman about the problem of the bath. But I want my daughter to go downstairs. I don't want her to see how much I need something to get in and out of the bath without being afraid. But I know that the bath chair, which is what I need, is a costly item and I must make my case convincing, so I must tell this woman. But my child is here and I don't want her to know how helpless I am. But I need the bath chair because I am so afraid of falling, falling and not being heard.

I know that Charlotte is no longer reading, that she is listening as I tell this stranger about my helplessness. I want to turn to her, to tell her that it is only this one thing, that she needn't worry. But I can't.

(1994, 16–17)

It has to be noted in passing that the careworker did not show adequate sensitivity to the interview context; she should have at the very least tried to deflect Charlotte's attention so that her mother didn't have to contend with the contradictory task of simultaneously persuading her of the need for the equipment *and* having to protect her daughter from witnessing her vulnerability at this point. Ellie O'Sullivan is worried about her husband's back, haunted by the traumatic memory of being left alone in the bath, and yet, at the same time, extremely concerned about what the effect of this dangerous knowledge might be on her daughter. Her physical needs, though absolutely pressing, seem momentarily to be placed on an equal footing with the need for her to appear as a capable mother. The constitutive ambiguity we see here is derived from the internalized expectation of what it is to be a mother, yet this internalized expectation is challenged by the physical needs of the impaired body.

Returning to Eva Peace, it is interesting to note that the constitutive ambiguity between disability and caregiving is rendered utterly invisible or at least not consequential *at the foreground of represented actions*. The contrast between represented actions and discursive dispositions is significant, because it is this that allows readers to ignore the contradiction, since the foreground seems to obliterate or at least conceal what is really the complex interlinking of the characters' actions and gestures with more subtle discursive significations. All we are allowed to see of Eva is empowerment without self-doubt, self-assertion without ambivalence, and a wholly coherent sense of identity that does not reflect the reality of the socialized domain within which disability finds its meanings. It is true that by noting this textual ambiguity I am by implication asking the realist text to be accountable in terms of its verisimilitude and that the representation be somehow "true" to the reality that it might purportedly be taken to reflect. But that is not the point I want to make here. The point is rather to highlight the fact that in recuperating a figure such as Eva for a discussion of the empowerment of women with disabilities, we have to properly take account of the totality of the artistic representation and not just the aspects in which she appears to be unproblematically empowered. Reading more closely, we find that there are different levels of "truth" to be explored, all of which are not necessarily coherent and mutually reinforcing.

And so we come to an odd detail about Eva. As noted earlier, it is never made clear how exactly she sustained the injury that led to the amputation of her leg. Rumor had it that she deliberately placed her leg on a railway track. The problem with this communal rumor is that it would have been manifestly impossible for Eva to determine the exact nature of the injury that would ensue from such a deliberate collision with a train *ahead* of the collision itself. It is not even clear from the text whether her left leg was amputated below the knee or above it, at mid-thigh. What is clear is that if she had deliberately placed her leg in the path of the train it would not have left her other leg in a shape to be admired. And yet we are told that "Whatever the fate of her lost leg, the remaining one was magnificent" (31). What posture might one adopt in surrendering a leg to a fast-moving train that would ensure the remaining leg would not only be undamaged but also magnificent? Is it not more likely that the damage would have extended well beyond the injured leg, perhaps affecting other parts of the body and causing major and irreparable damage? Far from being overly concerned with verisimilitude, these questions reveal the futility of seeking precise answers about Eva's disability. For that is the point: her missing leg is described in vague terms precisely in order to focus attention *away from it* as an object in itself. Its value is more symbolic than real; our attention is directed away from it and onto the other qualities that serve to characterize her personality. It is not for nothing then that "fewer than nine people in the town remembered when Eva had two legs, and her oldest child, Hannah, was not one of them" (31). The townspeople pretended to ignore it, and it was never spoken about unless "in some mood of fancy, she began some fearful story about it—generally to entertain children" (31). The stories she tells the children serve to mythify her disability. This mythification is conjoined to her quasi-deific qualities, thus suggesting that she is to be read not just as a real character, but as a symbol of something much larger and elusive. Once read in this way, the novel's elusiveness about the source of her impairment renders it the signal of liminality, thus placing the impairment itself on the borderline between reality and symbol. We are invited to interpret the absent leg both as the sign of a real and manifest impairment, and, *at the same time*, as the insignia of a quasi-mythical aspect.

In her killing of Plum, however, her quasi-mythical status is partially short-circuited by being conjoined to another dimension of ambiguity. In this case, her quasi-deific status as dispenser of life and death comes to coincide problematically with the constitutive ambiguity inherent in her role as disabled mother. This constitutive ambiguity—constitutive because it is inherent in her role as mother *and* as a person with a disability as such—is more or less in suspension until the point at which she kills Plum, when it suddenly forces itself to the foreground of her characterization and invites us to reinterpret her earlier deific status. The process of this textual inruption is itself quite subtle and has to be attended to carefully.

On returning from the war in 1921, Plum confines himself to his bedroom, doing as little as possible and foraying out sporadically only to get himself high on drugs. Eva hobbles into his room one day when he is asleep, douses him with kerosene, and calmly sets him on fire. She closes the door after her and hobbles back upstairs. To all intents and purposes, she is actualizing the implications of the quasi-deific status we have associated her with up to this point. However, of peculiar interest with regard to this horrific act is her response two chapters later to a question Hannah poses, singing the words like a small child saying a piece at Easter: "Mamma, did you ever love us?" The passage continues:

> Eva, who was just sitting there fanning herself with the cardboard fan from Mr. Hodges's funeral parlor, listened to the silence that followed Hannah's words. . . .
>
> "Now," Eva looked up across from her wagon at her daughter. "Give me that again. Flat out to fit my head."
>
> "I mean, did you? You know, when we was little."
>
> Eva's hand moved snail-like down her thigh toward her stump, but stopped short of it to realign a pleat. "No, I don't reckon I did. Not the way you thinkin'."
>
> "Oh, well. I was just wonderin'." Hannah appeared to be through with the subject.
>
> "An evil wonderin' if I ever heard one." Eva was not through.
>
> . . .
>
> "But what about Plum? What'd you kill Plum for, Mamma?"
>
> . . .
>
> Hannah was waiting. Watching her mother's eyelids. When Eva spoke at last it was with two voices. Like two people were talking at the same time, saying the same thing, one a fraction of a second behind the other.
>
> (66, 71; italics added)

The reference to words sang at Easter is not to be taken idly, as they provide allusions to Christian religious sacrifice, the sacrament, and so on. And it is also pertinent that Eva is at this point fanning herself with a fan from "Mr. Hodge's funeral parlor," the realist detail immediately importing a vague whiff of the morbid into the scene. In giving her answer, Eva speaks in two voices at the same time, almost as if articulating a self-division that makes itself manifest at precisely the moment when her maternal instincts are being questioned. The two voices represent a splitting and the very site of the constitutive ambiguity that emerges out of the coincidence of disability and maternal caregiving. Paying attention to the totality of both her gestural and verbal responses to Hannah's question, we cannot but notice that when the question is posed, Eva first makes as if to stroke her stump. But instead of doing this, she reorders the pleats in her skirt. The pleats immediately act as a form of concealment and at the same time as the metonymic displacement of the stump. The gesture then becomes a nervous reaction, setting up a discursive relationship between her views on motherhood and her physical disability. The two must then be taken by the reader as mutually defining and acquiring meaning from each other.

Her answer in the end is that she had wanted to prevent Plum from crawling back into her womb. She had dreamt of him crawling up the stairs as a full-grown man, trying to pry her legs open to get back into her womb. To prevent this from materializing in reality, she killed him. She said she had to keep him out so she thought of a way he could die not all scrunched up inside her womb, but like a man. In other words, she wanted him to die not infantilized, as was likely if he followed his drug habit, but heroically, as a man would die in a war. However, despite her answer, we may also interpret her act as not so much the unproblematic assertion of love in an attempt to save him from an unheroic death but rather as her way of expressing her anguish at not being able to save her son from what was clearly a path toward self-destruction. Plum's return produces a site for the intensification of her ambivalence as a disabled mother toward a son who is clearly in a deep existential crisis but whom she cannot save.[6] Her terrible act is then a futile attempt to remove him as a challenge to her capacity to love unambiguously. In other words, her son confronts her with the failure of her love, something she deals with by staging a heroic death for him and thus enacting directly her role of deity. Yet in acting as deity she also simultaneously accentuates the anguish of her role as a mother with disability, in this case signaled after the fact by her unconscious reaching for her stump when Hannah poses the terrible question. There is then an inextricable connection between her deific functions, her maternal articulations, and the ambiguities produced by the fact that she has a disability. By first recognizing that her son is heading for disaster and then proceeding to kill him in such dramatic fashion, Eva enacts the violent form of projection of an unruly part of her psyche outward in order better to manage and contain the constitutive ambiguities of being a disabled mother. This unruly part may arguably be connected to an absence, which in the novel is marked both by the loss of her leg and by the rumors of the violent way in which that loss is sustained. In other words, even though in the foreground of representation Eva portrays a veneer of calm, given the total economy of her discursive representation we cannot but link her subliminally to a form of violence. It is a violence "done" to her by the vagaries of dispossession and of which her stump is a permanent symbolic token. At the same time, this violence is also internalized as part of the duality of her psyche as a disabled mother. In the killing of Plum, these various dimensions of violence and the ambiguities that they bring forth are manifest in the singular tragic gesture.

The killing of Plum and Hannah's subsequent question come together as sites of the intensification of the constitutive ambiguity for the disabled mother. When, later in the novel, Eva jumps out of her second-floor bedroom window to smother her burning daughter's body with her own, she articulates the extremes of both sides of the disabled mother's ambiguous maternality. In the first instance, she takes Plum's life to save him from what she takes to be certain destruction; in the second, she takes a chance with her own life to save her daughter from the real threat of a fiery death. What joins both actions is not just the presence of fire in the death of the two children, but the fact that Eva moves from the extremes of infanticide to salvational self-immolation for the sake of her children. The two incidents mirror the internal necessity of extreme acts of love as definitive of maternality. And yet I want to suggest that the two extremes are a manifest enactment of the constitutive ambiguities that pertain to her role as disabled mother. The uneasy location of her character between realism and myth is then further intensified by the oscillation between the two opposing poles of motherhood and death. Both sides of the equation do not remain static as binary oppositions but coalesce restlessly around her, thus helping to define her liminality as multifocal (realism/myth; maternal love/infanticide) and indeed highly resonant for the ways in which we might interpret her character as a refraction of the contradictions inherent in the lives of disabled primary caregivers in reality. The central difference between Eva and Consolata in terms of the ways in which discursive effects are constructed around their disabilities is that in the case of the former, the narrative of *Sula* is essentially linear and sequential, thus placing what appears to be an ineluctable process of narrative unfoldment at the foreground of the text. This essential linearity encourages us to take the empowerment of the character at face value. *Paradise*, on the other hand, is scrupulously nonlinear and enjoins us to be alert to the shifts, turns, and restless movements of the text. It is this that gives salience to the structure of surrogacy we noted in our discussion of Consolata, even though, strictly speaking, we might be able to speak of degrees of the same discursive effects in both novels.

Negative Epiphanies in *Beloved*

Eva's killing of Plum puts her immediately in the company of Sethe in Morrison's *Beloved*, and, behind Sethe, of the Greek Medea. As with Eva, in the case of Sethe there is also a moment of the irrevocable coupling of motherhood and violence. Despite the similarity of the two women, there is something that Eva has that Sethe lacks throughout *Beloved*, and that is the sense of empowerment and entitlement that Eva possesses as a natural part of her character. For unlike Eva and Medea, Sethe's terrible choice is not the attempt to assert control over events; rather, it is the problematic and desperate attempt to exit her tragic history. Though ennobling, the effort to kill her own children as a means of helping them escape the horrors of slavery is also simultaneously the sign of her concession of defeat. Furthermore, unlike Eva, Sethe is arguably not in full control of her senses at the point of the infanticide.

There are three significant differences that need to be noted between *Sula* and *Beloved*. First is that *Beloved* references many more disabled characters at various points in the narrative, such as Baby Suggs, of whom we will have more to say shortly; Sethe's mother, who had a bit in her mouth so many times that her own smile had been replaced by a permanent smile; Nan, the one-armed woman who breastfed the children on the slave plantation; and Sethe herself. Sethe's disability falls under the category described by Rosemarie Garland Thomson as a mark of "formal particularity." The mark of the chokecherry tree on her back was placed there by the whip of the slaveowner. Thus *Beloved* gives us many more possibilities for interpreting disability than we find in *Sula*. Second, all the disabilities referenced in the novel are directly attributable to the system of slavery. In other words, slavery is shown to be overdetermining in terms of the effects it has on the bodies of these individuals and thus on their self-imaginings. But third, and perhaps most significant for our interpretation, is the degree of interiority that the characters are permitted in the narration of events. In *Beloved*, the third-person narration unfolds in close proximity to the consciousness of the characters themselves. Since all the characters, and especially Sethe, have been victims of the traumatic experiences of slavery, the narrative is concomitantly fragmentary and shifts constantly between the immediate represented foreground and the events that lie in the past but which constantly intrude into the consciousness of the present. With the exception of the eponymous heroine and, to a different degree, Shadrack, none of the characters in *Sula* are fully interiorized.

Sethe tries unsuccessfully to "keep the past at bay," for her past continually intrudes into her present and interdicts her very capacity to keep that past in quarantine:

Unfortunately her brain was devious. She might be hurrying across a field, running practically, to get to the pump quickly and rinse the chamomile sap from her legs. Nothing else would be in her mind. The picture of the men coming to nurse her was as lifeless as the nerves in her back where the skin buckled like a washboard. Nor was there the faintest scent of ink or the cherry gum and oak bark from which it was made. Nothing. Just the breeze cooling her face as she rushed toward water. And then sopping the chamomile away with pump water and rags, her mind fixed on getting every last bit of sap off—on her carelessness in taking a shortcut across the field just to save a half mile, and not noticing how high the weeds had grown until the itching was all the way to her knees. Then something. The plash of water, the sight of her shoes and stockings awry on the path where she had flung them; or

Here Boy lapping in the puddle near her feet, and suddenly there was Sweet Home rolling, rolling, rolling out before her eyes, and although there was not a leaf on that farm that did not make her want to scream, it rolled itself out before her in shameless beauty. It never looked as terrible as it was and it made her wonder if hell was a pretty place too. Fire and brimstone all right, but hidden in lacy groves. . . .

(*Beloved*, 6)

As we see from this passage, the third-person narrator is completely at one with Sethe's own consciousness. More important, however, is the fact that her perspectival sensorium seems to be suddenly intensified by what on the surface appear to be quite mundane details in her immediate environment: the plash of water, the sight of her shoes and stockings awry, and the sight of Here Boy. Suddenly, an entire scene that lies in the past obtrudes into the present and unfurls itself, as if it is no longer part of the past but coexists with the present. In a split second, her senses are accentuated, not in order that she might experience the present in all its sensual fullness, but that the present might reveal itself as a container of previous moments, as if defining a granulated reality.

The obtrusion of the past into the present is a form of interdiction or arrest of the present. For what it implies is that both past and present are abolished in an instant and that she experiences them with *equivalent immediacy*. Thus the relation of depth and hierarchy between the time frames of past and present cannot be experienced as such, but rather as shifting sides of the same immediate experience. There are two possible reasons we can adduce for this. One has directly to do with Sethe's trauma. Having lived a terribly traumatic past, it is no wonder that the negative affect of the trauma refuses to lie in the past but comes back to color the present. Sethe herself provides an explanation for this in what she describes to Denver as "her rememory" (35–36).[7] What is not so evident, however, is that these traumatic leakages produce a hermeneutical conundrum. Essentially, this is because the interdiction of the present by her traumatic past is in the form of what appear to be epiphanies. However, the function of these epiphanies is not to produce a sense of integration or wholeness, as epiphanic moments in literature are often assumed to do, but to generate disjuncture and fragmentation.[8] They are negative epiphanies. But as epiphanies they also leave an interpretative residue for the character and the reader, coming together to define the relationships between character and event, between past and present, and between narrative structure and content. It is the peculiar character of these negative epiphanies that allow Sethe to come to an interpretative intuition of the notion of rememory. Read in this way we might then reinterpret the entire "poeticized" sections in part 2 of the novel (206–217) as a serialization of such interpretative epiphanies for each of the three characters Sethe, Beloved, and Denver. The last two pages of the novel, where there is an incantatory repetition of the formula "It is not a story to pass on," is then the refusal of the invitation to interpret lodged in the string of epiphanies that have littered the text. For each element invoked in those closing pages—bad dream, a photograph, the stream, and the footprints— are phenomena that are saturated with the past. Yet rather than take up the invitation to interpret these phenomena, it is implied that the community must "remember to forget." In other words, there is a conscious decision not to allow the past to swamp the present via any such mundane details that are nonetheless pregnant epiphanies.

It is in focusing on the idea of negative epiphanies that we see that the text also ascribes a tragic interpretative position to Baby Suggs. Even though Sethe is close to Eva in their giving and taking of their children's lives, it is Baby Suggs who, having a physical disability, allows us to see in starker terms the constitutive ambiguities of motherhood and disability. Baby Suggs is herself connected to Eva Peace through a number of fascinating discursive links established between *Sula* and *Beloved*. A hip injury ensures that Baby Suggs "walks like a three legged dog" (140); furthermore, "her hip hurt every single day—but she never spoke of it" (139), recalling Eva's silence regarding her stump. When Eva leaves town for eighteen months to reinvent herself, she leaves her three children with a neighbor by the name of Mrs. Suggs. The number eighteen is itself not insignificant, as it is the number of years that it takes Beloved, the child killed by Sethe, to return as a young woman to live with her and Denver, her sister. To link her even more closely to Eva, Baby Suggs is also a figure of empowerment who tries to reclaim her body and share her "big heart" with others. Baby Suggs herself had a very problematic attitude to the many children she gave birth to as a slave. Apart from Halle, she refused to love any of the seven children she gave birth to through a variety of circumstances beyond her choosing.

The system of slavery is responsible both for her fractured body and her ambivalent maternal instincts. There is too much at stake in having to regularly witness her children, and indeed people whom she loved, being taken away from her. As we are told:

Anybody Baby Suggs knew, let alone loved, who hadn't run off or been hanged, got rented out, loaned out, bought up, brought back, stored up, mortgaged, won, stolen or seized. So Baby's eight children had six fathers. What she called the nastiness of life was the shock she received upon learning that nobody stopped playing checkers just because the pieces included her children. Halle she was able to keep the longest. Twenty years. A lifetime. Given to her, no doubt, to make up for *hearing* that her two girls, neither of whom had their adult teeth, were sold and gone and she had not been able to wave goodbye. To make up for coupling with a straw boss for four months in exchange for keeping her third child, a boy, with her—only to have him traded for lumber in the spring of the next year and to find herself pregnant by the man who promised not to and did. That child she could not love and the others she would not.

(23)

Here, the ambivalence she feels about loving any of her children (except for Halle) is a form of self-protection and is shared by most other women within the traumatizing system of slavery. Baby Suggs is witness to the one negatively epiphanic moment in the text that is shared by various characters simultaneously (Sethe, Stamp Paid, the four horsemen, and later, Paul D). In other words, Baby Suggs bears witness to a traumatic memory that is public as opposed to private. Witnessing Sethe's terrible choice presents Baby Suggs with a primal moment that focalizes and intensifies all the ambiguities of her own life as woman, mother, slave, and disabled person. As we are told: "They came in her yard anyway and she could not approve or condemn Sethe's rough choice. One or the other might have saved her, but beaten up by the claims of both she went to bed. The whitefolks had tired her out at last" (180).

The absolute ethical undecidability of Sethe's choice makes it impossible for Baby Suggs to operate under the aegis of the faith she had exercised hitherto. Her "faith, her love, her imagination and her great big old heart began to collapse" (89) after the event and she withdraws into a sequential contemplation of primary colors, almost as if trying to rediscover the primary colors of Creation itself.[9] In contrast to Sethe, who often has her perspectival sensorium intensified through the moments of traumatic leakage, in the case of Baby Suggs her epiphanic witnessing has the effect of shutting down not just her zest for life but her senses as well. Crucially also, though Sethe is frequently afflicted by the traumatic leakage of the past, the moment of her rough choice never enters her consciousness directly. She never "rememories" it. Even when Paul D asks her directly to say what happened, in answering she circles both him and the traumatic event itself: "Sethe knew that the circle she was making around the room, him, the subject, would remain one. That she could never close in, pin it down for anybody who had to ask. If they didn't get it right off—she could never explain. Because the truth was simple, not a long-drawn-out record of flowered shifts, tree cages, selfishness, ankle ropes and wells . . ." (163).

At no point in her account does she actually describe or indeed visualize the deed. It is almost as if she has suffered a strategic amnesia around it. Thus Baby Suggs's bearing witness to the event serves a double purpose. Not only does the event generate a hermeneutical impasse for her, but there is also the transfer of the event's negative affect even unto her soul. She is not merely a witness but a sacrificial carrier of the terrible knowledge that is born at that moment. In this way, the epiphanic moment leads to a splitting within the event itself (between the tragic actor and the tragic witness who is also the carrier of the terrible knowledge that is born) as well as within the psyche of the witness herself (Baby Suggs can neither endorse nor condemn the tragic act and so takes to her bed to contemplate primary colors).

Significantly, the epiphanic moments in which maternality is brought into question are only evident in relation to the physically disabled female characters in Morrison. There is no such epiphanic crisis for the nondisabled characters, or indeed for those with mental or cognitive disorders. There is certainly none for the men in her texts. In the cases of both Eva Peace and Baby Suggs, their respective physical disabilities are the discursive markers of a crisis of representation, an aesthetic nervousness as I am trying to elaborate in this study. Their sense of empowerment is undermined precisely by the nature of their fractured bodies. Nowhere else in Morrison's writing do we find empowerment so sharply conjoined to a sense of loss as we see in the lives of these great female bearers of the terrible knowledge that the coupling of maternality and disability brings with it.

As we noted in our provisional typology in chapter 2, the categories of disability as epiphany (5), disability as enigmatic tragic insight (7), and as normality (9) appear to be most applicable to Morrison's work. However, it is also evident that none of these categories is able to do full justice to the complexity of her writing. For in Morrison's work, whenever we encounter a disability at the level of content, it begins to proliferate various significations that shape themselves in a restless and oscillatory fashion that affects the overall structure of the narrative. The disability becomes like a fulcrum or nexus point that radiates variant processes of signification and of the transfer of such signification across various representational scales and locations. Thus, unlike the examples of bifurcation we saw in chapter 2 with regards to Disney's *Finding Nemo* and Bapsi Sidhwa's *Cracking India*, where the narrative directly contradicts the positive implications of the disability representation *at the level of the content*, in Morrison's work the splitting is best defined in terms not of bifurcation but of multivocality. Her texts are multivocal both in terms of the many positions that are adopted regarding disability as well as in relation to the manner by which any judgment we might come to regarding her disabled characters is obliged to take account of the various ethical options she presents that are not reducible to any easy hierarchy. There is thus an optimization of the process of coming-to-judgment as such. Toni Morrison makes it impossible, through her writing, for us to reach closure without constantly anticipating its alternatives. In this way, a putative ethics of reading is generated that aligns the literary to the social and vice versa. I shall have more to say on what this ethics might entail in the conclusion to this study.

5

WOLE SOYINKA

Disability, Maimed Rites, and the Systemic Uncanny

ROM MARY DOUGLAS'S DISCUSSION IN *Purity and Danger* (1966) we get a sense of the main ways in which ritual pollution, uncleanliness, and contagion are demarcated in various societies. As she shows, in the early historical stages of anthropological studies religions, and indeed entire cultures, were divided between those that attributed pollution to material circumstances (the proximity to dirt, blood, spittle, and other excrescences) and those that, irrespective of such material circumstances, saw pollution in terms of intentionalities and psychological motivations. Such social demarcations are still in different degrees as pertinent to modern societies as they are to so-called primitive ones.

Apart from the material/intentional divide on the question of ritual contagion, we should note a third kind of demarcation, which pertains to perceptions of social stigma. The shift in the meanings of the word "stigma" from its earliest definition as the external marks of either physical or social difference in classical Greek and Christian thought to its current usage to designate a spectrum of negative attributes of both physical and nonphysical kinds serves to show how much the body has historically been assimilated to varying grids of social symbolization (Goffman 1959).

Social perceptions define the anomalous and the polluted within a differential structure of sociocultural relations. The key to these relations is that the perception of pollution and anomaly is part of a shifting set of socially designated meanings. Additionally, the social perception of what is designated as anomalous is often assimilated to questions of power, or at least to that of the values and practices that undergird social decorum. These values and practices themselves get translated into hierarchical notions of moral entitlement and help define varying understandings of exclusion and inclusion within social groups. In extreme contexts such as that of the Third Reich, the stigma attributed to physical and mental disorders was connected directly to the question of the right to life.

The prime place given to ritual and ritual impulses in Soyinka's drama helps place the human body itself as the prime bearer of multiple ritual significations. However, what has not as yet been properly commented upon is that even as much of his work is centered on ritual, it is also the case that the ritual impulses get focalized in a particularly intense way upon the figure of the person with disabilities. The disabled character in Soyinka is often a cryptograph of the metaphysical and the anomalous. Outside of A Dance of the Forests, where the limping god Aroni and the terrifying esoteric Half-Child are to be read as direct spiritual challenges to the complacency of the human world, in the rest of his writing disabled characters within ordinary human interactions are never fully normalized. Rather, they retain a residue of liminality, whether this is liminality of metaphysical import, as in the case of Murano in The Road, or one that combines the metaphysical with more social psychological meanings, as we find in The Strong Breed, The Swamp Dwellers, and Madmen and Specialists.

Annemarie Heywood is right in pointing out that whether in his novels, poetry, or plays, Soyinka's essentially dramatic gifts are geared more toward antimimeticism than to any form of naturalistic representation. This does not mean that he does not produce straightforwardly naturalistic works. The Jero plays, The Swamp Dwellers, The Strong Breed, and even to a degree The Lion and the Jewel are good examples of such mimetic and naturalistic writing that center on predictable character psychology and motivation and proceed through a linear mode of unfoldment. The same disposition is evident in his "factional" works such as Aké, Isara, and Ibadan, all of which are auto/biographical. The problems for staging character and setting in his antimimetic plays relate as much to the question of how to generate a persuasive authentic range of expression for the largely politico-ethical messages that we find in them as for the more difficult one of finding the exact dramaturgic medium by which to carry cryptic and elusive ritual meanings. As Heywood goes on to note, Soyinka's antimimetic strand is marked by contrastive characterization and the tendency to frustrate any resolution to the conflicts that are set up in the action. The unfoldment of the action is supposed to compound the conflicts at various levels and to intensify the structural implications of misunderstandings between characters. Thus many of the plays, along with *The Interpreters* and *Season of Anomie*, end on an "intolerable open paradox," with at best a dialectical balancing of the multifariously contending forces that have been exposed over the course of the action (Heywood 2001, 2–43).

To read Soyinka's work through the perspective of disability, however, is to be obliged to attend in meticulous detail to the ways in which disabled characters either manifestly represent ritual anomalies, or, in what amounts to a partial qualification of the ritual impulse, institute significant disjunctures to the established protocols of the social domains in which they appear. What emerges as aesthetic nervousness in this work is underscored by an apparently irresolvable paradox tied to the peculiar relationship that is established between ritual dispositions and the process for the production of subjectivity and agency, a process that is in the last instance political. It is also manifest in the depiction of what I shall describe as the systemic uncanny, the process by which the chaos of fraught sociopolitical processes are translated into the negative affects of anxiety, fear, and even horror in the consciousness of individuals. I want to suggest from a reading of *The Strong Breed* (1964) that the aesthetic nervousness in the play resides in the counterpoint between the processual institution of ritual authority and the manufacturing of docility and compromise that is its flipside. This is especially pertinent to the unstable and shifting discursive positions given to Ifada, the cognitively impaired character in the play. On the other hand, using *Madmen and Specialists* (1971) I want to suggest that the apparently subversive position given to the disabled mendicants is undermined by the fact that they also represent the failed synthesis of conflicting ideological standpoints in the play. The mendicants may be productively read as the synthesis of an interrupted dialectical movement. *Madmen and Specialists* is also significant in that it is a refraction of specific historical conditions, namely those to do with the Biafran conflict and its aftermath. This historical context is important for evaluating what the play says about a postwar Nigeria and the constitution of the systemic uncanny. The systemic uncanny is also to be seen in an attenuated form in *The Strong Breed*, but it is the later play that allows us to productively correlate the content and form of the dramatic action to the chaos of historical conditions. Even though the two plays are sharply contrasted in their respective mimetic and antimimetic structures and the relationships that they establish between disability, ritual impulses, and issues of subjectivity and agency, taken together they allow us to see the suggestive and critical place disability occupies within Soyinka's work.

The Strong Breed: Disability and the Maimed Rites

The Strong Breed shares a cluster of thematic features with other Soyinka plays in which a relationship is established between disability, ritual contagion, and the quest for privileged insight by the nondisabled characters. It is a play that appears on first encounter to be fairly straightforward in its naturalism and seems quite easy to explain. As in many other plays with a similar ritual thematic, it turns on the Ogun heroic ideal, with its full paraphernalia of transitional abyss, ritual danger, and the need for heroic sacrifice in bridging the abyss between the gods and man.[1] As scholars of his work have often noted, the precise location of the abyss differs from play to play. Thus, in *The Road*, what we might describe as the transitional abyss lies partly on the external fringes of the dramatic action and at the confluence between the living, the dead, and the yet unborn. In this schema, Murano, the limping and speech-impaired character who has been rescued by Professor from a bad motor accident, stands as the keeper of the gateway to esoteric secrets. At least that is how Professor views him in his quest for the Word. The Word itself appears to carry quasi-Christian connotations but is also aligned to traditional Yoruba sensibilities about the conjuncture that Murano presides over. Murano thus combines the notion of ritual danger with that of spiritual insight in his singular person. Simultaneously, however, the sense of the transitional abyss is dispersed within *The Road* as an effect of alienated urban consciousness. This is to be seen in the circumstances surrounding the thugs and unemployed layabouts who form the bulk of Professor's reluctant group of followers. In their many conversations throughout the play about death on the roads of Nigeria and in their representation of the heroic ideal as inhering in the mastery of vehicles that traverse the asphalts of death, characters such as Say Tokyo Kid, Sampson, and Kotonu reveal a sense of the ritual abyss as intermeshed with the dispossessed conditions of their postcolonial urban identity.

In *The Swamp Dwellers*, on the other hand, Blindman comes south from the legendary northern clan of the blind bearing insights about the willpower required for conquering the infertility of the land of the swamp dwellers. His insights are of directly practical and instrumental value, so that when he offers himself as slave to Igwezu it is done in the hope of galvanizing the young man out of his feelings of anomie and into a disposition of self-mastery and decisive action. Here, even though there is an awed response to Blindman, the sense of contagion or ritual danger is not exclusively attached to his person. Rather, the determination of ritual danger becomes a political instrument controlled by Kadiye, the chief priest of the Snake of the Swamp, and is a means to his own self-aggrandizement and profit. That the period of interdiction against cultivating the swamplands is declared ended on the same day that Blindman arrives in the community of the swamp dwellers is not entirely insignificant. He seems to simultaneously mark the end of ritual pollution for the place he has come to visit as well as an inchoate sense of its manifestation within his own person. It is almost as if to suggest that he represents a ritual switchboard effect, on the one hand arriving just when the period of pollution is over, and, on the other, hinting at the fact that he bears in his being the nature and knowledge of ritual contagion. Blindman is discursively located in direct opposition to the implied aridity of ritual represented in the figure of Kadiye. Having walked a long way along the river from the blind community that had itself collapsed under the weight of disillusionment, Blindman represents a source of hardy Ogunian insights that might help transcend the limited purview of ritualized beliefs and practices encapsulated in Kadiye. The alliance between the disgruntled Igwezu, who challenges the authority of Kadiye, and Blindman is then that between the insightful Ogunian heroic outsider and the alienated proto-Ogunian insider.

The Strong Breed is distinctive in bringing together various threads that may be seen working separately in Soyinka's other plays. Thus we have a direct link between the stranger and ritual anomaly in the persons of Eman and Ifada. The link between the stranger and such ritual anomaly is particularly exacerbated around the character of Ifada, the cognitively impaired child who is seized upon by the community as a reluctant sacrificial victim. Furthermore, in the play the transitional abyss is very clearly demarcated as one that for the continued well-being of the community needs to be bridged by a sacrificial carrier. The complication, however, is that the choice of ritual sacrifice raises a series of ethical complications regarding agency, intentionality, and the status of the disabled as a perceived signifier of metaphysical disorder. It also raises the issue of the production of docility, which, as we shall elaborate shortly, is ultimately an issue inextricable from the exercise of political power and ritual authority.

From *The Strong Breed* we also get the dramaturgical representation of ritual contagion that needs to be demarcated and policed for the well-being of the society. Certain Greek concepts are particularly pertinent to interpreting both this play and *Madmen and Specialists*. As Vernant (1980) and others have shown, the link between dirt and pollution was not at all straightforward in Greek thought. What was most pertinent were the links between disease construed as evil and evil conceptualized as disease. For these pairs to be fully grasped, however, several interlinked concepts were understood in their relationality within a wider totalized discourse of purity, purification, contagion, and danger. Thus even though the term *katharsis*, highly suggestive in discussions of dramatic theater from Aristotle onward, generally means cleansing, what is to be cleansed might include menstrual blood and pathogens in the body as well as disturbing emotions in the soul. To achieve *katharsis*, Greek healers turned to *pharmaka*. *Pharmaka* (singular *pharmakon*) could be used to denote medicinal drugs as well as poisons, a notion that is pertinent, as we shall see, to the status of the herbs that the old women gather in *Madmen and Specialists*. What the sick hoped to be cured of was sometimes called *pathos* (as in pathology), but the term could include anything that happened to you or that you underwent or suffered. *Pathe* were not necessarily negative phenomena, ailments that had to be removed. The word is often translated as affection or feeling. Thus in Euripides' *Hippolytus*, Phaedra's *pathos* is manifested as emotional madness.

Significantly, however, the *pharmakon* need not be identified as something to be ingested. Thus spells or charms recited over a patient were also *pharmaka*. *Pharmakos*, on the other hand, was used to denote the scapegoat figure driven out of the community to bear off its pollution. The *pharmakos* was itself intensely negatively charged with associations of disease, death, and evil, while also bringing welfare to the community when it was driven out. It was thus viewed both positively and negatively. The many examples from Greek literature, including Oedipus, Philoctetes, Hippolytus, Ajax, and Heracles, give a good sense of the imaginative parameters of these terms and concepts.[2] The significant thing to be noted about all these terms, however, is that they formed a nexus of interrelated concepts, a semiotic of the sacred and its opposite, as it were. And because within the conceptual domain of ritual action all the concepts were intricately tied to one another, the representation of ritual pollution itself became multilayered and often even contradictory. This paradoxical situation is best conveyed by the term "sacred horror," which Durkheim (1912) used to designate the generic ambivalence of the idea of the sacred, especially in its automatic collocation with notions of contagion. As we shall see, the intricate multilayering of ideas of the sacred/polluted and the paradoxes inherent in them are pertinent to a reading of *The Strong Breed*.

At the most basic level, the play is about a town's quest for a sacrificial carrier, a *pharmakos* to mark their end-of-year festival. Among the elements of this festival are the displays of mummers and *egugun* masquerades, both of which are supposed to denote the connection between the world of the living and that of the spirits. Also, there is the requirement for the sacrificial carrier to undergo a period of "preparation" as part of the ritual passage. Part of the cleansing ritual involves the sacrificial carrier being taken to each compound to have him beaten up and thoroughly abused, a direct mimetic enactment of the bearing of the ills and negative feelings of the community. The frenetic activities that are enjoined within the framework of annual cleansing also mean that the sense of contagion has to be driven away through some form of mass participation, thus signaling a joining together of the townspeople within a ritual of communal *katharsis*. Because most denizens of the town know what is entailed by this, there is great reluctance to offer themselves as sacrificial carriers. Thus we are told that over the years the practice has been to choose sojourners among them to be the *pharmakos*.

In the play, the sense of liminal danger is felt everywhere; yet it also gets focalized in two distinctive ways, both of which come together to generate a form of contrastive signification of the sacred/polluted. The first avenue for this focalization is in the characters of Ifada and Eman. When the play opens, there is no clear indication that they are liminal characters, except in the sense that as strangers in the community they are already potentially marked in this way. However, there is an incremental accentuation of their liminal status to the point of there being no doubt that they are indeed mutually defining figures of contagion. The second set of liminal figures consists of the diseased Girl, who self-identifies as being permanently in a phase of ritual contamination, and the village community, which as a collective entity has entered a sphere of liminal danger by virtue of its end-of-year festival. A strong link is then established between ritual contagion and evil, on the one hand, and between disease and ritual contagion, on the other. However, the relationship between the two sets of figures is that between those that claim to themselves the exclusive power to nominate others as ritually anomalous (the Girl, the village community) and those that are so named and then have to decide whether to acquiesce or resist such a nomination (Ifada, Eman). In other words, ritual (de)nomination is also entangled with questions of subjecthood and power.

To add another layer to the question of nomination and agency, each of the nondisabled characters involved in the ritual passage—the Girl, the community-as-collective, and indeed Eman—self-identify at various points as carrying some form of ritual contagion. Eman starts off resisting such a self-identification, but when he reluctantly agrees to become a ritual carrier he appropriates this as an inescapable part of his destiny. It is only Ifada, the cognitively impaired child, for whom this is never a self-identified choice at any point in the action, but is solely an imposition or external projection upon his being. And yet, because of the way the play opens on a note of domesticity and ordinariness, with references to Sunma's intense anxiety regarding Ifada's place among them, Ifada's assigned status as the bearer of contagion is rendered almost natural, as opposed to being a forced imposition. The process of naturalization takes place *before* the rude violence of his seizure by the chief priest and his cohorts. At a very basic level, the play suggests that Ifada is "naturally" contaminated, and yet, at another, it makes us recoil from the ultimate implication of that naturalization, that is, that he could be seized upon violently and against his will as a sacrificial carrier by the sheer fact of his disability. But why this odd paradox? Why this peculiar and contradictory movement of transposition around the figure of the disabled person?

The affirmation of Ifada's "natural" contaminated status contrasts sharply with the slow disclosure of Eman's own status as a descendant of a long family line of sacrificial carriers in his home village. After he has agreed to take Ifada's place as carrier, his past is disclosed via a series of flashbacks in which, in the midst of the unfolding action of the chase presented on stage, there are pauses for him to step back into the memory of childhood conversations with his father, his tutor, and Omae, his deceased bride. The interweaving of his past and his present through the flashbacks serves to show how much he is a product of that past and completely entangled with it. Critically, however, in both the past and the present Eman is shown to exercise choice and agency, something that ultimately defines him as an ethical being rather than someone who mindlessly acquiesces in the dictates of communal verities. This is what emerges out of the conversation he has with his father about the task of the "strong breed." For him this means nothing once the affective links with his community have been effectively severed on the death of Omae during childbirth. Eman no longer feels connected enough to his community to follow in the footsteps of his father and become its official sacrificial carrier. However, because he comes from a line that has historically exercised the vocation of sacrificial carrier, it is also implied that he is not entirely free of potential ritual contagion, irrespective of his own views on the matter. Thus even in his case a subtle discourse of the "natural" subtends his identity and ultimately circumscribes his exercise of agency.

As noted earlier, the play opens on a domestic setting, with Sunma and Eman preparing to close their clinic for the evening. Eman is a teacher and a healer, and Sunma is his wife. It is the same night of the end-of-year festival, and one filled with untold danger. The danger is not relayed directly, but is registered as a vague but persistent sense of anxiety on the part of Sunma. She keeps insisting that they, or at least Eman, leave on the last lorry (the sounds of whose engine we hear in the background), to spend the evening at another location. To her exasperation, Eman will have none of it and nonchalantly dismisses her anxious requests. We are later to discover that this inchoate sense of anxiety was not entirely misplaced: as daughter of Jeroge, the chief priest, she knows fully well that Eman might be targeted as sacrificial carrier. However, we do not know any of this with certainty until much later in the action. Over the course of their argument, Sunma spots Ifada crouching underneath their window; he bears a basket of fruit he has brought for Eman. He has been trying all along to catch Eman's attention. Her reaction to the sight of Ifada is surprisingly violent:

> SUNMA. Just tell him to go away. Let him go and play somewhere else.
>
> . . .
>
> SUNMA. I don't want him here [*Rushes to the window*]. Get away idiot. Don't bring your foolish face here any more, do you hear? Go on, go away from here. . . .
>
> . . .
>
> SUNMA. He comes crawling round here like some horrible insect. I never want to set eyes on him again.
> EMAN. I don't understand. It is Ifada you know. Ifada! The unfortunate one who runs errands for you and doesn't hurt a soul.
> SUNMA. I cannot bear the sight of him.
> EMAN. But he does work. You know he does a lot of work for you.
> SUNMA. Does he? And what about the farm you started for him! Does he ever work on it? Or have you forgotten that it was really for Ifada you cleared the brush? Now you have to go and work it yourself. You spend all your time on it and you have no room for anything else.
> EMAN. That wasn't his fault. I should have asked him if he was fond of farming.
> SUNMA. Oh, so he can choose? As if he shouldn't be thankful for being allowed to live.
> EMAN. Sunma!
>
> . . .
>
> SUNMA. The sight of him fills me with revulsion.   (116–117)

Two things seem to be playing out here, neither of which serves to explain Sunma's startling reaction to the disabled child. On the one hand, she insists that he is a lazy good-for-nothing child on whom Eman is wasting precious time. On the other hand, there is the sense of revulsion, the feeling that he is somehow contaminated and indeed contaminating. The reference to him as a "crawling insect" captures this sense of revulsion. It also suggests that he is perceived as only partly human. It is worth repeating, however, that these reactions to Ifada are being registered *prior* to his being chosen as a sacrificial carrier for the community. He is being identified as contaminated as such and by virtue of his being disabled, and not merely because Sunma has an inchoate sense of his liminal status.

Curiously enough, the idea of Ifada's contaminated status is further reinforced from a completely different source shortly after the argument we have just seen. Ifada is nominated as a sacrificial carrier by the Girl, who is herself considered as contaminated because of her incurable disease. The Girl first comes to Eman's house to get a piece of clothing for her effigy, an object she pretends is a sacrificial carrier that will take away her unnamed disease. An overarching idea of ritual contagion is immediately foregrounded in and around her person. Eman is about to lend her his *buba* (a loose-fitting neck blouse) to put on her effigy:

EMAN. Here . . . will this do? Come and look at it.
GIRL. Throw it.
EMAN. What is the matter? I am not going to eat you.
GIRL. No one lets me come near them.
EMAN. But I am not afraid of catching your disease.
GIRL. Throw it.
[EMAN *shrugs and tosses the buba. She takes it without a word and slips it
    on the effigy, completely absorbed in the task.* EMAN *watches for a while,
    then joins Sunma in the inner room.*]   (119)

In the game that Ifada plays with the Girl shortly after this, he is the one invited to beat the effigy, as if to metaphorically take the place of the villagers who have to get rid of their ritual contagion. It is not insignificant that the girl reinforces the sense of his being anomalous by reinvoking the association with an insect that we saw with Sunma earlier:

GIRL. [*after a long , cool survey of Ifada.*] You have a head like a spider's
    egg, and your mouth dribbles like a roof. But there is no one else.
    Would you like to play?
[IFADA *nods eagerly, quite excited.*]   (119)

In the immediate context of this segment of the action, the notion of contagion is distributed equally between the Girl (as one who bears an incurable disease), Ifada (as one who carries an incurable cognitive disability),
and the effigy (as stand-in for the ritual carrier). What this tripartite
scheme of contagion signifies is the absolute transferability of the ritual
contagion and the speed at which it can be metonymically displaced from
one entity to another. Seeing this, it is obvious then that in lending the
Girl his *buba* Eman enters into the symbolic circulation of contagion. It is
a small step from this symbolic circulation to his decision to take the place
of Ifada as sacrificial carrier in actuality. Eman's destiny as descendant of
familial sacrificial carriers seems inescapable and is prepared for both by
the nature of the choices he exercises and by the semiotics of the sacred
and the profane as they circulate among the characters.

Eman's Christ-like self-sacrifice in taking the place of Ifada serves to
conceal another process that his standing in for the boy hints at in the
play, and that is the relation between the production of docility and the
threatened subversion of power. For the process of identifying and securing a *pharmakos* to take place properly, the community in the play requires a docile subject. As we have already seen, in the rituals enjoined for
cleansing the community a sacrificial carrier is required to whom (violent) things can be done. It is important in this regard that as much as
possible the townspeople get a subject that is not only culturally an outsider (and therefore that might be ignorant of the ritual mores of the
community), but one that is prepared to absorb the ritual violence "willingly," as the chief priest ominously puts it at one point. What is clear,
however, is that no ordinary human agent would be thus willing. Given
that Ifada's disability has marked him off as contaminated in the minds of
individual characters ahead of his identification as official ritual carrier,
there is the suggestion that, irrespective of his own agential position, he
is situated within a sacred semiotic as one who will always occupy the position of a subject to whom things occur rather than as a trigger of action
himself. This is so despite the fact that his running away from the chief
priest causes a commotion in the community and prompts an epiphanic
crisis for Eman. In prompting Eman's ethical epiphany, Ifada has only succeeded in instigating the process that would produce Eman in his turn as
the docile subject of his own particular lineage of sacrificial carriers. He is
fated to be thus and the self-examination that he undergoes is only so as
to deliver him more securely into the acceptance of his ritual role. In oth-

er words, the ritual processes of problematic (de)nomination and of the natural election of the *pharmakos* are represented in such a way as to obscure the true political nature of such processes. Rather, they suggest that a docile subject emerges organically from them. In this way the play seems on the surface to be about agency and the choice of destinies while discursively displaying a robustly conservative attitude to the structural location of the disabled character.[3] (We should pause to recall the pertinence of the categories of disability as null set and/or moral test and of disability as epiphany that we outlined in chapter 2).

The combination in Ifada's characterization of a discourse of docility and the possibility of epiphany for the nondisabled makes his role similar to that of Murano in *The Road*. Murano's presence is much more curtailed than Ifada's since he is referred to tangentially in the action and appears properly only at the end of the play. However, what makes the two of them similar is that Murano is also a docile subject. In his case, he becomes what the crazy Professor interprets him to be, while at the same time signaling the conjuncture between the real world and that of the ancestors. But Murano's signaling of this other world is not done consciously, at least not by himself. It is because he is the bearer of all the signs of disabled anomalousness, such as having a limp and being speech impaired, that he becomes the ritual gateway to threnodic secrets in a play that is partly about Ogunian rites. Thus, like Ifada, Murano is the bearer of excessive metaphysical signification and one to whom things occur by virtue of his location within the discursive economy of the text. And like Blindman in *The Swamp Dwellers*, Ifada also performs a discursive switchboard effect. He becomes the focal point for the radiation of different dimensions of ritual disquiet in the action. The manner in which the disquiet gets expressed through people like Sunma suggests that there is something systemically unsettling within the culture at large, but which gets articulated in the form of an inchoate sense of disorder around the disabled character. The play is insistent that we be left in no doubt about Ifada's contaminated and unsettling status. He is taken to breach the commonplace of everyday life by the very virtue of his disability. Because this is a play governed by a ritual thematic, his disability is automatically assimilated to a metaphysical understanding and interpreted as producing anomalousness as such. This then serves to obscure the disability, since it is never allowed to stand for itself but is made an object of metaphysical interpretative excess from the very beginning.

Even though the temptation to settle on an exclusive ritual interpretation of the play is strong (and in many respects would be quite satisfac-
tory), I want to suggest that the disquiet that Ifada's disability causes be
read in terms of the systemic uncanny. In brief, the systemic uncanny is
the translation of an inchoate sense of disorder into a negative affect that
is then lodged in the human consciousness and expressed in the forms of
anxiety, unease, and, in extreme cases, abject fear. I shall elaborate more
fully on this concept in the next section with regard to *Madmen and Specialists*, a play that allows us to see the concept in operation at a more
complex level. Both plays are central parts of Soyinka's continual creative
reflections on the nature and character of systemic disorders and the effects that these have on the production of subject positions for the disabled within an inherently confusing political realm.

Madmen and Specialists: Choric Arbiters of Arrested Development

Scholars of Nigerian literature generally agree that the Biafra War (1967–
1970) marked an epochal moment not just for interrogating the parameters of the Nigerian nation-state but also for the ways in which it might
be represented in literature (Ezeigbo 1991; Obafemi 1992). In a brilliant
1983 essay, Chidi Amuta illustrates how Nigerian postwar writings revealed a decidedly different generic temperament from all that had been
published prior to the war. Whereas earlier fiction had been marked by
the conventions of animist realism and an ethnic consciousness (exemplified by the accentuated place given to spirits, ghomids, and suchlike in
the work of Fagunwa and Tutuola), a nationally conscious realism moti-
vated by the desire to highlight the effect of the colonial encounter on
the viability of local traditions (Achebe) and, finally, by the progressive
literary excoriation of the political elites (Achebe, Soyinka, Ekwensi),
postwar Nigerian writing was marked by the quest for a strongly ethical
framework by which to propound an urgent new vision for the endan-
gered nation. For Amuta, this phase of Nigerian writing raised in a much
sharper way than hitherto the problematic question of the relationship
between specific historical details and their aestheticization in literature
and art, with various writers struggling to reflect upon the Biafra experience in their work without completely surrendering the ontological sta-

tus of the aesthetic domain. This was done with various degrees of success. In another essay, this time devoted specifically to Soyinka's postwar writing, Amuta argues that the war marked an important turning point in Soyinka's essentially idealistic and mythopoetic artistic temperament. Soyinka, he suggests, now adopts more of a "secular posture," attempting to "reconcile the horror of personal indignation and moral anguish with the communal responsibility of the committed artist" (Amuta 1986, 52). This is shown in the changed emphasis of work such as *The Man Died, A Shuttle in the Crypt,* and *Madmen and Specialists,* all of which came shortly after his incarceration from 1969 through 1971.

Amuta's suggestions on the twists and turns in Nigerian writing are generally apposite and insightful, but his remarks on Soyinka's work are slightly less to the point. For what is also evident in works such as *Madmen and Specialists* is that Soyinka does not so much depart from the essential ritual emphases of his earlier work as that the representation of ritual as organically deriving from a coherent context, whether real or imagined, is no longer considered possible. This is, however, not a theme entirely new to his work. An inkling of this is already to be found in *The Road.* We also find that he returns to a more secure affirmation of the links between politics and a mythopoetical mode of interpretation in his collection of essays *Myth, Literature, and the African World,* in *Death and the King's Horseman,* and in his adaptation of *The Bacchae* of Euripides, all from 1975. As I shall try to show, *Madmen and Specialists* occupies a special place in his oeuvre, in that it is the first time he confronts the full implications of personal and national dismemberment that he had been elaborating in a piecemeal fashion in earlier work.

Madmen and Specialists is the only play of his to securely place a group of disabled characters as central protagonists. Second, it is the only play, perhaps alongside *The Road,* in which the enigmatic open-endedness we find at the end is made fully integral and incrementally repeated as part of the dramatic action itself. The disabled mendicants exert a determining hold on the open-endedness of the action via a structure of interruptions. Often through songs, but sometimes also by way of tangential departures from the dialogue, they serve to render open-endedness endemic at the microlevel of the plot. The mendicants are choric arbiters (Heywood's term), but in ways that far supersede what is usually attributable to the choric function deriving from Greek and classical models. To understand the special status of the mendicants, we have to bear in mind their resemblance to choric arbiters in other plays by Soyinka, and, more importantly, to the degree to which they are cryptically situated at a conjuncture of the political and the metaphysical. And yet, contrary to Amuta's methodological focus on the play as providing direct correlatives to the historical situation from which it derives, I want to suggest that its impulses are so convoluted that it ends up both invoking the context of the war and completely obliterating it as a meaningful referent. In fact, the war is left securely in the background to the dramatized events and is not invoked specifically by name. Rather, it provides the occasion for a secularized allegory about the effect of mindless violence on the constitution of human subjectivity. It is also a play about biopower and the control of human bodies as such. In this regard the foregrounding of the disabled mendicants becomes even more important for understanding the play's variable and contradictory meanings.

The similarities of the disabled mendicants to other choric groups in Soyinka's theater are noteworthy. Parallels may be drawn between them and the Reformed Aweri Fraternity of Kongi's Harvest. Like the RAF, the mendicants provide humor, pantomime, nervous laughter, and satiric choric commentary, and like them they feed us with important information about the historical background to the action. The disabled mendicants differ from the members of the RAF, however, in that they provide what might be described as a neurotic center to the action, something that they manifest by the manner in which they bear their impairments and also through their various interruptions of the action. Even though at the beginning they are subjected to pejorative remarks from both Si Bero and Dr. Bero, it becomes increasingly evident as the play progresses that unlike what we saw in The Strong Breed, the mendicants are much more central to the overall ethos of the play than other characters' responses to their disabilities might initially lead us to believe. Also, as has already been noted, the mendicants frequently break out into song and dance, often for no apparent reason other than to interrupt the flow of the action and to redirect it momentarily toward themselves. Dende and the Reformed Aweri Fraternity in Kongi's Harvest have no such luxury. Furthermore, the group of choric arbiters in Madmen and Specialists is decidedly different from the one we find in Soyinka's adaptation of The Bacchae of Euripides. There the choric function is regulated by a classical ritual disposition, and the Bacchantes, now mixed with a group of slaves, are meant to influence our ethical responses to the action through the modulation of ritual rhythm that is so central to both the original Euripidean text and Soyinka's adaptation of it.

The formal features of the mendicants and the internal dynamic established among them are both significant for understanding the peculiar nature of their role in the play. The group is led by Aafa, who suffers from epileptic spasms, something that we suspect he sometimes manufactures to aid him in the getting of alms. At least that is what the other beggars accuse him of. But there is no doubt that the source of the original illness could be traced back to psychic trauma sustained during his stint as a chaplain on the war front. His description of the first time he suffered the spasms is illuminating in this respect:

> That's true. They told me there when it began, that it was something psy-cho-lo-gi-cal. Something to do with all the things happening around me, and the narrow escape I had. It's not so bad now. I still remember the first time. I was standing there just like this, blessing a group of six just about to go off. They were kneeling before me. Then— well, I can't say I heard the noise at all, because I was deaf for the next hour. So, this thing happened, no signal, no nothing. Six men kneeling in front of me, the next moment they were gone. Disappeared, just like that. That was when I began to shake. Nothing I could do to stop it. My back just went on bending over and snapping back again, like the spirit had taken me. God! What a way for the spirit to mount a man.   (54)

The understated way in which Aafa describes what happened should not detract from the fact that it was a severely traumatic event. Praying for the kneeling soldiers about to go off to the field, he hears what is obviously the sound of a coming bomb, and when he opens his eyes they have all been blasted out of existence. Curiously enough, he does not mention any injuries to himself, focusing only on the spasms that were the reaction to the shock. But there is no doubt too that the incident places him at the threshold of life and death. When he invokes God, it is no longer as a chaplain, but as someone who is suggestively situated on the boundary between the living and the dead. His pretend spasms are then the invocation of a form of the uncanny, the placement of his body upon the boundary that lies between the wholly human and the wholly mechanical, making him a liminal figure *par excellance*.[4] It is this also that lends

him his determinedly nihilistic tone, something which of course is produced by and subtends the general ethos of the war.

Each of the other mendicants has also suffered some nasty effect of
war. Goyi has a steel contraption inserted into his back, giving him a stiff
and mechanical gait much like a robot's;[5] Blindman has lost his eyesight,
but keeps the spectacles he had with him when the blast happened as a
souvenir of things past. Cripple seems the least sentimental of them all,
and among them functions as the voice of internal critique. What brings
them together as a group, as opposed to a collection of individuals, is their
having all been students of Old Man and his philosophy of As during
their various periods of convalescence in the military field hospital.

Their specific role as choric arbiters straddling several domains of signification is expressed in the drama in a variety of ways. When the play
opens, we find them casting dice, the stakes for their game being negotia-
ble parts of their own bodies:

AAFA. Six and four, good for you.
CRIPPLE. Your turn, Blindman. [Gives the dice and gourd to
    BLINDMAN.]
BLINDMAN throws. Five and five. Someone is going to give us fivers.
GOYI. Fat chance of that. [He throws.]
AAFA. Three and two, born loser. What did you stake?
GOYI. The stump of the left arm.
CRIPPLE. Your last?
GOYI. No, I've got one left.
BLINDMAN. Your last. You lost the right stump to me yesterday.
GOYI. Do you want it now or later?
BLINDMAN. Keep it for now.
CRIPPLE. When do I get my eye, Aafa?
AAFA. Was it the right or the left?   (7)

This exchange immediately invites us to read them as Fates, the only
qualification being that they never make any attempt whatsoever to predict or interpret the future except for how it might relate to their begging
for alms. However, we find as the play unfolds that their insights about
the background to the action and about other characters is not entirely
related to past events; the information they provide is sometimes also
premonitory. Such is the case in the reenactment of Bero's methods of

extracting information from his victims, which ends in Blindman's shooting pantomime: "I know what he means. (*He points an imaginary gun.*) Bang! All in the line of duty!" (11). The implication of this mimed shooting is later actualized when Bero shoots Old Man at the end of the play. The same can be said about Aafa's disquisition on vultures, an epithet he wholeheartedly claims for the group as a sign of the service they provide for the rest of the populace: "We clean up the mess made by others" (11). We later find that the mess he is referring to is the mess of human carnage due to the war, and that their participation in the cannibalistic feast set up by Old Man is a significant form of such "cleaning up." These two examples suggest that the mendicants' choric role is not solely connected to providing information, but is also designed as anticipatory of later action in the play. Thus their casting of dice at the beginning of the play also signals their role as portentous choric arbiters that can both provide information and hint subliminally at the future. And yet this portentousness is undermined by being completely intermeshed with the mundaneness of their everyday lives. The volatile proximity between everydayness and the portentousness is part of the definition of their collective liminality.

Critical to their discursive position in the play is the degree to which they are taken at different times as instruments of the will of Old Man and of Bero, father and son. Dr. Bero, originally a physician, switches to the Secret Service when he goes to the war front. This switch allows him to indulge his desire for total control over human bodies. His "laboratory" now becomes a laboratory of torture rather than of rational scientific and medical experiment. As an agent of the system, however, he seems peculiarly oblivious of its operating ideology. Contrastively, Old Man has an elaborate if quite contorted sense of the ideology that undergirds the system. Under psychological torture by his own son, Old Man cryptically identifies the parameters of As and manages to crystallize in his own demented way the dominant ideology of the war system. Having been put in charge of the rehabilitation of war wounded, he transforms his task to subversive effect by providing the disabled soldiers under his charge with the capacity to transcend the mind/body dichotomy implied by their maimed identities. His ideology of As is revealed in a fragmented and roundabout way throughout the play and may be taken as an encapsulation, at the level of ideological rhetoric, of the maimed identities of his charges. In other words, his disquisition upon As is a metonymic displacement to the level of ideology of the fact of the fragmented bodily identities of the mendicants themselves. Furthermore, his rhetoric of As also mirrors their highly neurotic and deconstructive mode of action within the play. The rhetoric of As both reflects the spoiled identities of the maimed and war wounded and produces them as objects of ideological disquisition.

The ideology of As is meant to retain an enigmatic aura that needs to be worked at laboriously but that can only be partially understood. The first difficulty with interpreting As is that it is the decontextualized first word of a well-known biblical statement: "As it Was in the Beginning, so Shall it Be in the End . . . " or, as Old Man puts it in another context: "As Was, Is, Now, As ever Shall Be . . . " (62). Naming As while separating it from its expressive context suggests another level of metonymic displacement, for not only has a part of the sentence been made to stand for the entire sentence sequence, but that part has been allowed to accrue to itself all the mystery and numinousness inherent in the originating biblical statement. It has also been transferred into the domain of political ideology and thus carries all the numinous and sacred potential of the statement into that of the political. As is then both an invocation of the promise of Godhead and an atrophied version of that promise. Thus, in the many instances in which As is mentioned in the play, it is meant to generate confusion and bafflement as to its real meaning. Since we have an unwitting exemplar of As and the System in the person of Dr. Bero, we realize that As is also meant to signal the replacement of the pastoral care that is one of the assumed tasks of medical and religious systems with the idea of mindless state brutality, whose most direct articulation is war. Significantly, however, Old Man's hospital is not diametrically opposed to Dr. Bero's laboratory as such, but is rather dialectically related to it. It represents an overlap and counterpoint to Bero's torture chamber, and each of them represents the instrumentalization of biopower (the control of human bodies and their desires) for different effects.[6] They come together as expressions of the microtechniques of such biopower within a mindless political system, one of whose main objectives is the production of docility.

Indeed, read in this dialectical manner, it is Bero who provides a simultaneous understanding and critique of his father's subversive tasks:

It's not his charitable propensities I am concerned with. Father's assignment was to help the wounded readjust to the pieces and remnants of their bodies. Physically. Teach them to make baskets if they still had fingers. To use their mouths to ply needles if they had none, or use it to sing if their vocal cords had not been blown away. Teach them to amuse themselves, make something of themselves. Instead he began to teach them to think, think, THINK! Can you picture a more treacherous deed than to place a working mind in a mangled body?

(37)

For Bero, readjustment to the pieces and remnants of the soldiers' maimed bodies should as a necessity involve rehabilitating them into economically viable units of labor. To his mind, autonomy is equated directly with labor potential and not to any fancy ideas about self-reflexivity. Note that the word "teach" in the extract above is attached both to the process of producing instrumental labor potential and to developing independent minds. However, Old Man is not merely interested in providing the wounded soldiers with the capacity for self-reflexivity. He also wants to make of them instruments of general subversion. Bero and Old Man then have one thing in common: they are both intent on perfecting a means by which to instrumentalize human bodies, even if the implications of Old Man's subversive rehabilitative practice seem quite different from the experiments of his son.

In Old Man's own description of the ideology of As, he does not limit it solely to a war mentality; As is supposed to be systemic rather than exceptional:

As Is, and the System is its mainstay though it wear a hundred masks and a thousand outward forms. And because you are within the System, the cyst in the system that irritates, the foul gurgle of the cistern, the expiring function of a faulty cistern and are part of the material for re-formulating the mind of a man into the necessity of the moment's political As, the moment's scientific As, metaphysic As, sociologic As, economic, recreative ethical As, you-cannot-es-cape! There is but one constant in the life of the System and that constant is AS. And what can you pit against the priesthood of that constant deity, its gospellers, its enforcement agency. . . . And even if you say unto them, do I not know you, did I not know you in rompers, with leaky nose and smutty face? . . . . then shall they say unto you, I am chosen, restored, re-designated and re-destined and further further shall they say unto you,

you heresiarchs of the System arguing questioning querying weighing
puzzling insisting rejecting upon you shall we practise, without passion—

(72)

The mendicants at this point interrupt his flow with one of their songs.
But what Old Man has told them is that there is no room for subversion
outside or beyond the system of As. Subversion must be understood as
immanent rather than transcendent. It is a practice of affiliation as much
as of attack, a guerilla tactic of alertness and the constant reconstitution
of positions. Thus the mendicants are all thoroughly implicated and are
of necessity subversives *through* their physical condition of impairment
and not in spite of it. It is this condition that helps them articulate the
dominant logic of war within their own bodies *and* to subvert this logic
by the resituation of their fragmented bodies as sites of thought. That is
the meaning of the curious reference Old Man makes to them as "the cyst
in the system that irritates, the foul gurgle of the cistern, the expiring
function of a faulty cistern." What makes them so dangerous is not merely their condition of disability, but the fact that they are capable of questioning the system, reminding its operatives of their shared humanity
(admittedly back in a period of childhood, when they were in "rompers,
with leaky and smutty faces"). Not only that, to self-identify as one that
questions is to automatically invite the system to settle upon you as one
on whom it might exercise its abominable practices for securing acquiescent and docile subjectivity. And we know from what we have seen of Dr.
Bero's activities that the "practice" is very far from pleasant. The whiff of
Orwell's *1984* is impossible to miss here.

The mendicants' proximity and indeed induction into Old Man's subversive ideology means that even though they bear the contaminating
stigmata of war, they also actively insinuate themselves into the discourse
of Power that might have completely Othered them and made them dis-
posable to the social. They thus help to define the problematic shifting
boundaries between purity and danger and inside and outside. Following
Old Man's lead, they challenge the most fundamental taboo that is to be
found in many human societies, namely, that against the eating of human
flesh. This taboo is rendered at least rhetorically void through the operation of a clever and sophistical argument in justification of cannibalism
by Old Man. Since all animals kill in order to eat but man kills only in
order to destroy, the only way for restoring man's superiority within the

scheme of living beings is for him not to waste (this word operating in more than one sense) but to partake of whatever he kills. Old Man's cannibalistic feast operates not by countering or even negating the mindless illogicality of war, but rather by extending that illogicality toward the annulment of all sentiment about what it is to be human. War wastes indiscriminately by killing man and destroying the environment, man attempts to counteract this by wasting not of human flesh, but the ultimate effect of the waste/waste-not dialectic is the dehumanization of man. In this way, Old Man accomplishes in the rhetorical domain what war does in the domain of the battlefield.

But then we come against an intractable paradox. Even though they are aligned to Old Man and are thus agents of subversion, the disabled mendicants are also shown to be operatives in the employ of Dr. Bero. They are therefore not merely compromised by being *in* the system but are actually servants *of* it. Their throwing of dice and waylaying passersby for alms when we first see them is only a cover for being able to spy on Si Bero and the group of old women who are the representatives of healing spirits and close to the natural rhythms of the earth. In the larger scheme of things, the disabled mendicants are instruments of a dastardly surveillance apparatus and therefore avatars of the negating aspects of As. Their quarrels with Bero are ultimately quarrels about remuneration and not about the ethical dubiousness of their task as spies. Furthermore, it appears that under instruction from Bero they have been willing accomplices in the enforced detention of Old Man. It is in the mendicants' odd discursive location as simultaneously *within* and *without*, *for* and *against* the system that we detect the parameters of aesthetic nervousness in the play.

Critics have conventionally seen *Madmen and Specialists* as entirely nihilistic and indeed dominated by evil. Ketu Katrak suggests that unlike previous plays of Soyinka that elaborated upon the Ogun heroic ideal, *Madmen and Specialists* has no transitional abyss that might require bridging by a sacrificial hero. The annulment of this transitional space is due to the play's dark meditation on the Biafran War, with no clear sense of hope of rescue from its nihilistic surface (Katrak 1986, 154–158; see also Jeyifo 2004, 141–144). In this account, the mendicants are read as inherently negative and coextensive with the evil that we see in Dr. Bero and, to some degree, in Old Man himself. However, to read the play in terms of the dominance of evil is to ignore the subtle ways in which it invokes a sense of liminality for the mendicants. This sense of liminality is admittedly not equivalent to what we find in *The Strong Breed*, *Death and the King's Horseman*, *The Road*, or even *Kongi's Harvest*, where Daudu and Segi jointly express the Ogunian ideal. However, the notion of liminality is still pertinent to a discussion of the disabled mendicants. As instruments both of Old Man's challenge to the order of As and of Dr. Bero's apparatus of torture and surveillance on behalf of the state, the mendicants are defined as doubly anomalous, once for carrying all the marks of physical disability and the social stigma that is involved in that, and another for being instruments of sundry irrationalities that proceed from opposite ideological directions simultaneously. They are anomalous in a physical and material sense because of their disability and, more importantly, because their standpoint is politically salient to the two contrastive factions as represented by Old Man and Bero. And yet, the two terms of their anomalousness are transcended by a third term, namely, the degree to which they act as a failed synthesis within a structure of dialectical mediation.

What is the nature of this failed synthesis? We have already noted that Old Man's military field hospital and Dr. Bero's laboratory are dialectically related. With respect to the disabled mendicants, however, the thing to note is that they do not represent a heroic ideal of any sort that might counter either Bero's or Old Man's contrastive ideological dispositions. Even among themselves their camaraderie is only partial and skin deep, as they are always quarrelling and disagreeing with one another, with sporadic threats of violence often at the fore.[7] This is particularly so with regard to Aafa, who detests having his opinions questioned at any time. Whenever any of the others appear to question his views on anything, even if indirectly, he launches into threatening language and behavior. The mendicants pause in their quarrelling only when they have to confront an external agent such as Si Bero, Dr. Bero, or Old Man. In this sense, they seem as a group to have assimilated the negative aspects of authoritarianism shared by both Old Man and Bero and are thus only a negative synthesis of the two representative standpoints. This assimilation is further confirmed by their discursive location within the triptych representational structure of the stage. Throughout the play the action oscillates between three spaces, as is outlined in the first stage directions: "*Open space before Bero's home and surgery. The surgery is down in a cellar. The level ground in the fore and immediate front space serve as drying space for assorted barks and herbs. The higher structure to one side is a form of semi-open hut."* Within this triptych structure, the surgery collapses the essences of both Old Man and Bero within itself—it is Bero's "lab" and the place where Old Man is held captive and from which he declaims his peculiar subversive logic—while the space before the house is where the mendicants ply their trade. The semi-open hut, on the other hand, is the abode of the old women, collectors of herbs and the representatives of a countervailing standpoint of healing set against the madness of the male characters. However, as the play progresses the triptych structure is contracted into a diptych, with only the oscillation between the old women's abode and the surgery remaining. This is conveyed by means of a play of lighting, with different parts of the stage being illuminated to show the switch in scene from one to the other. The mendicants are completely assimilated to the space of the surgery, and thus, strictly through the disposition of the spatial logic of the play, to the overlapping irrationalities of Bero and Old Man. The external space that they previously occupied has been completely annulled. Even though a group with their own internal dynamic and contradictions, they are ultimately not an independent entity as such, but only meaningful as they are constitutively assimilated to the dominant logic of biopower that governs the system.

This assimilation to the dominant is further revealed in the degree to which, even while challenging the negative epithets about disability launched at them by other characters, they sometimes echo the same atrophied perceptions among themselves. Again, Aafa is the main culprit. At one point he makes a lunge for Goyi's crotch:

GOYI. Where? I am lost.
AAFA. Where? I'll show you, dumbclod. [*He lunges for* GOYI's *crotch.*]
GOYI. [*protecting himself.*] No!
AAFA. Why not? You got any more use for it?
BLINDMAN. Maybe he wants to continue the line.
AAFA. What! This crooked line? It would be a disservice to
   humanity.   (14)

This is only partly in jest, because the threat of violence is repeated at various times toward others. At any rate, the remark about the disservice to humanity reveals a well-known fear of the nondisabled about the danger to society of disabled people's capacity to reproduce themselves.

Critically also, apart from the speech that Blindman and Aafa make toward the end of the play, the mendicants are generally portrayed as clowns rather than as particularly insightful interlocutors. In fact, what is described as "thinking" minds in mangled bodies is to be taken strictly on faith only; we only discern their "thinking" when they are repeating, as if by rote, the main tenets of Old Man's teaching. In other words, whether in the hands of Old Man or in that of Dr. Bero, they would have ended up as automatons, concerned mainly with how to eke out survival in their disabled condition. Unlike characters such as Brother Jero, Professor, Elesin Oba, and even Eman, who as characters mobilize, orchestrate, and subvert a variety of ritual idioms as a means of triggering the self-examination of society (Jeyifo 2004, 83–119), the mendicants in Madmen and Specialists do not produce any such questioning outside the framework that is established for them by others. Despite their being used as instruments of subversion sharpened through induction into the ideology of As they are really only docile subjects. Docility here is not to be interpreted as mere passiveness; rather, it is the fact that they are ultimately characters to whom things occur and whose disposition is to acquiesce in the dominant. Their lack of self-reflexivity is to be discerned in the eagerness with which they desire to go on the promised circus tour, where they would presumably have been part of a freakshow. Thus, the following stage directions are telling about their disposition toward being objectified as spectacle:

> Si Bero approaches, carrying a small bag from which protrude some twigs with leaves and berries. The Mendicants begin their performance as soon as they sense her approach. Blindman is alms collector, Goyi repeats a single acrobatic trick, Aafa is the "dancer." Blindman shakes the rattles while Cripple drums with his crutches and is lead singer. Blindman collects alms in the rattles.   (8)

Considered in this way, their many songs throughout the play may be reinterpreted as part of their extended "rehearsal" for their role as clowns in the world's pantomime of forms. The play is framed by an unendingly repetitious ritual action paced entirely by interruptions, and in that respect it differs markedly from The Strong Breed, which, though also focused on rit-

ual, is steadier in connecting character dilemma to overall ritual unfoldment. Thus the mendicants end up providing an assimilable spectacle
rather than a stubborn singularity that would have to be taken into account as such in the implicit dialectical movement suggested by the play.
What we see, then, is that an integral poetic ritual action, as represented
by the mendicants, attempts to transcend both the empiricist (Dr. Bero)
and idealist (Old Man) impulses of the play only to collapse into the arrested idiom of a failed mediation. All the dramatic ratios within which
the disabled mendicants are located—dialectical interplay between characters, triptych/diptych spatial structure, contrastive and overlapping ideologies of the instrumentalization of human bodies—point to the fact that
they represent such a failed synthesis.

The Systemic Uncanny

But how does a play whose immediate historical and material context is
a war of secession and that is written by one of the most self-avowedly
political of African writers end up so compromised in its vision? Why
does it choke on the possibility for subversion that it outlines? And why
does this failure center on the depiction of disabled characters? I would
like to answer these questions by returning to Freud's notion of the uncanny and to my own remarks on the subject in previous work.[8]

Pertinent to my reading of Freud's discussion is the idea that the uncanny cannot be thought to derive solely from ruptures within the familial saga. This is what Freud implies in his reading of Hoffman's "The
Sandman" and in his remark that Nathaniel's anxiety about his eyes is
really a code for the fear of castration by his father. I share the Kleinian
view that castration anxiety should be seen as the fear of bodily dismemberment as such and that it is connected to an ultimate understanding of
death (Klein 1997, 30–31, 45, 135). However, I want to qualify Klein by
insisting that this fear is assimilated under certain conditions to the general sense of a systemic disorder. She provides room for this qualification
in her 1948 paper "On the Theory of Anxiety and Guilt" (Klein 1997,
25–42). Here Klein attends to the oscillatory relationship between a primary internal danger and danger perceived as coming from the outside.
This throws up the problem of objective versus neurotic danger, and she
explains the mechanisms involved by distinguishing between depressive

and persecutory anxieties for individuals. It is evident that the systemic uncanny as I understand it may be composed of both depressive and persecutory vectors, though I wish to emphasize the essentially persecutory dimension of feeling a threat to the sense of self that comes from perceptions of social chaos. Even if the fear of dismemberment is evocative of the primal anxiety relating to the child's original projection/introjection of the mother's breast, the systemic uncanny may be more directly connected to chaotic events of a social or political nature. It is the conversion of the sense of a systemic disorder into a negative affect that marks what I describe as the systemic uncanny. In the face of persistent physical and social violence, either triggered by acute political chaos or the general collapse of the social order, a process of internalization of these perceived disorders takes place. In such instances, the self is presumed to be constantly under threat, whether this threat ever materializes or not. The internalized translation of disorder does not, however, remain merely internalized, but gets cathected into inchoate senses of guilt, inexplicable terror, or a general sense of disquiet that may or may not be consciously traceable to a direct source. On this reading, the uncanny overlaps with post-traumatic states, and may sometimes be said to be an attenuated effect of these. The process of translation of negative affects in such states from the perception of external disorder into an internal sense of disquiet sits between interiority and externality and cannot be explained exclusively with reference to the familial saga of much psychoanalysis. Ultimately, the systemic uncanny is to be understood in the Kleinian idiom of oscillation, however moving not from the dynamic relations between the child and the mother's breast and into the consciousness, but from the perceptual surface of fragmented and chaotic details of social life and into the psyche. The fragmented social details then get re-vivified and in their turn gain energy from the psyche such that the social phenomena themselves seem to embody the uncanny as such. The systemic uncanny may be social as well as personal, public as well as private. Even though the force of the systemic uncanny is best discerned as deriving from intense conditions of chaos and confusion and may become attenuated or even dissolved completely with time, within the political domain the range of negative affects inherent in the systemic uncanny may also be present under apparently peaceful conditions, when individuals sense that a threat to their well-being is persistent rather than transient and is directly associated with the state and its apparatuses. This is inarguably the case under totalitarian regimes in Africa and elsewhere, where people are known to disappear or suffer all kinds of brutalities unleashed by the state security apparatus.[9]

What I describe here as systemic, however, is essentially open to historical analysis, even if it may also be productively understood synchronically in terms of a wide-ranging discursive ensemble. Furthermore, it must also be remembered that every culture has a way of translating the uniqueness of epochal events, whether these are negative or positive, into a general transcendent value. As Bernard Cohn (1987, 45) puts it in another context:

> We write of an event as being unique, yet every culture has a means to convert the uniqueness into a general and transcendent meaningfulness through the language members of the society speak. To classify phenomena at a "commonsense" level is to recognize categories of events coded by the cultural system. An event becomes a marker within a cultural system. All societies have such markers, which can be public or private. . . . *In many societies ritual transforms uniqueness into structure.*   (Italics added)

If we take "structure" in Cohn's formulation to mean the commonsensical and predictable generated by the codes of a cultural system, then with regard to war the translation of the uniqueness of such a traumatic event into a transcendent value will also rely on ritual, whether such ritual is of the state variety (commemorative marches, monuments) or of a more literary-aesthetic articulation (drama, music, and dance that carry a war thematic). The literary-aesthetic domain allows members of a society to recall the traumatic and negative affectivity of war within a constrained space that they can be distanced from even as it is consumed and participated in. Art is thus a way to mediate the strong emotions of a society.

Even though they retain a space for the assertion of the usefulness of ritual and cultural values, the images of ritual that Soyinka gives us in his plays often imply a challenge to the commonsensical and the predictable. It is this that allows Olunde to take the place of Elesin Oba as sacrificial carrier at the end of *Death and the King's Horseman* and Say Tokyo Kid to stab Professor at the end of *The Road*, when he blasphemously attempts to convert the *egungun* masquerade into an instrumental epistemological template. Similar observations might be made of *The Lion and the*

Jewel, Kongi's Harvest, The Beatification of Area Boy, and *The Strong Breed*. In each instance, the strength of cultural values is strongly asserted even when much of the action has been devoted to questioning them. *Madmen and Specialists* is markedly different from all these in that there is absolutely nothing commonsensical and predictable about the play. Quite the opposite. It is a study in deconstructive techniques, and, as we saw, full of interruptions, sharp changes of tone and direction, the failed synthesis of a dialectical movement, and the mirroring and collapse of various polarities of signification both in terms of characterization and in the depiction of stage spectacle. In this way, as we noted earlier, the play is in its overall dramaturgical expression a translation of the systemic disorder that might be said to be pertinent to an understanding of the Biafra War itself. In this translation, the disabled mendicants take center stage. And it is around them that we see the contradictions of aesthetic nervousness. For what we see is that they replicate typically negative depictions of disability (disability as moral deficit/evil) while also suggesting a certain choric energy and the capacity to proliferate interpretative impasses within the text. Their status as a failed synthesis between opposing ideological standpoints also makes them problematic characters that are rid of the capacity to mean anything that is not ultimately assimilated to the dominant, even if this dominant is itself in a state of confusion and flux. Thus, as in many other depictions of disability, the mendicants provide the occasion for a meditation on the tragedy of war, rather than being the heroic protagonists for a way out of the impasse produced by war mentality.

Perhaps what is more important, however, is that the mendicants' problematic discursive location may also be interpreted as encapsulating the emotional chaos in the mind of the author himself following his incarceration during the war. It is almost as if, being himself traumatized by incarceration, Soyinka seizes upon the mendicants as a means of articulating his own loss of direction and his incapacity to establish hierarchies between the values espoused by the two sides in the Nigerian civil war. The espousal of a preference for either side would of course have been extremely difficult, since like many others he interpreted the war as revealing the fundamental incoherence in the foundation of the Nigerian nation-state as such, something that he had depicted in the earlier *A Dance of the Forests*, a play originally commissioned to commemorate Nigeria's independence in 1960. As part of an antimimetic dramatic action, the disabled mendicants are ciphers of an emotional impasse in the mind of the author articulated via a fragmented dramaturgical idiom. In this respect I would endorse Jeyifo's (2004, 141–142) view that the plotlessness of *Madmen and Specialists* well captures "war psychosis as an analog of (dis)organized social life," only adding that the disorganization is also in the mind of the playwright himself. In *Madmen and Specialists*, Soyinka is no longer able to stand at any point outside the system to manufacture an artistic critique of it. He has been too emotionally affected by the chaos to be entirely free from it. It is interesting to note, then, that *Death and the King's Horseman* and *The Bacchae* of Euripides, both of which followed four years after *Madmen and Specialists*, do not have the same fragmented idiom. Both of these later plays are more secure in their uses of ritual and were written and produced during his stay in England between 1975 and 1977, when he presumably had a chance to distance himself from the chaos of the war. *Madmen and Specialists* was produced the very year in which he was released from prison, following on closely from *The Man Died*, the prison notes that detailed his anguished state of mind during the period of his incarceration. It may thus be argued that *Madmen and Specialists* is the play that is emotionally closest to the sense of chaos brought on by the war upon the playwright's psyche and in that respect is not a play just about the civil war but also about the anguished theater of the author's own mind.

To read his work in this way may be interpreted as falling into the trap of an overly convenient psychoanalysis of the author's mind, something that is open to serious question and which I would wish to repudiate completely.[10] What I want to suggest is something even bolder and that goes beyond an ordinary attempt at psychoanalyzing the author. I want to suggest that the disabled characters in Soyinka's work encapsulate most securely his own predisposition toward enigma, open-endedness, and dramaturgic experimentation, and that they are the ones that allow him to properly explore the boundary between the political and the metaphysical, a boundary that is central to all of his creative writing. The disabled characters are thus the objective correlatives of a chaotic postcolonial world as well as being the ciphers of the author's creative predispositions. On this premise, I would like to argue that disability is as significant to his writing as is the Ogunian aesthetics that have been so painstakingly elaborated by him and his critics as paradigmatic. The full significance of this additional paradigm is only made visible when we take detailed account of the disabled characters he gives us as part of his dramaturgic schema.[11] In that respect, reading Soyinka through a disability studies paradigm rescues him for use in a different kind of social commentary than the one with which he has normally been associated. In this we would be doing justice to his stature as the foremost playwright and most fearless political and social commentator on the African continent today.

6

J. M. COETZEE

Speech, Silence, Autism and Dialogism

So FAR, THE INTEREST OF THE PREVIOUS CHAPTERS HAS been mainly on physical disability. Whenever I have turned to a discussion of mental and psychological states, as was the case with Molloy and Consolata, it was to re-situate their physical impairments within the parameters provided by their highly elaborated states of consciousness. I want to turn now to cognitive as opposed to physical disability, with a special focus on the representation of the autistic spectrum in literary writing. But in turning in this direction I will also be raising certain theoretical questions regarding narrative itself. Whereas in chapter 1 I suggested that disability may be taken as providing *structurally constitutive points* for narratives of social deformation in general, I now want to supplement that proposition with a more subtle and complex one, namely, that the nature of the representation of cognitive disorders such as autism allows us to see the acute contradiction that is established within narrative between an implied interlocutor—shown here as a surrogate for the wider social domain—and the silent or inarticulate character who seems to opt for silence in negotiating the vicissitudes of social existence. The autistic character provides us with a template for seeing the relationship between speech and silence, and between the domain of cognitive disorder and that of social relations, where everyone is arguably spoken for within a social semiotic that cannot tolerate anomaly (much less silence). In placing the implied interlocutor in a dialogical relationship to Coetzee's autistic Michael K, I will be bringing to the foreground a thematic thread that has run through the previous chapters, particularly in the discussion of Molloy, Hamm and Clov, the Mendicants, and, to a lesser degree, Consolata and Baby Suggs.

Benita Parry (1996) offers some useful insights about the relationship between speech and silence in Coetzee's work. Essentially, her argument is that inarticulateness is distributed in his work in such a way as to imply a hierarchy among various Others, and that this implied hierarchy rehearses the ways in which the power to (self-)represent is dispersed within the colonial archive. Even though white women are less powerful than white men in this discursive arrangement, they are at an advantage over racial others. Parry suggests that Coetzee goes as far as imitating women's writing in his elaboration of recalcitrant women who seize the center of the narrative and unravel patriarchal codes of writing (Magda, Curren, Susan Burton); on the other hand, he aligns the racial other's inarticulacy or silence to implications of the ineffability of noncanonical knowledges (Michael K, the Barbarian Girl, Friday). Her conclusion is that despite troubling the generic features of white South African writing (the pastoral fable, the novel of liberal humanist crisis, etc.), Coetzee inadvertently replicates the same system of hierarchies that have bolstered the white colonial archive.

Parry's reading is based first on a structuralist interpretation of the relationship between silence and speech. This assumes that the silenced are to be understood primarily in relational terms and that such relationality defines a series of repeated active/passive positions that are productively understood when all Coetzee's apparently marginal figures are read together. Second, she outlines the ground of the formal features of speech and silence as being ultimately related to the specific history of South Africa and to Coetzee's place, as a white man, in it. The relationship between elements in his texts is then a refraction of larger discursive relations within South African history, so that his is both a subversive account of such a history and a replication of its construction of race hierarchies. Her critique is highly suggestive both for its particular insights and for the process by which she aligns literary interpretation to a materialist analysis. One thing that Parry does not note in her account of speech and silence in Coetzee's work, however, is that there is also a coincidence between inarticulacy, racialization, and disability in the writing. All the inarticulate "other" characters he gives us carry physical and cognitive impairments of various sorts. These impairments cannot be separated from their role as inarticulate and spoken for. The question posed in Coetzee's work more generally about who has the power to narrate, though clearly connected to the ambivalent interrogation of the colonial archive, is ultimately also inseparable from bodily questions. Furthermore, these inarticulate racial others also represent the convergence of disabling physical and social conditions, even if Coetzee is careful to foreground only the physical ones. Thus Michael K has a harelip but is inarticulate also because he is an underclass colored person in apartheid South Africa, Friday was possibly once a slave and is certainly mutilated and without a tongue, and the Barbarian Girl is tortured into blindness by the Empire's security agents for the mere reason of being a "barbarian." In all these instances, the inarticulacy *and* disability of his nonwhite characters performs an insistent invitation to interpret while frustrating the possibility for interpretation at various levels, thus generating what we noted in chapter 2 as a form of hermeneutical impasse. This dialectic of invitation and frustration is demonstrated most strongly in *Life and Times of Michael K*, *Waiting for the Barbarians*, and *Foe*, though it can also be seen in operation disconnected from the characterization of disability in *In the Heart of the Country* and *The Age of Iron*.[1]

To speak of silence in a literary text seems somewhat tautological, since the words we read are always evoking ideas in our own minds. The words thus "make a noise" despite the presumed silence of the inarticulate characters. Furthermore, there are many types of silence that make the issue of inarticulacy both variegated and suggestive. Leslie Kane (1984) enumerates the following typology of silence:

The dumb silence of apathy, the sober silence of solemnity, the fertile silence of awareness, the active silence of perception, the baffled silence of confusion, the uneasy silence of impasse, the muzzled silence of outrage, the expectant silence of waiting, the reproachful silence of censure, the tacit silence of approval, the vituperative silence of accusation, the eloquent silence of awe, the unnerving silence of menace, the peaceful silence of communion, and the irrevocable silence of death. (Kane 1984, 14–15)

More significantly, as she goes on to point out, "non-participation in the speech act symbolizes withdrawal from temporal, spatial or social reality" (19). Thus silence is of variant signification and may have quite startling implications.

The inarticulate character is silent only within the context of the specific representational domain in which they are found; otherwise "silence" is practically impossible. This uneasy fit between a character's elective silence and the rupturing of silence that the text insinuates on their behalf and around them may also be glossed more fully if to Parry's structuralist and materialist analysis we add two other terms by which to understand the nature of speech and silence in Coetzee's writing, namely autism and dialogism. Autism seems to me particularly relevant to a discussion of characters such as Michael K, the Barbarian Girl, and Foe not because they illustrate broad aspects of an autistic spectrum, but because of the scrupulous silence they enjoin upon themselves, which carries a hint of their extreme discomfort with extant forms of social communication. All these characters carry physical marks of "formal particularity," to turn to Rosemarie Garland Thomson's felicitous term, which I have referred to more than once over the course of this study. Physical marks of formal particularity signal the disability of the characters and may be read in physical, cognitive, and ultimately social terms (Thomson 1997, 119). In the particular case of Michael K, as we shall see later, it is impossible to escape the impression that his silence is part of a wider autistic spectrum.

Focusing on the literary representation of autism allows us to raise the question of silence in a particularly productive way because, in reading silence as connected to cognitive *and* physical conditions, we are obliged to attend to all that remains unstated and merely suggested. Furthermore, the autist's silence generates a multiplicity of significations that cannot be encompassed solely within a reading of content or theme. Silence/autism and dialogism have to be seen as related and indeed dialectical pairs rather than as separate terms, for in the representation of inarticulacy an implied interlocutor is invoked whose role is to provide an ethos of continual dialogism and thus to maintain the process by which the silent character's nonsocial musings are inflected in a manifestly socially significant way. But the role of the implied interlocutor is much more exacerbated in a text dealing with a person with autism, since the elective silence of the autist is constantly balanced against the intrusions of sociality concealed within the discursive template of the implied interlocutor. Indeed, I would like to suggest that the status of autistic silence is to be read within individual texts as more variegated in the ways in which the relationships between character(s), narrator, author-function, and implied external sociopolitical contexts are displayed and negotiated. For even though it can be argued that *all* literary characters, whether disabled, autistic, or not, in the end interact with an implied interlocutor, the point I am making here is that for the disabled, that interlocutor may be an aggregation of attitudes of Garland Thomson's "normate" such that the structure of interlocution in such texts may be sharply differentiated from representations that are not focused on disability. I will have more to say about this later in the discussion.

Of Autism and Dialogism

But first, what is autism? In filmic representations of persons with autism, a composite definition of autism is deployed that includes features such as extreme discomfort with the unfamiliar, echolalic and monotonic speech, difficulty understanding social cues, unusual preoccupations, pronounced lack of affect, and auditory hypersensitivity.[2] However, in real life autism has a broader symptomatology and is diagnosed on the basis of abnormalities in the areas of social, adaptive, and communicative development and imagination, together with marked repetitive or obsessive behavior or unusual narrow interests. Autism is determined both by neurological features and by observable behavioral symptoms. People with autism may have an IQ at any level. As a rule, if a person with autism has an IQ in the normal range or above, they are said to have "high-functioning autism." If, on the other hand, a person meets all of the criteria for high-functioning autism except for communicative abnormality/history of language delay, they are said to have Asperger's syndrome. An individual with lower functioning autism is likely to be classified as severely disabled, since they would necessarily exhibit acute forms of cognitive and sometimes even physical retardation. Children and adults with high-functioning autism (HFA) and Asperger's syndrome may show the following features:

1. Greater involvement with objects and physical systems than with people;

2. Lower tendency to communicate than other children;

3. Tendency to follow their own desires and beliefs rather than paying attention to, or being easily influenced by, others' desires and beliefs;

4. Showing relatively little interest in what the social group is doing, or being a part of it;

5. Showing strong, persistent interests, sometimes stretching for months only to be switched to new, equally intense interests;

6. High degree of accuracy in perceiving details of information in addition to higher rates of recall than others;

7. View of what is relevant and important in a situation may not coincide with others' views;

8. Fascination with patterned material, be it visual (shapes), numeric (dates, timetables), alphanumeric (license plates), or lists (of cars, songs, etc.);

9. Fascination with systems, be they simple (light switches, water taps), a little bit more complex (weather fronts), or abstract (mathematics);

10. Exhibiting a strong drive to collect categories of objects (e.g., bottle tops, train maps) or categories of information (types of lizard, types of rock, types of fabric, etc.);

11. Preference for experiences that are controllable rather than unpredictable;

12. And finally, whereas in lower functioning autism the autist understands almost no metaphors, so everything is taken literally, in Asperger's syndrome they learn the meanings of idioms one at a time, almost as if they are compiling a database of nonliteral sentences and their meanings, which makes them seem more able to cope with figurative language. This is still subtly different from how non-AS people use language.[3]

Since autism is made up of both physically discernible behavioral features and aspects of mental responses, the project of identifying autism in writing that does not explicitly set out to present itself as dealing with that condition is an elusive and fraught process. My application of an interpretative framework drawn from an understanding of autism is designed to highlight specific features of texts that seem pertinent to literary representations of the condition, whether the writers explicitly set out to represent an autistic condition or not. The framework provides a way for illuminating details that normally get ignored or assimilated to other categories of interpretation. In fact, once we begin to think of such silent characters as illustrating aspects of the autistic spectrum, we begin to see how widespread autism features in literary writing.[4] I want it to be noted that in the discussion that follows, I do not mean to imply that the autistic condition is by any means uniform and generalizable across the board. For ease of reference, I shall be using the terms autism and autistic spectrum interchangeably, not in order to sidestep the task of isolating each specific example for analysis in its own right, but to suggest the main parameters of an analytical category that will hopefully be picked up and further elaborated by the community of disability scholars and others.

Dialogism in novelistic discourse raises a different set of issues that I want to suggest are pertinent to the understanding of how autism is situated in literature generally and more specifically in relation to Coetzee's writing. Commenting on the polyphonic nature of the opening passage of Dostoevsky's *Crime and Punishment*, Bakhtin (1984, 61) states that "the dialogized interior monolog . . . is a brilliant model of the *microdialog*: every word in it is double-voiced, every word contains a conflict of voices." As always with Bakhtin, when he uses the term "word" he is really referring to utterance as it pertains to a communicative environment. The word/utterance is first and foremost social. As he states later: "The other person's word is not reproduced, it is merely implied, but the entire structure of the speech would be completely different if this reaction to the implied word were not present" (162). In Bakhtinian thought, every word implies the residue and echo of an anticipated response, such that the word/utterance is inescapably dialogized within itself. As extrapolated from his comments on Dostoevsky, even first-person novelistic accounts proceed on the basis of the incorporation of an interlocutor. This interlocutor is sometimes an unstable interlocutor, such as the implied addressee of a diary, journal, or report, who is in turns sympathetic or antagonistic to the writer. Thus, in *Problems of Dostoevsky's Poetics* Bakhtin explores in detail the various ways in which the interlocutor, whether polemical or otherwise, is incorporated into the structures of novelistic discourse, helping to shape the narration of the character's consciousness by always implying an addressee to even the most mundane and silent hopes, fears, desires, and vague ideas.

As will be recalled from previous chapters, the invocation of a skeptical or polemical implied interlocutor for the disabled characters proves highly productive in stipulating their addressees and how these addressees lead to various types of symbolic relationships in terms, for example, of the attempts at evasion of normality (Molloy), the illustration of the impulse to control the narrativization of the past (Hamm), the modulation of the consequences of the split between divine and erotic templates for the task of self-understanding (Consolata), or the design and dissemination of the effects of a systemic uncanny (Soyinka's mendicants). However, all these disabled characters form a collectively distinct class from the autist by virtue of the fact that they are all far from inarticulate or silent. No one would associate Hamm, for example, with inarticulacy. As we shall soon see, the same cannot be said for Coetzee's Michael K. Michael K's implied interlocutor is produced by his silence even if there is also the insinuation of a form of social rupture to that silence.

We are obliged to make a number of qualifications then in transferring the Bakhtinian model for an exploration of the representation of the autistic spectrum in Coetzee. As we noted a moment ago, in Bakhtin the "word" is always split between an addresser and an addressee, both of whom are by implication human subjects. This is so even when Bakhtin is writing about all the elements within the communicative nexus (word/addresser, addressee/social context, and the overall inflections of communication) in generic terms and without specific characters in mind. But what if the addressee/interlocutor is not a human character at all, but rather a structure of societal and cultural expectations not attributable to any single source? What if the interlocutor within the dialogized word is not an individual but an effect generated by the specific discursive structure of dialogism contained in the text itself? These questions and what they imply are directly pertinent to exploring the relation between speech, silence, autism, and dialogism. We have to note first of all that whereas the concept of the dialogized interior monologue may be generally applied to most modernist and postmodernist novels, in the case of the representation of the autistic spectrum the point of interest is not so much that the thoughts of the autist are dialogized and oriented toward an addressee, but that this orientation is performed *against* the autist's desire for absolute social silence and separation from social intercourse. For there is ample evidence in novelistic discourse that even when characters are silent they talk to themselves in their own minds and often actively anticipate direct and not-so-direct social responses. They may even from time to time cultivate solitude as a conduit for getting deeper access into their own sense of themselves prior to reemerging into social interaction. The main difference between an autist and another character that chooses to cultivate their solitude-in-silence is that the autist elects silence as a way of completely disavowing or at the very least sharply attenuating social interaction. The autist's orientation to social silence is also augmented by the intense attention they bring to bear on objects, abstract patterns, and systems; these may all be perceived in their separateness and distinctive-ness from the realm of human interaction. Furthermore, the autist devel-ops gestures and precise ritualistic and repetitive physical movements as a means of sharply indicating their withdrawal from the domain of ordi-nary human interaction. Thus the central clues to whether a character depicted in a piece of writing illustrates aspects of the autistic spectrum or not is the degree to which they (a) elect silence as a natural and organic part of their being-in-the-world; (b) display an insistent focus on objects, patterns, and abstract systems; and (c) develop repetitive gestures, ac-tions, or motions that represent a ritual of partial withdrawal from the so-cial realm. As we noted earlier, in literary texts the autist's silence, though elective, is concomitantly riddled by the contradictory pressures of the di-alogized novelistic discourse. This seems to go against their wish to re-main undisturbed within their silence. I want to recommend that the in-trinsic reading of silence as a characterological choice set against the interruptions necessarily instituted by the structures of narrative be seen as taking place primarily from the assumed perspective of the autistic character. Such a reading takes the autist's implicit orientation toward si-lence as a starting point from which to grasp the significance of all the levels of narrative discourse within which the autistic spectrum takes shape. My argument here is that the autist's silence must be taken as hav-ing an effect on the entire domain of the narrative discourse while also being produced and sustained by it.

Autism Versus Metaphor

Another dimension that complicates the literary representation of au-tism is the degree to which metaphorical discourse, or indeed metaphor itself, undermines the assumed verisimilitude of representations of the condition. The nature of this problem may be gleaned from Matthew Belmonte's (2005) fine argument regarding the relationship between autism and literary representation. Arguing that certain neurobiological features of persons with autism bear direct comparison with the impairment of associative processes that are central to narrative thought, Belmonte suggests that the autist's essentially inventorial cognitive predisposition (listings, patterns, a focus on mechanical or other deterministic systems, etc.) is directed toward nonsocial phenomena as a protection against disorder. The autist's efforts at meaning-making are essentially related to a narrative problematic: "In autism, when failures of neural connectivity impede narrative linkage, when each element of a scene or a story exists in isolation, the surrounding world can seem threatening and intractable. Autistic withdrawal into repetitive behaviours and scripted interactions can be read as an effort to gain control over such arbitrariness and unpredictability" (Belmonte 2005, 11). In Belmonte's highly suggestive account, the impulses behind the person with autism's repetitive behavior is the same as the impulse governing the narrative drive in the first place. Both have to do with the desire to organize reality so that it may be epistemologically ordered and understood, even if, as in postmodernist writing, this understanding depends upon a preparedness to surrender the comforts of predictability. As Belmonte concludes, persons with autism may be described as "human, but more so."

It must be noted, however, that metaphor and metaphorical discourse raise a peculiar problem for taking autistic processes as analogous to narrative impulses as such. As has been pointed out by many scholars of the condition, those on the lower-functioning end of the autistic spectrum tend to have difficulties with interpreting metaphor. Metaphorical discourse hides too much while revealing a labile surface in little. The discourse's elusive surface produces various levels of meaning, such that the person with autism is no longer able to entirely predict the precise significance of the language that they are confronted by. The problem of metaphor and metaphorical discourse for the person with autism is raised quite forcefully in Haddon's *The Curious Incident of the Dog in the Night-Time*, where Christopher states an explicit preference for simile as opposed to metaphor. To his mind, metaphor is untruthful. At one point, however, he seems to inadvertently succumb to the allure of metaphor. This comes in his description of the policeman at the station: "He also had a very hairy nose. It looked as if there were two very small mice hiding in his nostrils" (22). This is arguably a metaphor (nostrils as mouseholes and vice versa), and Christopher's attempt to deconstruct it and to show that the figure of speech he has just used is not metaphor but simile because it "really did look like there were two very small mice hiding in his nostrils" (22) fails to persuade. Had he seen two real mice nestling in the nostrils of the policeman, he is not likely to have described it so calmly. He would have found the sight expressly odd and unsettling and, given what we had already seen about him, would have raised some serious questions about it to the policeman himself (rather than just thinking about it in his own mind). In other words, even the decidedly autistic Christopher cannot entirely escape the reach of metaphor. But it is inescapable not because Christopher is a person with autism, *but because his condition is being represented from within the domain of literary discourse itself.* A real person with autism may be able to conduct their social relationships without any recourse to metaphor, but it would be hard to find a literary text without any metaphor whatsoever. This point can be pressed even further when we interpret the dead dog that triggers the investigative action of *The Curious Incident of the Dog in the Night-Time* not as an ordinary dog but as a literary device suggestive of the ritual scapegoat we encountered in the previous chapter. We are told on page 4 of the novel that the dog was leaking blood from its forkhole wounds. Thus as soon as Christopher hugs the dog to his body he takes on the ritual aspect of the dead animal and becomes its walking surrogate within the text. And it is evident on reading further that Christopher is indeed the ritual *pharmakon* for various familial and social disorders in the text. These are encapsulated in the reportedly strained relations between his parents, the low-intensity violence of his father deriving from his frustration and anger, the unsociability of the neighborhood, and, finally, the economic decay of an impoverished Swindon.[5] It is Christopher's pursuit of who killed the dog that progressively reveals all these levels of social disorder. By acting as a detective, he inadvertently becomes both the key to unearthing familial and social contradictions and the direct sacrificial carrier of the effects of these contradictions. The text thus metaphorizes him even while trying to produce the entire narrative in scrupulously realist terms (that is, eschewing any explicit metaphorization of people, events, and environmental details). Thus we can say that whereas Belmonte points out that autism shares similar impulses with the narrative drive, it is also clear that narrative as such undermines the possibility of a pure articulation of the autistic spectrum.

As will be recalled from our discussion in chapter 1, a close reading of disability requires that it be situated within the totality of representation and not treated as a discrete and isolated element within the literary discourse. The autist's dispositions tend to raise implications for the entire narrative text in all its dimensions. In cases where the autist is a central character, this is even more significant. There is no way of demarcating between the autistic "zone" and the nonautistic "zones" of such texts. Every zone is mutually constitutive and implicated. And in such a literary interpretation we find that metaphor sets the limit to what we might wish to attribute to the temperament of the autistic character as opposed to the representation in its entirety.

The Structures of Dialogism in Coetzee's Earlier Work

In a similar way to Beckett, on whom he based his doctoral dissertation, Coetzee illustrates the variable incorporation of a skeptical interlocutor into the processes of thought of his central characters and how their orientation to this interlocutor dialogizes their consciousness. A brief discussion of these will clear the way for seeing how the technique applies to *Life and Times of Michael K*. There is a fascinating similitude in Coetzee's work between characters such as Magda (*In the Heart of the Country*), David Lurie (*Disgrace*), and Paul Rayment (*Slow Man*) in the ways in which they constantly interrupt themselves to qualify their thoughts and feelings. For Magda, these interruptions emanate from an insistent sense of narrativity, that is, both the incitement to narrate and the fact of being narrated through her diaries. They also come from the elusive place of representation in the face of the violations of the female self discernible within the South African pastoral tradition in general.[6] For David Lurie, the self-interruptions derive, among other things, from his faulty understanding of what pertains to an epic Romantic action, seen in his case in the refusal to sign the apology recommended by his university authorities after accusations of raping a student have been brought against him. Lurie's dialogized self-interruptions also come from his

fraught perception of what it is to be a white man living in a postapartheid era with concerns about the necessity of reparations for the past.[7]
It is not a context that he either fully understands or indeed endorses.
Magda and David Lurie are both characters that are fundamentally afflicted by "second thoughts." Contrastively, in the case of Paul Rayment,
who has had his leg amputated after a car runs into him while he is riding
his bicycle, the regular process of internal dialogism that we see in relation to Coetzee's nondisabled characters is redirected into a secondary
and quite unexpected path that serves to illustrate a degree of aesthetic
nervousness.

Paul has had to suffer the ignominy of being looked after by various
caregivers, most of who treat him like a child. This is until he is sent
Marijana, a Croatian immigrant who has come to Australia with her husband and three children. Her expertise and robustness in caring for both
him and his house begins to stir feelings first of admiration and then attraction in the otherwise cautious Paul, until he can take it no more and
declares his love for her. After his declaration there is an awkward pause
after which Marijana leaves abruptly with the little daughter she normally
brings along to the house with her. We are left in suspense as to what will
happen next. This is the close of chapter 12. At the beginning of chapter
13, something quite strange happens: Elizabeth Costello enters the text!
Readers of Coetzee will recall her from *The Life of Animals* (2002) and
Elizabeth Costello (2003). She is not a pleasant character. What is she doing in *Slow Man*? Beyond the obvious postmodern trick of the intertextual hemorrhaging of characters from one text to another and the attendant
problematization of the ontological status of the characterization that
this implies, Elizabeth Costello represents something much more complicated with respect to the structures of dialogical interlocution that may
be discerned in Coetzee's writing. For not only does she insist that Paul
Rayment is a figment of her own writing (that is, that she wrote him into
being), but she comes to act as his conscience *in the same way that the
structure of dialogical interlocution we have seen operating in his own mind
produces the work of conscience earlier in the narrative.*

Within Paul's mind, his approach to almost everything, whether it be
his amputated leg, his not having had children, the history of Croatia, his
memories of the affair he had after separating from his first wife, and so
on, are always without exception hedged round by clichés and stereo-

types. He is a "slow" man not just because of his amputation, but because he has always been a fastidious man careful to "maintain the decencies." He is utterly unadventurous. Thus we are told:

> All in all, not a man of passion. He is not sure he has ever liked passion, or approved of it. Passion: foreign territory; a comical but unavoidable affliction like mumps, that one hopes to undergo while still young, in one of its milder, less ruinous varieties, so as not to catch it more seriously later on. Dogs in the grip of passion coupling, hapless grins on their faces, their tongues hanging out.
>
> (45–46)

Note the references to foreign territory, illness, and animals in trying to establish the parameters of passion, almost as if by such stereotypes to distance himself from it. With regard to Marijana and her family, he can think only in terms of stereotypical characteristics, even when he has known the various family members over a period of time and has had the opportunity to assemble a more complex idea of their "normality":

> The ease between the two of them [Marijana and Miroslav, her husband] tells all—that and Marijana's laughter and the freedom of her fingers in his hair. Not an estranged couple at all. On the contrary, intimate. An intimate relationship with a row every now and again, *Balkan style*, to add a dash of spice: accusations, recriminations, plates smashed, doors slammed. Followed by remorse and tears, followed by heated lovemaking.
>
> (253; italics added)

Paul regularly uses such unexamined clichés to describe Marijana and other members of her family in his own mind (34, 42, 51, 64, etc.). In thinking about the trick that Elizabeth Costello has played on him to get him to sleep with the blind Marianna, he reflects: "Blindness is a handicap pure and simple. A man without sight is a lesser man, as a man without a leg is a lesser man, not a new man. This poor woman she has sent him is a lesser woman too, less than she must have been before. Two lesser beings, handicapped, diminished: how could she have imagined a spark of the divine would be struck between them, or any spark at all?" (113).

Paul Rayment's shocking attitude to disability derives from his normate response to impairments in general, revealing how difficult it is for him to accept his current condition. But it is also of a piece with the many clichés and stereotypes he falls back on regularly in his encounters with what is strange and unusual within his social environment.

When Elizabeth Costello enters the text and chastises him for expressing his attraction to Marijana and in her place suggests the blind Marianna instead, we see her role as actualizing the set of cautionary clichéd dispositions that have already been amply evident in the mind of Paul himself. Costello expresses her irritation at his sentimental excess thus:

> But who are you to preach second thoughts to me? If you had only been true to your tortoise character, if you had waited for the coming of second thoughts, if you had not so foolishly and irrevocably declared your passion to your cleaning lady, we would not be in our present pickle, you and I. You could be happily set up in your flat, waiting for visits from the lady with the dark glasses, and I could be back in Melbourne. But it is too late for that now. Nothing left for us but to hold on tight and see where the black horse takes us.
>
> (228)

In other words, she is reminding him of how far he has strayed from his "natural" characteristic of caution. And notice the "us" she smuggles in, invoking not complicity but the fact that they are supposed to be of the same mind and disposition, in this case quite literally since, as I have been arguing, she springs up full-bodied from his mind and vice versa. This is a sure sign of the aesthetic nervousness in the terms I have been suggesting in this study. For why does Coetzee need to deploy this post-modern trick to ensure that Paul has the mirror image of his own fastidiousness in the form of a character from another novel? And why is this particular corrective required for what are completely normal feelings and desires? Why are the desires of the disabled man coded as illicit at this point, when he could very well have been left to struggle with his emergent desires and negotiate their meanings with the object of his attention like many other nondisabled characters in such a situation would be allowed to do? Since Costello steps into this novel from another one, it is almost as if the text is anxious that we do not make the mistake of misinterpreting the status of the intervention. She imports a range of implications derived from her characterization in the previous Coetzee novels in which she has featured. Thus she introduces an already formed template of possibilities via which her character and the relationship established with Paul Rayment and with any others in the text might be interpreted. Seeing that she emerges in the text when Paul, the disabled man, has just declared his amorous attraction to a nondisabled and married woman, there is the suggestion that Elizabeth Costello enters to "rescue" him from a transgression. Her role, in brief, is to intensify the structure of skeptical interlocution available in Rayment's mind in order that the free play of his emergent sexual desires is stemmed and arrested.[8]

If the structure of dialogical interlocution is seen to be central to Coetzee's writing to the point where a postmodern trick is used to produce the skeptical interlocutor as an intrusive character within Slow Man itself, a focus on his representation of the autistic spectrum shows the dialogical interlocution in a more subtle and complex light. As we noted earlier, in literary representations of persons with autism since the autist is noticeably reluctant to communicate with others unless this is absolutely inescapable, the implied interlocutor and indeed the rest of the text is always also assimilated to different pressures on silence. The implied interlocutor becomes both a product of the autist's silence and its archenemy, since the interlocutor is also entangled with the dialogized social domain that the autist desires to disavow through his or her silence. And since the autist's silent thoughts generate symbolic "noise" within both the wider representation and in our own readerly minds, a fundamental epistemological problem is raised regarding how we assess the status of the literary character with autism. Are they really silent, or is this silence the residue that remains from the interactions of the various discursive levels of the text? For there is no doubt that in the process of reading we align ourselves with different parts of what we read—character, narrator, spatial dynamic and temporal flows, and so on—as products of the modulations of the narrative, and that our shifting perspectival alignments are what generate the meanings that we take to be significant in what we read. One of such meanings is silence. Thus we find that in the literary text illustrating aspects of the autistic spectrum there is an unbridgeable gap between the represented inarticulacy of the character and the echoes that are raised by the other discursive dimensions of the text.

Autism and the Discriminations of Silence in
Life and Times of Michael K

Three difficulties immediately make themselves manifest once we turn our attention to *Life and Times of Michael K* and attempt to read it as a literary representation of a person with autism. First, though he is depicted as generally of a quiet and withdrawn disposition, Michael K begins to show autistic tendencies only after his mother dies. This is about a third of the way into the text. Second, his internal monologue is nothing if not filled with various figures of speech of both a metaphorical and other nature, thus distinguishing him in a significant way from real-life persons with autism. And third, because of the ways in which aspects and images of his internal monologue coincide with the perspectives of the third-person narrator, he is made directly amenable to various metaphorical interpretations both by other characters within the text and by readers of the novel. He becomes an archetype of contrastive metaphorical and indeed ethical interpretations.[9] It is mainly around his extreme silence that the autistic spectrum in the text is built, and it is the silence that we need to focus upon in evaluating his location on the spectrum and what implications this raises for the novel in general.

On the second page of the novel, we are told that Michael K's job as a gardener had given him a measure of solitariness but that "down in the lavatories he had been oppressed by the brilliant neon light that shone off the white tiles and created a space without shadows" (4). The "oppression" seems to be simultaneously a form of attraction, thus providing the mildest hint of an autistic tendency. However, it is not until the death of his mother several pages later that he begins to display clear signs of social withdrawal pertinent to an autistic condition. On his mother's death at the hospital, there is an odd contradiction between the frigid emotional response in his own mind and the many repetitive enactments of infantilization and bewilderment that he exhibits toward the people and events around him. This contradiction is captured most succinctly in the contrast between the gesture of pinning a black strip on his arm and the thought about his mother that accompanies this ostensible sign of mourning: "He tore a black strip from the lining of his mother's coat and pinned it around his arm. But he did not miss her, he found, except insofar as he had missed her all his life" (34). A bit earlier, we are told that while wandering about in the hospital with no clear purpose the day after her death, he climbs into a great wire cage containing soiled linen and sleeps there "curled up like a cat" (32). As we shall see later, this is the first of many references to sleep that we find in the novel. Coinciding also with his mother's death is the depiction of his struggles to interpret the codes behind what people say to him. Thus:

> "Your mother passed away during the night," the woman doctor told him. "We did what we could to keep her, but she was very weak. We wanted to contact you but you didn't leave a number."
> He sat down on a chair in the corner.
> "Do you want to make a phone call?" said the doctor.
> This was evidently a code for something, he did not know what. He shook his head. (30–31)[10]

His attempts to gauge what response people want when they speak to him is reminiscent of the depiction of Christopher Boone's similar struggles in *The Curious Incident of the Dog in the Night-Time*.

It is Michael K's endemic silence then that provides the most significant clues to the ways in which he might be taken as an illustration of the autistic spectrum. There are a number of interrelated dimensions to this silence that form a coherent pattern. We are told early in the novel that after his birth and the initial shock of the sight of his harelip, his mother kept him away from other children and took him to work with her. He sat on a blanket year after year watching his mother carrying out her chores and "learning to be quiet" (4). Silence is also inculcated in him by the ethos of Huis Norenius, a school for "variously afflicted and unfortunate children." Significantly, Michael K's father is never referred to directly in the entire novel. In his mind, the father-function is taken up by the twenty-one rules on the door of the dormitory at Huis Norenius, the first one of which is "There will be silence in dormitories at all times" (105). The implicit parental attributes given to the rules at Huis Norenius means that the institution joins his mother in creating silence for him as familial and normative. He is begotten in silence (absented father) and brought up in silence by his birth mother and his surrogate, institutional father. Even though from this early account it would seem that silence was imposed upon him as a parental and educational injunction to good behavior, it is also evident that the injunction to silence is further assimilated to his own desire to avoid social interaction of all sorts. The fact that the institutional father is a system of rules that have to be obeyed at all times means that there is a suggestive assimilation of Michael K's sense of self to a system of predictable codes of social behavior. The Huis Norenius rules, underpinned by the obligatory and foundational code of silence, form the deictic basis of the relationship of his personal sense of self and its relationship to the selves of others. Since the deixis of self and other is also played out within his dialogized internal monologue, the place attributed to the implied interlocutor is also the place where his elective silence is constructed as well as undermined. Read differently, the rules of the school may also be seen as the assimilation of the space of absence to the Law of the Father. This Law is partly responsible for generating the dialogized interlocutor to whose implicit perspective Michael K's thoughts bear an orientation. Thus the implied interlocutor of Michael K's thought is both the generalized system of socializing rules of behavior first invoked by Huis Norenius and the code of an implicit and unacknowledged masculinity. This implicit code of masculinity is revealed in the novel incrementally.

Silence is so natural to Michael K that at points in the narrative it even permeates the ontological foreground of the representation itself. His response to persistent questioning from the doctor at the Kenilworth camp is silence, but one so absolute that it becomes objectified to the doctor as a pure sound associated with death: "There was a silence so dense that I heard it as a ringing in my ears, a silence the kind one experiences in mine shafts, cellars, bomb shelters, airless places" (140). Three of the elements in this list invoke places of the potential negation of life, whether this negation is due to economic exploitation (mine shafts), war (bomb shelters), or an environmentally threatening location (airless places), so that Michael K's silence becomes evocative of the *unheimlich*, of homelessness and the uncanny. Earlier in the novel, this *unheimlich* silence manifests itself as a narrative problematic. In warding off the robbers that attempt to steal from him and his mother at a point on their journey to Prince Albert, the event as it is narrated has a peculiar soundtrack that does not really match his menacing gestures. We get a multiple focalization of sound and silence:

They were accosted by a pair of passers-by who, coming upon a man of meagre build and an old woman in a lonely place, concluded that they might strip them of their possessions with impunity. As a sign of this intention one of the strangers displayed to K (allowing the blade to slip from his sleeve into his palm) a carving knife, while the other laid hands on the suitcase. In an instant of the flash of the blade, K saw before him the prospect of being humiliated again while his mother watched, of sitting on the floormat with his hands over his ears enduring day after day the burden of her silence. He reached into the cart and brought out his sole weapon, the fifteen-inch length he had sawn from the axlerod. Brandishing this, lifting his arm to guard his face, he advanced on the youth with the knife, who circled away from him towards his companion while Anna K filled the air with shrieks. The strangers backed off. Wordlessly, still glaring, still menacing with the bar, K recovered the case and helped his quaking mother into the cart with the robbers hovering not twenty paces away.

(25–26)

In the flash of the blade, he has a flashback to an earlier cycle of humiliation and waiting that starts from the beginning of their journey when they were turned back at a military checkpoint. Significantly, the flashback also calls up an attempt to block out the accusatory loudness of his mother's silence. The only sound in the entire described sequence with the robbers is of his mother's shrieks. Anna K's shrieks act as a metaphor for the accusatory loudness of the remembered silence and a metonymic displacement of the sounds he should have been making in warding off the robbers. There is thus the foregrounding of a silent reel of ritual menace and repulsion for the narrated actions set against the background of what is essentially a bifurcated soundtrack, one from the memory of the loudness of his mother's accusatory silence and the other from her present shrieks. But why does K not say anything or make any sound whatsoever, even as a means of registering his obviously strong emotions in warding off their attackers?

The silence here registers a larger narrative problem, which has to do with the way in which Michael K has assimilated an interlocutor—the Law of the (Absent) Father—into his consciousness. This interlocutor does not have the same status as the skeptical interlocutor of *Slow Man*, who, as we saw a moment ago, is materialized in the person of Elizabeth Costello to mirror back to the central character the essential lineaments of his own thought. Michael K's interlocutor in these sections is also markedly different from what we find with Magda, David Lurie, or even with Susan Barton in *Foe*. In each of the earlier Coetzee novels, the characters' internal monologues are oriented toward specific social and cultural templates by which they evaluate their senses of self. In contrast, the significance of Michael K's implied interlocutor lies in the fact that it is the voice of a Judgment or Opinion that comes from the subliminal trace of a social memory (the school rules) and is also simultaneously derived from an implicit judgment of masculinity (the Law of the Father). There are thus sediments and bifurcations to his interlocutor that nonetheless seem to be effaced because he imagines himself existing determinedly *outside* of social discourse. As an autistic character, his silence may be elective, yet his implied interlocutor is multiply socialized and assimilated to a familial template whose effect is to naturalize the place of the interlocutor and render him unobtrusive and thus even more effective.

An inkling of the masculinist character of K's implied interlocutor is provided in the flashback to humiliation and the cycle of waiting that we encountered a moment ago. It is essentially the flashback to a judgment, but it is a judgment that, given the highly attenuated mode by which Michael K expresses his own masculinity, is left truncated and incomplete. Why should he feel *humiliated again* before his mother if not because he thinks that he is failing in the view of this implied interlocutor? When later on in the novel he thinks of a family on the run with their property in a barrow such as theirs, the image that he calls to mind is of a man, a woman, and two children, thus implying a normative familial setup (106). The figure of dependable masculinity is never too far from the surface of K's mind. Tellingly, this dependability is tied to notions of courage, something that at one point he seems interested in claiming, even if obliquely and indirectly. After his mother's death, a soldier at a checkpoint stops him and relieves him of his mother's purses. With a mixture of threats and mockery, the soldier takes out the money from the purses and puts it into his pocket. He peels off a ten rand note and flicks it in Michael K's direction. It is meant as a "tip." The narrative continues:

> K came back and picked up the note. Then he set off again. In a minute or two the soldier had receded into the mist.
>
> It did not seem to him that he had been a coward. Nevertheless, a little further on it struck him that there was no point in keeping the suitcase now. (38)

Why did it *not seem to him that he had been a coward?* We recall that apart from his mother's ashes, K has shown no attachment to any of their paltry itinerant possessions. The basis of his thought after his encounter with the soldier is that of an Opinion that does not seem to derive its authority from any evident source. The thought about not being a coward is followed up not by a reflection on what cowardice might or might not constitute in him, but by the practical gesture of shedding the paraphernalia that might in the future expose him to attack. The deictics of the interaction with the implied interlocutor—his I in a dialogical relationship with the Interlocutor's You—leads him to modify his action without a return to the interlocutor for verification or validation. The often repeated pattern in K's mind is thus of an apparently stray thought that is also a Judgment or Opinion and is indistinguishable from his own views. This Judgment or Opinion then triggers a sequence of further thoughts or actions without recourse back to that implied interlocutor. What then is this interlocutor but the voice of the Law of the (Absented) Father, which in this text has been assimilated to rules and regulations governing acceptable (masculine) behavior? Michael K's many rebellions against the system can then be interpreted as emerging out of the interactions between his thoughts and the Judgments and Opinions of this internalized implied interlocutor. The central effect of these interactions is the production of a particular form of subjectivity that is both subversive of the dominant and yet also acquiescent in certain codes of masculinity. Admittedly, this code stands in sharp contrast to the mindless military codes that dominate the war system depicted in the novel. But it is a code of unacknowledged masculinity all the same.

At one point, Michael K self-reflexively observes a thought emerging in his own mind and renounces responsibility for it, blurring the distinction between himself as character, the third-person narrator, and the author-function governing the narrative. It has to do with the extermination of unwanted beings at the Jakkalsdrif camp:

> If these people wanted to be rid of us, he thought (curiously he watched the thought begin to unfold itself in his head, like a plant growing), if they really wanted to forget us forever, they would have to give us picks and spades and command us to dig; then, when we had exhausted ourselves digging, and had dug a great hole in the middle of the camp, they would have to order us to climb in and lay ourselves down; and

when we were lying there, all of us, they would have to break down the
huts and tents as well as every last thing we had owned upon us, and
cover us with earth, and flatten the earth.... .

It seemed more like Robert than like him, as he knew himself, to
think like that. Would he have to say that the thought was Robert's
and had merely found a home in him, or could he say that though the
seed had come from Robert, the thought, having grown up inside him,
was now his own? He did not know.   (94–95)

The idea of the mass grave invokes the Nazi camps in which Jews were
exterminated (Dachau is mentioned elsewhere in the novel). When he
renounces the thought as not his own but Robert's, it is also partially the
renunciation of the mediating role of the narrator. Since the knowledge
suggested here is qualitatively different from any such referents in the
novel and ties the narrated events to a well-known historical register of
annihilations, the moment also invokes the narrator as a historically
knowing subject, perhaps even proximate, at least at this point, to the
real Author behind the text. The background of war in a South African
context is represented in the novel as being more allegorical than real,
since historically such a war was waged against racial others and their
supporters, whereas in this novel active insurgency seems to be disconnected from race. Making the reference to mass graves is directly evocative of a specific historical context beyond South Africa and is a piece of
knowledge that lies well out of the reach of Michael K as we have come
to understand him thus far. Not concluding the thought either way signals a retreat from closure, leaving the implications of ownership hanging. Are the thoughts his, Robert's, or the narrator's?[11] Coupled to K's
elective silence, then, the partialness and inconclusiveness of the dialogized interlocutor at such points also suggests the discursive entangle-
ments between the character and the narrator within the novel. In each
such entanglement, the elective silence of the autistic character is undermined by the structures of dialogism, even if, as we have come to see, the
dialogism is scrupulously assimilated to the mind of the character himself
and naturalized as a dimension of his own consciousness.

Several times in the novel, Michael K is depicted sleeping.[12] K thinks
of himself "not as something heavy that left tracks behind it, but if anything as a speck upon the surface of an earth too deeply asleep to notice
the scratch of ant-feet, the rasp of butterfly teeth, the tumbling of dust"

(97). The desire not to leave a trace also informs his decision to erect only a makeshift abode on his return to the Visagies farm; he desires something that would not "tug at the heartstrings" (101). Yet this desire to leave no trace is undermined by the persistent attempts on the part of others to assimilate his story to a larger semiotic context. His autistic silence gathers meaning in spite of itself from the domain of war and violence that provides the superscript for the broader social context of his existence. The semiotic excess of his silence is partly driven by the ease with which he is made amenable to metaphorical interpretations. In such instances, the "traces" that he invokes are manifestly those of fable and parable. Significantly, these parabolic and fabular associations appear regularly as descriptions by the narrator of Michael K, as K's own self-description, and, most crucially in part 2, in the first-person journal narration of the camp doctor. For the camp doctor, for instance, Michael K represents the opportunity for a spiritual epiphany:

> You ask why you are important, Michaels. The answer is that you are not important. But that does not mean you are forgotten. No, not forgotten. Remember the sparrows. Five sparrows are sold for a farthing, and even they are not forgotten. (136)

> Did you eat locusts? Your papers said you were an *opgaarder*, a storage man, but they do not say what it was you stored. Was it manna? Did manna fall from the sky for you, and did you store it away in the underground bins for your friends to come and eat in the night? Is that why you will not eat camp food—because you have been spoiled forever by the taste of manna? (150–151)

> Your stay in the camp was merely an allegory, if you know that word. It was an allegory—speaking at the highest level—of how scandalously, how outrageously a meaning can take up residence in a system without becoming a term in it. Did you not notice how, whenever I tried to pin you down, you slipped away? I noticed. (166)

Sparrows, locusts, and manna all reference biblical stories.[13] K's potential for allegorization means he oscillates between an inside and an outside of material significations. The doctor sees this as "scandalous," by which we can assume that the elusiveness of K's potential meanings is a worry for the war semiotic that dominates the narrative. More important, it also means that the war semiotic that seeks to name adversaries and to convert the mundane into a self-other structure of antagonism is superseded by a mode of signification that is spiritual and not limited to any particular historical context. It is in K's amenability to fabular and parabolic interpretation that he becomes "scandalous."

The standard critical view of Michael K's silence is that he is a spiritual being and by that status poses a challenge to the status quo of war. Two difficulties with this interpretation are that (1) even while thinking of himself through associations with insects and animals, he never actually assents in his mind to any form of spirituality, and (2) he shows a remarkable knack for violence toward animals. At the start of his stay on the Visagies farm, he brutally drowns a goat in the hope of getting food to quell his raving hunger. The effort is exhausting and he is not certain whether it was worth the trouble. However, the event presents him not with an occasion to reflect on the lives of animals, but only to learn the lesson not to kill animals of that size: "The lesson, if there was a lesson, if there were lessons embedded in events, seemed to be not to kill such large animals. He cut himself a Y-shaped stick and, with the tongue of an old shoe and strips of rubber from an inner tube, made himself a catapult with which to knock birds out of the trees. He buried the remains of the goat" (57). K seems to be essentially a predator killing animals, insects, and birds for survival; at no point does he surrender to any form of sentimentality in relation to these creatures. And at no time do they trigger a spiritual impulse within his own consciousness. This implies a form of splitting around his person. On the one hand, he performs all the predatory instincts of a carnivore without any sentimentality. Yet on the other, the silence and frailty of his person allows others to interpret him as bearing a resemblance to the lives of animals and therefore of carrying an excess of religious connotations. Like animals, insects, and birds, he is not of the human world. Thus the various points at which he is described as being asleep are supposed to mark his otherness from the world and proximity to that of animals. And yet this association with animals also means he is subhuman; the fog of stupidity that he refers to at least twice over the course of the novel references his animalhood yet registers his recoil from that ontological state.

If we go back to our earlier discussion of masculinity in the novel and rethink it in the context of the semiotic of war, we see that Michael K

evades the masculine code of war yet transposes its more violent dimensions onto his relations with animals. His attitude to animals and birds
and the fact that he refuses the influx of sentimentality toward them
means that they are treated in his mind as serviceable objects without
significance beyond their objecthood. It is almost as if the text is suggesting that the evasion of the *antagonistic* semiotic of war leads to the erec-
tion of an *agonistic* relation to animals. This is never fully conscious and
at any rate is somewhat attenuated by the fact that he frequently refers to
himself as a small animal or insect. It is, however, the threatened similitude between the violence imposed by war and the violence he visits
upon animals that unsettles the disparity between him and the dominant
semiotic order. Yet similitude is not the same as symmetry. For the brutal
effects of war as represented in the text (the creation of prison and labor
camps, the mindless violence inflicted on the citizenry, the effects of itin-
erancy and sexual predatoriness as seen in the last part of the novel) are
not of the same order as K's violence against animals. For one thing, the
war machine is aimed at reconstituting social relations as such. Coetzee is
careful not to make explicit what these social relations might look like,
but written in a South African context it is clear that the effects of state
violence are aimed at propping up a dastardly system of racial segregation.
Contrastively, K's violence against animals is depicted as being necessi-
tated strictly by the needs of survival. The real problem raised by his violence in my view is the contradiction that it institutes between his violent
instincts as a person and the animal metaphors that cluster around him
and that render him amenable to allegorical interpretation. In other
words, the contradiction is between his historicity as a hungry man and
the possibility of his dehistoricization and dissolution into the form of fable, parable, and allegory.

In fact, the implications of the contradiction between allegory and
historicity may also be discerned in the degree to which the text blurs the
social conditions that are really generative of Michael K's disability and in
its place foregrounds an intense focus on the character's consciousness.
For Michael K is a working-class colored man and one of apartheid's dispossessed. The fact that his mother had to work as a cleaner and carry
him with her on her rounds is revealing of their class background. Historically, the internal militarized struggles during apartheid were conducted
by the ruling white regime against people of color and their supporters.
Yet at no point in Michael K's internal monologue does he think in color

or class terms. There is not the vaguest whiff of any such thoughts. Furthermore, society—in terms of full-fledged social relations marked by the tensions of hierarchy and attenuated by the codes of civility or otherwise—does not exist in the text. In *Life and Times of Michael K*, the social microcosm is represented either through the unit of the family (K and his mother), on the farm (K and the Visagei boy), or in the work camps. In all these instances, the image of society is miniaturized and truncated. Each unit of sociality within the novel could be taken out of context and interpreted as presenting a discrete and self-sustaining symbolic nexus of signification. Society as such is abrogated. To add to this, Michael K is political only in a broadly allegorical sense of standing outside of the dominant patterns of signification. He has no Fanonian anger or angst and no racialized double consciousness, despite being victimized at various points by a war machine that he wants none of. To all intents and purposes, his situation could conveniently be interpreted as the allegorical template of an existential inarticulate condition under a regime of violence. Race and class could be left out of the account without any distortion of the interpretation.

The particular narrative disposition of the contradiction between history and allegory and the individual and society is one that applies to a reading of all of Coetzee's texts, as Derek Attridge (2004) and others have adroitly shown. But for the particular focus of this study, the contradiction is also relevant from the view of the representation of disability, in this case, autism. For if the autist is so easily assimilable to an allegorical reading, in what ways does this repeat the very well-known social practice of interpreting people with disability as ciphers of a metaphysical or transcendental meaning? In other words, how does the potential for immediate allegorization of the disabled character in literary writing frustrate the process by which they might be properly viewed as illuminating the social contradictions that circulate around people with impairments? I will attempt to provide a set of provisional answers to these questions in my conclusion. For now, let us continue in the South African context, but this time turning to the history of Robben Island and the intersections between corporeal difference, disability, and the ideologies that underpinned colonialism and apartheid in that country.

7

THE REPEATING ISLAND

Race, Difference, Disability, and the Heterogeneities of Robben Island's History

I N *The Repeating Island,* ANTONIO BENITEZ-ROJO'S MAGNIFICENT book on the Caribbean, he argues persuasively for seeing the Caribbean as not having a center.[1] In his words, it is "not a common archipelago, but a meta-archipelago and as meta-archipelago it has the virtue of having neither a boundary nor a center" (Benitez-Rojo 1992, 4). By enumerating an elaborate cultural and geographical inventory for the Caribbean that takes in various times and places, Benitez-Rojo illustrates the degree of the Caribbean's decenteredness and also supplies us with a way of thinking about islands as crossroads. The point to take from his reflections is that the archipelago's boundaries are not solely geographical; its identity is inescapably entangled with various other cultural locations that are dialogically and historically connected to it. This helps define the Caribbean's symbolic capacity for repeating both familiarity and alienation.

While not invoking the same degree of the Caribbean archipelago's significance in contemporary cultural understanding, Robben Island generates something of its own peculiar symbolic resonance because of the strong association it has had with apartheid oppression and the resistance against it. As Oliver Tambo put it in 1980: "The tragedy of Africa, in racial and political terms is concentrated in the southern tip of the continent—in South Africa, Namibia, and, in a special sense, Robben Island."[2] Richard Marback (2004) has suggested that the island is a special rhetorical space produced by the complex interaction between spatial experience and rhetorical authority deriving from its political associations. Holding up the island as a metanarrative and rhetorical space runs the risk of telescoping its history to coincide firmly with the period when it held apartheid's famous political prisoners, such as Nelson Mandela, Govan Mbeki, Ahmed Kathadra, and others. This culturalist and presentist perspective is indeed the one that Marback takes in his article, proceeding as if the "spatial experience" that was born out of the intersection of race and politics was only to be found in that slice of the island's highly politicized and symbolically charged history. Crucial though this procedure is for the project of postapartheid nation building, such a politico-culturalist approach ultimately serves to obscure a richer and more variegated history, something that has been pointed out repeatedly by historians of the island. For despite serving as a place where criminal and political undesirables were detained from at least the 1650s, it was from the mid-nineteenth century a place where the sick poor, persons with leprosy, and lunatics were also kept. Indeed, the General Infirmary of Robben Island operated as one of the instruments of colonial public-health policy from 1846 to 1931, when the last of its three medical institutions—the hospital for people with leprosy—was closed down. The hospital for the chronically sick had been shut down in 1891, with the lunatic asylum following suit in 1931.

Going against the greater prominence given to the recent history of the island by cultural critics and commentators, I want to suggest a more wide-ranging discussion of the links between various historical moments, but through a focus on the lives of particular disabled persons whose lives were intrinsically related to the history of the island. Rather than dismiss the status of the island's rhetoricity, I want to intensify it, but in doing so reroute it through the lives of these disabled figures. In other words, I want to take both the totality of its history and the rhetoricity of its space seriously as points for productive cross-fertilization. What happens when we try to read the history and literary representations of the island through a perspective generated from a focus on disability? And what if, in highlighting the island's associations with various forms of disability we intensify those associations in order to situate the island not as an icon of political struggle but as the place where the social boundaries of embodied otherness (in terms of race, gender, class, *and* disability) were set out and sometimes contested? As has amply been shown elsewhere, colonial and apartheid ideology stipulated notions of undesirability that were ultimately derived from perceptions of essential difference. In a way, these perceptions were grounded in the corporeality of the body as such. Thus stipulations of undesirability placed in close and volatile proximity ideas of illness, deformity, insanity, and criminality, sometimes interweaving the various terms and leaving none of them entirely stable. The central methodological implication for me here is that it is not enough just to attempt to excavate the fullness of Robben Island's known history. Rather, that known history has to be inflected to show how much issues of corporeality and embodiment helped to fashion the history and ultimately fed into the logic of apartheid. In the case of Robben Island, what has been "repeated" historically are the denominations of bodily difference and how these have been incorporated into racial and other hierarchies. I am, of course, not the first person to be making the link between bodily difference and the evolution of apartheid ideology.[3] However, the specific question of corporeality and embodiment on Robben Island and how the island provided the historical vector for the focalization of these issues has not as yet been fully explored. Without attempting an exhaustive analysis, I want to proffer the present effort as the outline of a research agenda for further debate.

This chapter differs from the previous ones in this book in a number of respects. First, it is more explicitly concerned with a specific place and its long history than any of the previous chapters. It engages with a discipline other than the literary while deploying a literary understanding for the reading of history. This interdisciplinary venture will take off with an analysis of Athol Fugard's *The Island*, a text that, though set on Robben Island, is unlike the ones that have been dealt with so far in that it is not concerned with disability as such.[4] The issues that are raised in Fugard's play seem more pertinent to a discussion of citizenship and the political imaginary than of aesthetic nervousness as has been elaborated so far. That being said, it is useful to recall Fugard's observation that Robben Island has been the most important absent presence in the lives of South Africans: it is real, visibly present in the sea just off Cape Town, and yet until the fall of apartheid was hardly ever spoken about (Vadenbroucke 1985, 126). Because of its political salience as an apartheid prison, it thus became the spectral figuration of the fraught political domain in which South African lives were lived. I propose to use the play as a way of de-centering the essentially political narrative that has dominated represen-tations of Robben Island by focusing on the theme of multiple rehearsals of the self encapsulated in the action of the play and how these provide a different means for thinking about the history of the island. What will emerge from this reading of Fugard's play is a sense of the island's hetero-geneities, which are at once spatial, rhetorical, ideological, and political. Furthermore, I wish by this recourse to a dramatic performance to help keep in view the materiality of bodies-in-action. This is something that has been raised in an attenuated way in our earlier discussions of Beckett and Soyinka. It is easy in reading a play (as opposed to seeing it per-formed) or a historical account to think of human beings as disembodied abstractions. A dramatic performance, on the other hand, places us in the presence of material human bodies sighing, losing their temper, fall-ing down, rising up again, wringing their hands in despair, laughing, and invoking a world of reality through gesture and action. A dramatic perfor-mance also produces a form of perspectival depth, since we are always meant to recall that the stage is a microcosm of a wider social universe that rings the action unfolding before us. Indeed, with regard to *The Is-land* the John and Winston of the play are really John Kani and Winston Ntshona, South African citizens who ran the real risk of being impris-oned should they have transgressed the many laws regarding theater, per-formance, and race in their country (Wetmore 2002, 197). While there are acute ontological differences between a dramatic performance and a historical account, what I wish to call attention to is the need to imagine the people we read about in the history of the island as persons within a particular universe of action.

Following this recourse to imagining historical figures as men and women in action, I will also be attempting a series of open-ended specula-tions about what might have been the feelings of three such figures whose freedom was at various times curtailed by virtue of their being placed on Robben Island. This kind of speculation is something that a traditional historian would feel extremely nervous about undertaking. The figures I have in mind are Autshumato (known as Harry by the Europeans) and Krotoa (named Eva), both of whom were associated with the island from the 1650s, and Franz Jacobs, who organized a leper rebellion there in the 1890s. In doing this, I am blatantly reading history as I would read literature—in this case drama—and moving from the one to the other and vice versa. As I stated in *Calibrations: Reading for the Social*, literary representation is intelligible only as part of a network of reciprocal determinations (Quayson 2003, xxii–xxiv). By this I sought to point out how the extrapolation of reality effects out of the literary-aesthetic domain depend upon the successful assembling of resemblances between its categories and those that appear elsewhere and in apparently unconnected contexts. Jealousy was the concept that I used in the discussion there but there are several such categories with which it might be fruitfully replaced. I now think that the notion of reciprocal determinations is also useful for interpreting the history and rhetoricity of a place such as Robben Island. For it may be argued that the meaning of any element that is invoked in association with its history is not fully comprehensible unless read alongside all the many other meanings that the island has held before and which in the contemporary public context seem to have been subsumed under the pressures of state-making. It is the notion of reciprocal determinations that allows us to invoke a literary text such as Fugard's *The Island* in trying to reorient our reading of the relationship of the island to the processes of corporeal differentiation that underpinned much of South Africa's history. Reading a text such as Fugard's in terms of the reciprocal determinations that pertain to the history of Robben Island is then an invitation to read the play against the full spectrum of the island's variegated history. The focalization should work both ways, because once the play is taken as an element within the island's signifying chain of reciprocal determinations it should also have a bearing on how the other elements of that rhetorical or signifying system are taken to operate. On this reading, no element of the island's history can remain entirely intact and secure from imaginative reinterpretation.

The Island and the Vicissitudes of Self-Fashioning

Readers of Athol Fugard's *The Island* will recall the point toward the end of scene 1 when John mimes a telephone conversation with one of his old friends on the mainland. Both he and Winston have returned to their cell after a hard day's work on the lime quarry undertaking the pointless task of filling in and emptying out a wheelbarrow onto each other's mound of sand. Though we cannot tell what exactly is being said on the other side of the line, we are able to piece together bits and pieces from John's end of the conversation: he asks about his friends and tells his interlocutor about their hard life in the Robben Island prison and the difficulties they are having with Hodoshe, the blatantly sadistic prison warden. He finally asks for a message to be passed on to his wife, Princess. Winston sneaks in a request for a message to be passed on to his own wife too, but by that point in the telephone conversation the two friends are less than enthusiastic about carrying on the charade. The stage directions state that "the mention of his wife guillotines Winston's excitement and fun. After a few seconds of silence, he crawls back heavily to his bed and lies down. A similar shift in mood takes place in John" (206). Even though the word "guillotine" signals decapitation, the fact that it is coupled with a description of John's "crawling back heavily" suggests that it also has resonances of emotional dismemberment and disablement. It is interesting to note, however, that the force of the word "guillotine" comes from reading the stage direction, whereas in performance the actor's rendering of the effect of the conversation upon him would return us to the level of his body and its gestures. Thus even though in reading the stage directions the word might be taken as operating at the level of metaphor, we have to visualize the sudden deflation of the two characters' egos and the return of their bodies to the harsh realities of incarceration. The mental and the physical are overlaid upon each other, and the moral issue of the loss of freedom and how one must act with regard to that loss is translated unto the bodies of the characters on stage.

There are several things that have been suggested by this point in the play and that are more or less encapsulated in the telephone conversation itself and the two men's gestural reactions to it. First is the obvious point about their nostalgia for freedom. But their nostalgia is not just for freedom, but for freedom as it is connected to their past as freedom fighters. In other words, the nostalgia is for a particular form of freedom, which is ultimately defined by their being political beings first and foremost. Second is that the telephone conversation is only one point in the various modalities of the taking on of roles that is also at the heart of the play. For as will be recalled, they are rehearsing their parts in a special production of Sophocles's Antigone, in which Winston will play Antigone and John, Creon. Getting Winston to believe in the efficacy of the suspension of disbelief is only one part of John's troubles in trying to persuade his cellmate to rehearse his lines; what is more pressing is the fact that Winston is going to have to dress in drag and perform the role of a woman, something that elicits a strongly negative reaction from him. By the time of the telephone conversation, the two men have gone through a series of adopted roles, most of which have no bearing on the Antigone play they are rehearsing for. The phone conversation is but the final and most dramatic of these adopted roles in the first part of the play.

Overarching the thematic of nostalgia for freedom and the rehearsal of various roles is something of much greater significance for the overall dynamic of oppression and resistance that is revealed in the play. This is the thematic of what, following Giorgio Agamben, we may refer to as bare life, the life of he who can be killed but not sacrificed. As Agamben points out in *Homo Sacer* (1998), the biological life of those situated on the periphery of the political order is precisely that which defines that order in the first place. It is the instantiation of the exception that allows the invocation of sovereignty; the excluded example helps to define that which is included. Thus the exception is the limit case that folds into itself both the logic of the dominant order and its definition of what is exclusionary to that logic. For Agamben, the bare biological life of the subject is the precise instantiation of the logic of the political system, since that biological life is meaningless outside the discourse of the polity itself (he turns to Aristotle and the Greeks to explore this point). What should be of interest to us here, however, is not solely his discussion of the bare life of the *homo sacer*, since, as he acknowledges it, the research agenda he pursues has already been laid out by Hannah Arendt and Michel Foucault, but the example he gives of the concentration camp as one of the foci for understanding the rule of the exception. He defines the camp not "as a historical fact and an anomaly belonging to the past (even if still verifiable) but in some way as the hidden matrix and *nomos* of the political space in which we are still living" (166). Agamben speculates on the genesis of camps, suggesting they might be traced to the 1896 Spanish effort in Cuba to suppress local insurrection or to the camps into which the English herded the Boers at the end of the nineteenth century. Both these are instances of states of emergency linked to colonial wars that then engulf the entire civilian population. However, as will be shown later in the discussion of both Krotoa and Franz Jacobs, Robben Island was at various points in its history an articulation of a "state of emergency" and was routinely used as a place to which socially and politically anomalous types were kept separate from normal society and used to define the exception.[5]

Returning to Fugard's play, we see that the bare life of John and Winston is defined across a range of practices of the self that they perfect in their incarceration, some of which we have seen in their adoption and rehearsal of roles. Their "nakedness" as prisoners is rehearsed before the imaginary audiences of their wives, comrades, and other political interlocutors on the mainland. It is this that gives the telephone conversation such poignancy and significance, for their naked identities are worked out both between themselves and in the anticipation of the reactions of various imagined and real others. This seems like an obvious point, yet since the gamut of other depicted characters outside of John and Winston is strictly evoked via the reminiscences and projections of the two characters on stage, the idiom of the drama becomes one of the refraction of anticipations. It is these anticipations that worry Winston. He can tell exactly how the other prisoners will respond to him as Antigone. It is for John to persuade him that beyond the laughter that he will provoke there will also be a space for listening and that it is this that he must wait for in enacting the role of that classical female rebel.

Commentators have noted that Fugard draws on a tradition that can be traced back to Beckett. Certainly, the intensity of the relationship between the two prisoners is evocative of the world of Estragon and Vladimir in *Waiting for Godot*, which as we saw in chapter 3 shares with other Beckett works the dialogism of an implied interlocutor. *The Island* shares with *Waiting for Godot* the themes of anticipation and waiting, since John is later in the play informed that his ten-year sentence has been commuted to three, leaving him with a mere three months of incarceration to bear. This in itself becomes the occasion for the two prisoners to rehearse the various situations that they imagine would be pertinent to John's arrival home among his family and comrades. One significant dramaturgical difference between Beckett's and Fugard's play, however, is that in *Waiting for Godot* the two tramps do not enact multiple identities. Even though they imagine different situations, Estragon and Vladimir do not alter their essential personalities to match these situations. They are not characters rehearsing the identities of other characters in different scenarios. The situations that they invoke flow directly from their (vaguely) remembered pasts and the future they anticipate in waiting for Godot. The only radically different situation to theirs is provided when Lucky and Pozzo enter the play, where the responses of the two tramps to the fresh pair provide different trajectories for interpreting their own condition. In Fugard's play, on the other hand, John and Winston proliferate scenarios and the responses that they might adduce in anticipation of putative interlocutors. This makes the play a medium of heterogeneous mediations of the self, since the effect of the proliferation of scenarios and the rehearsals attendant upon those scenarios is (a) to multiply other interlocutory selves and (b) to engender new modes of address in relation to such interlocutory others. I would like to suggest that it is this medium of heterogeneities that gives the play its insightful and radical edge and not the enactment of the trial of Antigone that all things seem to lead up to and that in fact closes the action.

The trial of Antigone in The Island is a major interpretative telescoping of what happens in Sophocles' play. In the Sophoclean Antigone, there is no trial in any straightforward sense of the word. What there is is a major clash between Antigone and Creon and a lengthy debate about the rights of the family as opposed to those of the city. Recall, at any rate, that Creon is Antigone's uncle on her mother's side and that she is betrothed to Haemon, his son, and things become somewhat more complicated than in Fugard's rendition. In telescoping the meaning of Antigone into the relative rights of the state versus those of the citizen, Fugard is drawing inspiration from a tradition of interpreting the play that can be traced at least to Hegel. In his own account, Hegel was to note that the essential form of a tragedy depended on certain inescapable collisions, but that these collisions were not necessarily the collisions of directly opposed ethical conceptions of the citizen, but rather conceptions that essentially participated of one another. Thus, writing about the mutual entanglement of the oikos (familial) principle with the polis (political) principle in Greek tragedy, he suggests that "the opposition . . . is that of the body politic, the opposition, that is, between ethical life in its social universality and the family as the natural ground of moral relations" (Hegel 1998, 39; italics added). The dialectical interplay that Hegel stipulates is between a form of social universality, essentially an abstraction, and a natural ground of moral relations that must perforce be concrete and immanent within the microcosm of interpersonal relations (i.e., the family). We must qualify Hegel's terms slightly in order to account for a different kind of dialectical pairing, particularly so as the ethics of a social universality in a place like South Africa were seriously called into question because of the uneven political domain within which such a universality might have been articulated. In other words, social universality cannot be taken for granted under conditions of oppression; the social universal is itself a ground for contestation and struggle.[6] And since the domain of interpersonal relationships both offers the grounds for working through morality and is itself produced by the essential logic that dominates any system, that domain then takes on a coloration from the problematic social universal that is being shaped under the impress of unfreedom.

To recapitulate our discussion so far: *The Island* allows us to (a) keep in the foreground of our minds the materiality of bodies-in-action, (b) focus upon the multiple rehearsals of the self that take place against a horizon of anticipations, (c) perceive the essential lineaments of the struggle between social universality and the interpersonal and familial grounds for the elaboration of morality, and (d) keep in view the oscillating relationship between the depicted foreground of the action and the wider social and political background that frames the action. All these are in varying ways pertinent to our discussion of the lives of Autshumato, Krotoa, and Franz Jacobs, to whom we will turn after the next section.

Heterogeneous Histories

One significant way in which the history of Robben Island may be reread is in the manner in which it provided multiple refractions of social relations unfolding on the mainland. Harriet Deacon (2003, 154–155) sees the history of the island as thoroughly entangled with that of the expanding colonial frontier of the Cape itself:

> One can map the expansion of the colonial frontier in South Africa by tracing the origins of political prisoners who were sent to Robben Island. . . . Robben Island was used to police internal boundaries on which rested the power and safety of the colonial state: employer-employee and master-slave relations, political activity, criminality, white poverty, infectivity and unreason. Internal boundaries could be seen as new frontiers of control.

We find here echoes of Benitez-Rojo's claim about the decentered nature of the Caribbean islands, except that in the case of Robben Island its apparent decenteredness was intimately connected to the policing of political and social boundaries on the mainland. Such boundaries were tied to internal distinctions among the Europeans themselves and between whites and blacks, but in such a way that the encounter and contact between the two races led to a constant need to police all boundaries, internal and external, geographic and symbolic. Robben Island became the site upon which these boundaries were mapped out both through the incarceration/medicalization/segregation of human subjects and the specific spatial locations of the different institutions that were placed on it. Shifting social inflections were attributed to all the material and symbolic vectors on the island and had an effect on how people on the mainland (both white and black) viewed those on the island and vice versa. Earlier in the same piece, Deacon refers to the island as the "mother node" of colonialism, since it was a safe haven from which colonists established and defended their interests on the subcontinent itself. The term "mother node" has more potential than just signifying a geographical toehold from which various colonists launched themselves onto the subcontinent. According to Deacon's own account and those of other Robben Island historians, three discourses remained pertinent to its history from the very beginning. Briefly put, these discourses were those to do with labor (work), the carceral economy (prison and the process of losing one's freedom or having it somewhat curtailed in spite of one's wishes to the contrary), and the value of the island as a last line of defense for the Cape. Not to be ignored also was the discourse of disability. In practice, the discourses of labor and of the carceral economy were always entangled and mutually reinforcing, since the variant populations that found themselves on the island were often there not out of their own volition; they also had to work hard in an often difficult and isolated environment. Indeed, we may even argue that there is no phase of the island's history when matters of work *and* imprisonment were not at the forefront of everyone's minds. In the lives of the historical figures we shall be looking at, it is instructive to speculate on what effect the shifting and policing of boundaries had on their subjectivities and their sense of embodiment. Some of this is to be found tangentially in the documents that were written about them, such as in court and hospital records, the journals of colonial officials, parliamentary and newspaper reports, and in the reflections of missionaries over the years about the various disabled groups on the island.

But first, a brief history of the island itself. Robben Island is a "low lying lozenge of rock and sand, guarding the entrance to Table Bay" (Deacon 1996a, 1). It is generally accepted to have been unpopulated at the time Bartolomeu Diaz arrived there in 1488 on one of his trips in search of routes to the East Indies. For two hundred years after that, it served as a refreshment station for sailors, being rich in seals and penguins and having a good supply of fresh water as well as a natural harbor. With the arrival of the Dutch East India Company (DEIC) at the Cape in 1652, new uses were soon defined and progressively implemented for Robben Island.

The layout of buildings reveals the spatialization of difference and how this was imposed upon the landscape of the island itself. The earliest dwellings were situated on the northeastern end of the island in 1654, to control the sandy anchorage and beach at that point. However, this part of the island has also repeatedly been associated with imprisonment. The Dutch prison was established just behind the beach in 1657 and was also designed to house staff and slaves as close as possible to the predominantly male black and white prisoners who found themselves on the island. The first apartheid prison, dating from 1960, was also located close to this landing place. Contrastively, the highest point on the island, which lies to the south, was associated with the security of the island from the period of the DEIC in the 1650s. The most significant structures there were the prison village, which grew incrementally with the addition of a church, a parsonage, and class-differentiated housing in the 1840s, and the lighthouse, dating from 1863. With the establishment of the medical institutions for lepers, lunatics, and the chronically sick, from 1846 the south buildings were recycled, placing all the medical institutions within the perimeter of the village. Crucially, however, as Deacon (2003) shows, over the next century the village itself was shaped "symbolically and physically" as a "whites-only domestic space." By the turn of the twentieth century, asylum staff were assessed for "whiteness," with applicants deemed too black being sent back home to the mainland (Deacon 2003, 157). The spatial differentiations on the island continued in the late nineteenth century, with the relocation of the leprosy patients to just outside the village perimeter, the boundary between the leprosy hospital and the village being called "Boundary Road," which the lepers were not allowed to cross. This followed the heightened fears of leprosy contagion in the 1890s.

As has already been noted, the history of Robben Island is inextricable from happenings in Cape Town. Apart from the Dutch, the early settlers on the Cape were Germans, Poles, Flemish, French, and Portuguese. Slaves were also brought in from East Africa, India, Ceylon, and the Malay archipelago, with several of those from the Malay archipelago being political exiles and historic figures in their own right. However, among the early Dutch themselves there was a mix of company workers from the higher echelons of society and others of somewhat shadier backgrounds, who had been either coerced or had found themselves unhappily having to work for the DEIC. According to de Villiers (1971), many of such men had been sentenced for petty crimes in their motherland and sent to work for the company at the Cape.[7] Indeed, many accounts found in the journal of van Riebeeck, the first Dutch governor of the DEIC, had to do with stemming the tide of drunkenness and criminality among the settlers. A mutinous demand for food by soldiers of the company in the 1680s led to the arrest of the four ringleaders and sentences of hanging, flogging, or being placed in irons for twenty-five years of hard labor. The four men were invited to draw lots on who should live and who should die. In another incident, a free woman who with her servants stole and slaughtered two cows was sentenced to be tied to a post with a halter round her neck and the hides of the two cows upon her head. She was furthermore flogged and branded (de Villiers 1971, 27). These apparent infractions and the punishments that were visited upon the unfortunate people who committed them defined an ethos of extreme volatility and violence, particularly as the disciplinary regime among the Europeans was designed to instill order so as to make the settlers a stronger group in dealing with the Khoikhoi, whom they depended upon for trade and sustenance but who were also perceived as posing a constant threat. The threat of imminent attack was always on the minds of the settlers and fed directly into the disciplinary regimes imposed upon them. An executioner was even appointed by the company, with handsome pay for meting out various kinds of punishments for different offenses (de Villiers 1971, 27). In this early process of creating a disciplined society among the settlers, company workers were soon being banished to Robben Island for all manner of infractions. The association of convicts with the Cape and, by later extension, Robben Island had already been made much earlier by the English. In 1611, an idea had been mooted by Thomas Aldworth, a member of the English East India Company, for the transport of one hundred convicts a year to the Cape to establish a colony. A much lower number was transported in 1615, but the experiment was discontinued when the English realized that neither the terrain nor the Khoikhoi were hospitable to the convicts (Penn 1996, 11–12).

A figure who encapsulated both the shifting social boundaries internal to the settlers as well as the problematic relationship between them and the Khoikhoi was Autshumato, otherwise known as Harry. Autshumato was the "leader" of a group of Khoikhoi lacking cattle herds and who lived close to the Table Bay area. They were Goringhauqua, but were known to the Europeans as Strandlopers or Watermen. The English had taken Autshumato to the East Indies in 1631, where he learned English and was returned to act as their agent and translator in southern Africa.[8] At his own request, Autshumato asked to be sent to Robben Island with some of his followers and for subsequent years he spent varied lengths of residence there. Nigel Penn (1996) suggests that this request was partly to gain security from the hostile Peninsular Khoikhoi and also as a means of controlling the extensive resources of penguins and seals on the island. Autshumato was important to European sailors because he could monitor all the ships entering the bay and light signal fires to notify those wishing to forward or receive letters. He was at once highly regarded and much feared by both the English and later the Dutch. Indeed, the first explicit Dutch meditation on the possibility of using Robben Island as a place for political convicts is found in the journal of van Riebeeck in November 1652, barely six months after he had arrived to set up a settlement for the DEIC:

> We are half afraid that the aforesaid Harry—being very much attached to the Saldanhars nowadays whereas formerly they used to be his ene-mies—instead of acting in our favor, may be brewing mischief. . . . If he is brewing mischief, it would not be inconceivable for him with his wife and children, together with all the Watermen, to be taken to Rob-ben Island with sweet words and left there, so that we might trade more peaceably and satisfactorily with the natives of Saldanha, who appear to be a good type of people. About all this time will show us more.[9]

Autshumato drifted in and out of favor with the Europeans over the course of the nearly twelve years that he acted as an interpreter for them. It is not clear whether van Riebeeck was aware that Autshumato had himself used Robben Island as his base some years previously, so that banishing him there was not necessarily going to be a punishment as such. What is evident from this journal entry, however, is the idea of the curtailing of his freedom, such that even if Autshumato had felt comfortable being on Robben Island with his followers previously, now it was going to be a place not of freedom but of interdiction. Also noteworthy is the subtle rhetoric of potential enemies and friends, which then institutes the requirement of clarity of action from people such as Autshumato. He is thought to be "brewing mischief," which could mean anything from not interpreting properly to actively undermining settler interests for his own profit. An opposition is set up in van Riebeeck's mind between Autshumato and the natives of Saldanha, who appear to be a "good type of people," that is, cattle-rearing natives they could do business with and who would not give them too much trouble. In the long term, van Riebeeck was proved to have been overly sanguine in his calculation of the cooperation of the cattle-rearing Khoikhoi, since Autshumato played settler and local Khoikhoi against each other to his own advantage. He was first and foremost a pragmatist; some would even say a politician. This brings to mind the case of Wangrin, another colorful character in local-settler relations from French Senegal. As Amadou Hampaté Bâ shows in *The Fortunes of Wangrin* (1999), Wangrin was a very astute and manipulative player within the French colonial bureaucratic apparatus from the late nineteenth century to the 1940s. He was an interpreter who, due to his indispensable role in mediating the contact between his people and the French colonial bureaucrats in Senegal, was able to play one against the other to his own profit. He was a masterful colonized Machiavel and, read against other better known Africans in the service of colonial bureaucracies, provides an interesting perspective on the ambiguities of the formation of the colonized administrative elite. Like Wangrin, Autshumato might be argued to be materializing the behavior of the trickster figure of African folktales, with practical consequences for both the settlers and the local Khoikhoi. The shifting scales of power and authority upon the social environment triggered by the coming of the Europeans must have struck him forcefully. He was partially assimilated to their worldview by virtue of having been taken to the East Indies and taught to speak English. And yet he must also have been always conscious of the fact that he was "white but not quite," to cite Homi Bhabha's felicitous formulation, someone who raised anxiety among both the natives and the Europeans precisely because of his status of insider/outsider to both camps. His self-fashioning or the rehearsal of his various selves was transposed onto a shifting set of social relationships in which his place was liminal and often fraught with danger.

Krotoa's Nervous Conditions

The shifting fortunes and positions of Autshumato touched on other people, both European and native, with the most poignantly significant being that of Krotoa, or Eva to the Dutch. Krotoa had extensive kinship ties with several Khoikhoi groups. Autshumato was her uncle, who, as we know, was one of the Goringhauqua. She had another uncle from among the Chainouqua, a mother with the Goringhauqua, and another "mother" with the Cochoqua. In addition, her sister, who was formerly the wife of Goeboer, the Chainouqua chief, was seized in war and became the most important wife of the Cochoqua chief Oedasoa, who was himself a very significant person in the life of Krotoa and the affairs of the Dutch (Elphick 1985, 106–107). Most of these groups were cattle herders and at various times entered into trade relations with the Dutch. Like Autshumato, Krotoa's significance to the settlers derived mainly from her role as interpreter. She learned to speak Dutch fluently and was also proficient in Portuguese. As Elphick (1985, 103–104) notes, the Dutch relied on their early native interpreters "not only for translations, but also for geographic and ethnographic information and for advice on the making of policies relating to the Khoikhoi." The place of the interpreter was thus overdetermined by the often contradictory political needs of different factions. In her case, as we shall see shortly, she had to mediate among various competing factions, sometimes attempting to further particular local interests as opposed to others, but at all times, it seems, trying to protect the interests of the settlers above all others.

Krotoa was brought to live with the van Riebeecks in April 1652, when they first came to settle at the Cape.[10] She was brought up in their household, taught their language and lifestyle, and trained in Christian ways. She was increasingly relied upon as an interpreter, the other two being Autshumato and Doman, a person from another ethnic group that had been taken to Batavia to be trained by the Dutch. The writer of van Riebeeck's journal always cast aspersion on the two men's command of the European languages (English for Autshumato and Dutch for Doman), and it is evident that Krotoa's facility in Dutch was much prized by the settlers. However, it did not take long for her to get into trouble with both Autshumato and Doman; in the case of the latter, the enmity was mutual and unrelenting, since Doman did everything to undermine the settlers' authority and knowledge of the local terrain. The entry for August 22, 1958, gives us a good hint of the intensity of the hatred between the two:

> Doman, the interpreter, who is a rascal, tries to thwart the Hon. Company in everything and is thrice as bad and harmful as Harry ever was throughout his life, as we discover daily, and as Eva testifies. She states openly that he is the chief opponent of the Hon. Company; he calls her a lickspittle, or flatterer, and makes her odious among her own people by saying that she speaks more in favour of the Dutch than the Hottentots. When she comes to interpret, he calls out: "See, there comes the advocate of the Dutch; she will tell her people some stories and lies and will finally betray them all," and anything which will serve to make her odious to them.[11]

This enmity appears to have come from many causes, but not to be dismissed perhaps is the fact that Doman may have been trying to bully her because she was in his eyes a mere girl and enjoying too much status by being so close to the van Riebeeck household.

On September 23, 1658, Krotoa left the fort on a trip to the interior. This has been interpreted variously. For Malherbe (1990, 23), she may have left out of frustration for not being able to intercede in her uncle Autshumato's final banishment to Robben Island earlier in the year. Elphick (1985, 107), on the other hand, suggests that, having reached puberty at age fifteen or sixteen, she may have been returning to her relatives to undergo the ceremony prescribed for every Khoikhoi girl of her age. What is not clear is why the van Riebeeck's allowed such a prized interpreter to leave for a ceremonial practice they are not likely to have either understood or approved of. Whatever the reasons for her departure, this trip proved to be a turning point in Krotoa's life. She first went to visit her mother, where she suffered the unhappy incident of being robbed and beaten up, apparently without her mother coming to her aid. After this she left to visit her sister, who was by now married to Oedasoa, the Cochoqua chief. Krotoa made a great impression on them and was reputed to have effected the cure of her sister from a bad fever with days and nights of prayer. She also sought to persuade Oedasoa to visit the fort and begin trading with the settlers. Things took a dramatic turn later during her stay, when Oedasoa was badly injured by a lion. Krotoa held herself responsible for the accident. Oedasoa and his men had been hunting for wild horses and trying to shoot elephants for their tusks on Krotoa's "repeated exhortations." The horses were of more use to the Europeans than to the Khoikhoi.[12]

Her uncle's accident had a great effect on her, for she subsequently returned to the colony on December 30, expressing the wish to "learn more of our religion." This was apparently on the suggestion of her brother-in-law and her sister, who had both learned so much through her that "they could feel in their hearts that what she told them of God and His service was true."[13] Krotoa subsequently moved regularly between the fort and the interior, but the fort became her main abode and place of residence in the following years.

The events that were to lead to the first Dutch-Khoikhoi War of 1658–1659 had been taking shape earlier. In February 1658, the DEIC released a number of their employees from their contracts so they could become free settlers at the Cape. These freeburghers were to raise livestock and hence relieve the company of its reliance on trade with the cattle-rearing Khoikhoi. They were also to grow crops that would hopefully free the colony from its dependence on Batavian rice (Elphick 1985, 220). It quickly became apparent to the Khoikhoi and particularly to Doman, who was at pains to find means of resisting the Europeans' encroachments, that access to pastureland and water was going to be a very serious issue with the institution of the new policy. Doman broke away from the colony and formed a militia that attacked the fort. The immediate trigger for the war, however, was the settlers' seizure of some Khoikhoi as hostages in June 1658 in retaliation for the theft of some of the colony's herd; the hostage-taking policy appears to have been suggested or at least endorsed by Krotoa. At the same time, during the war, she sought to establish an alliance between Oedasoa and the Dutch, partly as a way of strengthening the hand of his Khoikhoi ethnic faction against the others that had been dealing with the settlers. The later part of 1659 found her moving regularly between the fort and Oedasoa's encampment, which had been set up not far from the fort. Neither side seemed entirely to trust her; at any rate, despite every sign of an alliance being made, Oedasoa vacillated and at the last moment refused to join forces with the Dutch against the other Khoikhoi.[14] The Dutch thought Krotoa contradicted herself extremely badly in several respects regarding Oedasoa's intentions and clearly suspected her of some underhanded dealings.

If Krotoa's unfortunate adventures among her sister and brother-in-laws' people and her status as interpreter during the war hinted at a trajectory of reversal in her life at the fort, her marriage in 1664 to Pieter van Meerhoff marked a decisive downward turn in her fortunes from which she was not to recover.[15] Her marriage was preceded by a number of events that could only have caused her much distress. Her sister died in July 1660, and in May 1662, the van Riebeecks left the colony after ten years at its head. Their last act before leaving was to have her baptized into the Dutch Reformed Church, giving her the name Eva. Though the baptism must have been a welcome coming-to-fullness of the religiosity she had exhibited hitherto, it cannot also be denied that the loss of the van Riebeecks, who had treated her as one of their own and indeed often protected her against the skepticism of both the Europeans and the natives, must have been a dire blow. At any rate, the new commander, Zacharias Wargenaer, took a colder attitude toward her. She was married to Pieter in April 1664, a marriage contracted partly for political reasons, as Wargenaer calculated that her marriage to one of them might fortify the alliance between the Dutch and her people, and partly, it appears, to accommodate the two children she had had in 1663 by the Europeans. The journal is silent on who the father(s) might have been, the only hint being that the children may have been by sailors who often came ashore at the Cape.[16] Pieter was a young and highly valued surgeon. However, his value to the company did not prevent them from placing him at a distance from the colony due to his marriage to a black girl. He was sent off to Robben Island along with Jan Wouterssen, the first Postholder, who also happens to have married a black girl. Conditions on the island were very harsh, and more importantly, Krotoa, by being sent off with her husband, had been effectively separated from the social and political center of the colony. She took to heavy drinking and once alarmed her husband by passing out and knocking her head badly on the ground. She was sent to the mainland for treatment and subsequently went back and forth between the island and the colony. Matters were not helped when her husband joined a slave-hunting expedition heading for Madagascar in June

1666. Eighteen months later, word returned that he had been killed by the people he was trying to enslave.

Krotoa was allowed to return to the fort, but it did not take long for her to get into trouble there. Her behavior was considered deeply embarrassing to the settlers. She was once so drunk that she swore interminably while sitting at the commander's table. She was severely reprimanded and threatened with the removal of her children if she did not mend her ways. After the incident at the commander's table Krotoa ran away, leaving her children behind. On another occasion, she was found sitting naked on a sand dune at the beach with a pipe in her mouth. As hopes of getting her cured of her ailment receded, she was banished to the island in September 1668.[17] She died in 1674 at the age of thirty-one, or, as the journal entry put it: "finally she quenched the fire of her sensuality by death . . . affording a manifest example that nature, however closely and firmly muzzled by imprinted principles, nevertheless at its own time triumphing over all precepts, again rushes back to its inborn qualities."[18] We will have more to say on this blatantly racist linking of the native to animals in a moment.

Elphick and Shell (1979, 184) suggest that in the early period of Dutch settlement, a number of processes took place that served to progressively erode the boundaries between the Khoikhoi and the Dutch. These included (1) the incorporation of the Khoikhoi into the European-dominated society as wage laborers subject to Dutch law; (2) the conversion of slaves and free blacks to Christianity or Islam; (3) miscegenation and intermarriage among groups; (4) the manumission of slaves and the consequent emergence of an important group, the free blacks; and (5) cultural exchanges among groups. A number of things emerging from the account of Krotoa's life suggest that she was in many ways placed at the interstices of these various processes, particularly the dimensions noted in Elphick and Shell's categories 1, 2, 3, and 5. We must note, however, the degree to which Krotoa's sense of "family" must have been thoroughly split between the mores and sentiments of her adopted family of the van Riebeecks and that of the Khoikhoi she clearly identified with, making the question of her "assimilation" to European culture highly problematic. All historians who write about her have noted her strong attachment to Autshumato, unreliable though he appeared to be in the eyes of the Europeans. When he was finally banished to Robben Island, she sought an occasion to visit him there. The seas were so rough that their boat lost direction and did not touch the island for another twenty-four hours. Krotoa was so seasick that the others thought she was going to die, "but she recovered completely when the sea calmed down."[19] We have already noted how shaken she was when Oedasoa, her brother-in-law, was bitten by the lion. She did everything she could to persuade the Dutch to enter into dealings with him and was a constant emissary between the two parties. And she clearly also had very strong bonds with her sister. Krotoa's joy knew no bounds when she had the opportunity of being reunited with her sister during her embassies between Oedasoa and the Dutch. It is reported that on the first occasion she was practically speechless with elation: "At the first meeting of these two women joy prevented Eva from addressing the other, and for the same reason she was unable to serve as interpreter for our people. She perpetually had her arm round the shoulder of her sister, Oedasoa's wife, a sign that they had great pleasure in each other's company. Eventually she was able to talk."[20]

Recalling Hegel's proposition about the family as furnishing the primary ground on which moral relations are established, we can speculate that these attachments to dual notions of "family" must have posed some confusion in Krotoa's mind. Having been brought up in the language of the Dutch and living so intimately with them, she could not have missed their real opinion of the Khoikhoi, her people. Throughout the journals, there are countless references to the suspicions that the settlers had about the natives. They were described as scheming, dirty, hungry (especially the Standlopers), and full of mischief. And the early freeburghers expressed their deep-seated hatred for the natives with whom they now openly had to vie for pastureland and water resources. At the same time, it was also clear to her that the European settlers provided a not inconsiderable cache of what Pierre Bourdieu (1991) refers to as symbolic capital. Many of Autshumato's machinations and the internecine plottings and counterplottings of the various cow-herding tribes on how to augment their standing with the Europeans proved beyond a doubt how useful it was to be associated with the settlers. And since she already had the special privilege of their language and direct access to the van Riebeeck household, she sensed how important the white family was to her own standing. This familial duality must have affected her sense of self in ways that can only be guessed at. How must she have felt knowing that she was treated as exceptional while all around her her people were being described as mischievous and uncivilized?

Her growing religiosity was also another crucial yet divisive part of her sense of identity. As we saw from the journal entry discussing her death, her Christianity was no insulation from the settler perception that as a native she was close to a bestial and irredeemable nature. This discourse of irredeemableness no doubt became stronger on the departure of the van Riebeecks. But it would be hard to imagine that she did not face such racist taunts from time to time at the hands of some of the company workers when they were drunk or particularly fearful of what it meant to have a native such as her so close to them. Her Christianity gave her no absolute protection. Her tragic demise could be partially related to the psychological schisms that her Christian/native self gave her, especially when she began to fall out of favor with the more powerful of the settler community; it did not help either that her new husband took off on several expeditions into the interior, leaving her bereft on the island. Her effective banishment to Robben Island, first with her husband and, after his death, on her own, was proof positive of the perception of her irredeemabilty and her peripheralization in the eyes of the settlers. In 1671, Sara, another girl who had spent most of her life among the Europeans as a servant and a concubine, committed suicide at the age of twenty-four. And a Khoikhoi man baptized as Frederick Adolf and taken to Holland in 1707 led a life on his return that was deemed so immoral that he was banished to spend the rest of his life on Robben Island (Elphick 1985, 203). Clearly, the early Khoikhoi converts who found themselves in the service of the Dutch suffered immense psychological pressures. We would not be wrong in speculating that Krotoa must have suffered a nervous breakdown over the course of her life, something for which she had no recourse and probably no one to turn to for help; her severe alcoholism from about 1664 onward is a sign of her desperation.

Some historians have speculated on whether Krotoa had sexual relations with either van Riebeeck or with one of the other settlers prior to her marriage to Pieter, the idea being that there must have been a practice of concubinage that she could not have escaped. For Yvette Abrahams (1996), Krotoa personifies the widespread rape of black women by the white settlers, whereas Julia C. Wells (1998) proposes that van Riebeeck may have had intimate relations with her, particularly as there is evidence that he admired the physicality of native women. Her marriage to Pieter was then part of a highly complicated set of symbolic exchanges in which Pieter won out by virtue of his having had a four-year relationship with her and sharing some of her own impulses toward advancing settler interests among the local populations. All these speculations must remain at the level of tantalizing possibilities. What is also evident, however, is the way in which the records try to separate the issue of her maternality from that of her sexuality and then blur her sense of agency in negotiating her various roles. The issue of who she had her first two children by or indeed how many children she had in all is never quite clear. Furthermore, with the coming of Wargenaer she is repeatedly referred to as a "vixen" and a "prostitute," references that did not feature in the van Riebeeck journals. In other words, her fall from political grace appears to have coincided with the increasingly negative and sometimes quite virulent references to her sexuality. These references were designed to emphasize her physicality (as a hypersexual woman, therefore requiring management and control) against her intellectualism (in her role as interpreter, upon whom they depended heavily).

We must pause for a moment on the reference to her sitting naked on the beach with a pipe in her mouth. For the "nakedness" of her body had many connotations. From the journal entry of January 12, 1656, we are informed that Eva (Krotoa), who is "clad in clothes, has lived some time in the Commander's house, where she has learned some Dutch."[21] This was one of the earliest references to her in the documents. However, as Malherbe (1990, 8) points out, the reference to her being clad in clothes was highly significant, since it was an important index of her status in Dutch eyes. Subsequently, on her trips away from the fort she was to stop at the edge of the settlement and change from her European clothes into native skins. On one occasion when she reached the edge of the fort, she dressed up in hides and sent her old clothes back home to the van Riebeecks, with the assurance that "she would in the meantime not forget the Lord God, Whom she had learnt to know in the Commander's house."[22] The evocation of her religiosity at the precise moment when she was donning the outward signs of her native affiliation must have been designed to assuage any doubts that the Dutch may have had about her allegiance to their cause. However, it is also evident that the question of clothing marked a not insignificant threshold for her. Thus when she strips naked and puts a pipe in her mouth to sit alone at the beach it is a clear sign of her rebellion against being garbed in the signifiers of either Westernization or nativeness. In this, she was, even if problematically, claiming her naked body as her own. And yet, at the same time her nakedness at the beach should be taken as a sign of her distressed mental state. The sea was a particularly poignant reminder of the ebb and flow of the relationships (sexual and otherwise) she had established with the sailors that came to the Cape. Since these sailors were there only for short durations, her relationships were of necessity ephemeral ones. But how are we to know if she did not actually fall in love with one of these sailors and desire to go to the mother country that had brought forth the van Riebeecks? What conversations did she have with the sailors? What shores did she question them about? What stories of mishap and adventure did they regale her with? What yearnings did she express to them? And what, in the end, passed through her mind as she sat naked on the beach with a pipe in her mouth?

Recall, finally, the category of disability as inarticulable tragic insight that we elaborated in chapter 2 in relation to tragic figures such as Cassandra, Io, Ophelia, Baby Suggs, and others. Like these literary figures, Krotoa suffered a nervous condition that was symptomatic of the fact that she bore an inexpressible tragic knowledge. We cannot tell whether she managed to express this to those closest to her. What, for example, must she have told her children about herself and the circumstances of her living with the Europeans? What we do know is that her alcoholism and later nervous breakdown marked the downward spiral of a highly intelligent and active woman. Since she never speaks in her own voice in the colonial records, all we can retrieve are the traces that other people leave about her. Yet even from these traces we can piece together the gradual ebbing of her vitality, her growing solitude, and what must have been her terrifying loss of standing both among the Europeans and her own people.[23]

A larger question presents itself if we resituate Krotoa in relation to *The Island* and John and Winston's rehearsals of multiple selves: what were some of the selves that Krotoa sought to rehearse in her short but highly eventful life? She was first and foremost an interpreter between two cultures, one of which was clearly intent on dominating the other. The selves she rehearsed depended on her judgment as to what was more pressing for her identity, and this was by no means either straightforward or predictable. She rehearsed the roles of interpreter, servant, wife, lover, mother, and ambassador. Also, as someone who was celebrated for her ethnographic knowledge of the local landscape and its people, she acted as a translator of the depths behind the visible. The elusive ethnographic knowledge she shared with the Dutch was only partially an ethnography; it was also the map of the shifting scales of her self-understanding as they were encapsulated in the knowledge she had about her own people. Krotoa was clearly a lonely woman, but one caught in the interstices of a colonial world whose social boundaries were in a state of flux and for whom the historical moment provided an excess of cultural signification. From the point of view of the Europeans, she presented an anomalous and confusing category. She represented the structure of simultaneous attraction and repulsion for them. Thus, as we saw a moment ago, a veritable discourse of wildness and unruliness was projected onto her body as a means of policing it. The settlers had worries about social reproduction both in terms of the reproduction of family structures as well as the reproduction of social relations. Thus, for them someone like Krotoa presented a confusing category for social reproduction in the new realm: she was a veritable slave yet a baptized Christian, a Christian yet a chronic alcoholic, married to one of them yet apparently promiscuous, acculturated in European ways yet also reflecting the behavioral patterns of the less savory European characters on the settlement. She swore in public and threw up, often walked out on her two children, and exposed her nakedness to the elements. Krotoa then may be taken as representing the tragic intersection of gender, race, mental illness, and unruly "otherness" that would be manifested in different dimensions and scales throughout the later history of Robben Island. She is historic in that sense.

Racial Segregation and the Leper Rebellion of 1892

The history of racial segregation in South Africa is full and complicated, with the nineteenth century providing the highpoint of the process. Intra- and interinstitutional segregation in Cape Town became increasingly racialized after 1890 (Deacon 1996b). From the 1900s, racialized metaphors of illness and health concerns came together to produce medical legislation that in its turn was used to justify segregation. As Baines (1990, 77) put it: "In the colonial context, the social metaphor of disease became a particularly effective means of maintaining political pressure for Africans to be kept away from white residential areas." Thus, by the late nineteenth century public health legislation was used to encourage and later justify stricter residential segregation in a number of colonial towns (Deacon 1996b, 289). The intersection of race with disease was intensified by the public health discourse of contagion, which, depending as it did on the discovery of bacteria as the transmitters of disease in the 1870s, led to the European stance that black culture and social life explained the etiology of most diseases.[24] Leprosy, in particular, was definitively linked to uncleanliness, and uncleanliness in its turn to black habits and lifestyles. After 1883, the fears about the dangers of contracting leprosy from the urban small trader or black farm servant were increasingly rife among Europeans, and the black migrant or urban immigrant was cited as the origin of the germ. In an 1896 book entitled *Handbook on Leprosy*, Samuel Impey, doctor at the Robben Island leper hospital, attributed the spread of leprosy entirely to various black groups, the most prominent of them being the "Bushman" (Deacon 1994, 61–62).

On the founding of the General Infirmary on Robben Island in 1846, racial segregation was established for the chronically sick, the lepers, and the insane patients that found themselves there. The infirmary was originally set up as a custodial institution for the unemployable sick poor by John Montagu, colonial secretary at the Cape in the 1840s. However, his push for the infirmary sought to encompass other categories of people as well. His original proposal was to make use of the "free" labor that able-bodied convicts could provide. This would involve evacuating the mainland prisons and the old Somerset Hospital of lunatics and the chronic sick. All these groups were to be sent to Robben Island and placed in the old convict buildings there. Montagu set up a special Medical Board to ratify his scheme in its totality. The fusion of the discourse of labor with that of illness and incarceration had important implications for how the lepers were viewed and in turn viewed themselves. Most of the lepers sent to the infirmary in the early years were from older leper hospitals such as Hemel-en-Aarde and Sunday's River. Several of them were in the final stages of their illness and all but three of those from Hemel-en-Aarde had died or left by 1861. The total number transported to the island in 1846 was fifty-four, with the number remaining consistently below one hundred until 1892, when it rose to 413. By 1915, the number of lepers on the island had risen to 613 (Deacon 1994, 66). Crucially, in the first few years the gaps caused by early deaths or discharge were filled predominantly by farm laborers through the request of magistrates and district surgeons. Indeed, as late as 1887 lepers were discharged from Robben Island on the basis of being time-expired convicts. In this sense, as Deacon (1994, 67) suggests, "prior institutionalization was an advantage, as the term of the legal prison sentence took legal priority over the term of the disease." In other words, there was an overlap within official attitudes toward persons with leprosy and convicts, with the capacity to work being the supervening category for both. Race played a part in the institutional attitudes to the lepers, lunatics, and sick poor on the island in as far as it determined their specific geographical location in the various wards vis-à-vis the white and wealthier patients (most of the black patients were poor), and also in the type of diet that was given to the different categories of patients there (Deacon 1996b; 2001).

The 1891 Leprosy Repression Act and the Amendment Act of 1894 effectively removed all civil rights from persons with leprosy. They were no longer allowed to leave the island, vote, kiss or otherwise touch their visitors, or prosecute adulterous wives under existing colonial law. In the eyes of the law they were "as good as being dead" (Deacon 1994, 70). It is within this ethos of putative incarceration that the first leper rebellion on the island took place. This was spearheaded by Franz Jacobs, who had been admitted to the leper hospital in 1887. A "colored Afrikaner," he was a well-educated Dutch Reformed Church member and teacher and also acted as a catechist for the lepers in general. Jacobs had originally opted to go to the infirmary of his own volition, stating that he did so because he thought that if he separated from his family his wife would have a better chance of finding work. His was a pragmatic response to the social stigma that attended families with lepers. At first, Jacobs and the other leprosy patients were able to visit the mainland, but following the Leprosy Repression Act these were cancelled. Toward the end of 1892, Jacobs led a group of black male lepers to protest their treatment on the island. He wrote letters to the Cape government, the attorney general, and the Queen of England, complaining that they had been banished from society and treated like common prisoners. He complained that he himself had been incarcerated on the island for five years and eleven months, and that before the Act of 1891 had been allowed to visit his wife, five stepchildren, and two children in Woodstock on the mainland. He argued on behalf of the lepers that they had been collectively "left on the Island as people who were dead" and protested the differential treatment that was meted out to black and white lepers. They were forced to work to get tobacco rations, their food was poorly prepared, and their clothing was inadequate. Jacobs made the specific argument to the Queen that since she had freed the slaves in 1834, she should also be able to free the lepers in 1892. He pointed out that they were British subjects but did not enjoy the requisite freedoms pertaining to this status.[25]

When no positive response from the authorities was forthcoming, Jacobs then began a campaign of disobedience and noncooperation, threatening in a letter that if their demands were not met there would be "war and riot" on the island. The lepers threatened to break into the female wards and also to attack the village and rape the women there.[26] Whereas Jacobs invoked the discourse of rights within what might be seen as a much larger idiom of human rights for the lepers through unorthodox means, the authorities were at pains to represent him as someone whose mental capacity was suspect. In other words, that Jacobs was really insane and that his requests were driven by a sense of ego over-aggrandizement. Governor and High Commissioner Henry Loch wrote in a letter to Lord Marquis stating among other things:

> Jacobs, who is said to incite discontent . . . wanted, when removed to the Hospital in CT, to be sent back to RI, where he said he was more comfortable, and would behave well, and when it became necessary a second time to bring him to CT, he expressed a preference for it. This, and the style of his letters to the Queen, support the opinion that he is not quite sane. A religious lunatic probably. No need to publish these papers as "this question" has not attracted public attention in this country [i.e., England].[27]

Jacobs' claim that the lepers were being treated worse than convicts was dismissed by the authorities as nothing but a "figurative expression." Samuel Impey, who as we recall was the island doctor at the time, was of a much darker opinion, stating:

> Franz Jacobs . . . is a ring-leader amongst them and instead of being pampered deserves the cells. He now demands amongst other things the following, viz., Cruet Stands, Finger Glasses, Table Napkins and delicacies of all kinds. Yesterday they rose against the nurses and refused to have their wounds dressed by them, and if the nurses had

not very wisely desisted from attempting to dress their wounds, there would have been bloodshed as they threatened to strike them with crutches.[28]

Impey asked for a contingent of armed constables for the protection of hospital employees. He was worried that the lepers might join with convicts on the island to overpower the convict guards and cause mayhem. After a period of seclusion from the other lepers, Jacobs was later to recant his accusation. Following the leper agitation, several government delegations visited the island to ascertain things for themselves, with a group of members of Parliament visiting in July 1893 and publishing a report favorable to the viewpoint of the lepers. The colonial government made improvements to the hospital food, issued free passes to visitors, and brought in a Dutch Reformed Minister for them. Jacobs himself was removed to the Somerset Hospital on the mainland to be placed under close surveillance, and although he returned to Robben Island briefly in 1893, he died later that year.

Sally Swartz (1999) has argued in relation to the retrieval of women's psychiatric records in colonial South Africa that the inherent discursive shape of such records militates against the historian's understanding of such women as unique individuals. Patient case histories frequently followed the same trajectories and made no concession to the differences among individual patients; they were considered as cases, not persons. We might suggest that it is not just women who suffered this form of obliteration from the colonial record. Any person designated as ill, whether physically or mentally, was immediately inserted into a particular discourse that entailed the institution of a curative regime. These regimes were not just "scientific." They were often reflections of beliefs in particular disease etiologies, limited medical knowledge, and cultural (read racial, class, or even gendered) stereotypes that themselves fed back into the medical discourse and helped to shape the "case" in question. Thus when we read the ways in which the official discourse interpreted Franz Jacobs' rebelliousness as a sign not of moral indignation but of madness, we must note that his leprosy was being globally extended to encompass the workings of his mind. As disability scholars have frequently argued, such globalization is a typical social response to disability, in this case exacerbated by being produced within a particularly situated colonial discourse that sought to dismiss and pathologize the entire rebellion. However, in the case of Jacobs it is also clear that the authorities had to contend with someone whose sense of self had been formed by his religious education as well as his understanding of wider historical processes by which he could interpret both his own position and that of the Europeans. His recourse to the language of abolitionism pointed to the fact that he was making a larger moral appeal, in which the lepers' unsatisfactory conditions might be seen as analogous to other kinds of struggles that had successfully marshaled popular moral indignation against acknowledged evil practices.

Referring again to John and Winston in Fugard's *The Island*, we should speculate on what selves Franz Jacobs was rehearsing at the interface between the collectivity of lepers, on the one hand, and the colonial authorities, on the other. His leprosy was to him no grounds for being treated less well than his white fellow lepers. More significantly, his ailment was suspended in his mind by virtue of his appeal to his sexuality and familial impulses (he wanted to see his wife and family first and foremost). The appeal to these impulses served to normalize him, for the implication carried in it was that he was like any of his more fortunate and presumably enlightened European interlocutors. And yet we cannot ignore the fact also that Jacobs oscillated between claiming his rights as a human being and threatening to deploy methods and instruments that could only be said to detract from the humanity of others (the threat to rape the village women, for example). Certainly, by the time he "recanted" his accusations to the authorities he had rehearsed a broad spectrum of subject and agential positions: agitator/spokesman, claimant of right to dignity/threat to the dignity of others, British citizen/colonial subject, bondman/free. Unfortunately, it is the nature and intensity of these oscillations as they were worked out in the mind of someone like Franz Jacobs that we will never be able to retrieve from the archival record. What we can retrieve is the fact that he was bold enough to launch an attack at an offensive piece of legislation that sought to shackle him and others with all the means at his disposal, limited and problematic though they turned out to be.

From the wider perspective of this study, what is perhaps most pertinent is the degree to which the lives of people like Autshumato, Krotoa, and Jacobs in their relationships to Robben Island helps to expose the overall discourses and practices by which the exception was established as a means of delimiting the boundaries of normality. All three instances serve to show that in the delimitation of boundaries several vectors of identity were brought into volatile proximity. Race and the social tensions that developed around it in the encounters with colonialism was just one of them. Also significant were the representations and later contestations of the intersections of illness and disability (both mental and physical), sexuality, and embodiment. As this brief discussion of Robben Island's history has sought to show, it is the body itself in its naked corporeality that is at the heart of social and political nervousness in real life. To read the history of Robben Island rhetorically through the lives of the three historical characters we have encountered is to point out a fruitful way in which literary and historical analysis may intersect to illuminate the ways in which reality subtends the literary-aesthetic domain and the ways in which the literary-aesthetic field refracts reality. Ultimately, my hope is to have provided a means by which to awaken our consciousness to the general question of justice, one that in the final instance cannot be divorced from the bodies we occupy and whose variant forms are to be seen around us in the world of persons with disability.

CONCLUSION

IN QUEST OF THE
ETHICAL CORE

O N July 6, 2006, the Centre for Democratic Development (CDD) in Accra organized a public lecture as part of events to celebrate the passing of Ghana's Persons with Disability Act. It had taken twelve years of active work by various disability advocacy groups and the CDD to get the relevant parliamentary committee to consider the bill. It had been a long struggle full of unanticipated twists and turns. Chaired by renowned Ghanaian Professor of Linguistics Kwesi Yankah and arranged under the general rubric of "Language and Attitudinal Change: Beyond Disability Legislation," the event gave me the opportunity to share some of my work with a mixed audience composed of members of the Ghana Federation of the Disabled and various disability advocacy groups in the country as well the Parliamentary Committee on Employment, Social Welfare, and State Enterprises, the media, and people with familial interest in disability issues.

My talk focused mainly on outlining the salience of insights from the social model of disability and linking these to a discussion of the endemic cultural and linguistic attitudes that had served to demean persons with disability and often render them either invisible or easily assimilable to negative cultural and social stereotypes in the country. Among Ghanaians in general, three elements have underpinned such negative attitudes. First is the cultural correlation drawn between notions of physical wholeness, beauty, and cultural status. In Akan culture, for example, it is often insisted that an aspiring chief or queenmother must be one "without blemish." This translates into an infrangible barrier against persons with disability ever becoming chiefs or queenmothers irrespective of their other cultural qualifications. It is also not unknown for families with persons with disability to suffer in the marriage market because of the stigma attached to severe impairments. The second element underpinning such cultural attitudes is the link drawn between bodily wholeness and economic autonomy. In a city such as Accra, this idea is given visible propping by the fact that the vast bulk of beggars on intersections and street corners are persons with various kinds of disability, thus making the link between the two almost natural in the minds of the nondisabled. Indeed, a local Akan saying, "*e ti se bafa ne fom*" (it is like the cripple [*sic*] and the ground), which is used to convey the inseparability between two entities, derives from the observation that persons with severe motor impairments are often seen dragging themselves on the ground, begging for alms at street corners and elsewhere. Thus the impairments are naturalized as part of the social landscape and given validation through the implicit prejudice contained in such sayings. Another Akan proverb, recalled to the audience by Kwesi Yankah, has it that "*Onyakopon nim odwan a o be ye dwan tro enti na omaa no eni baako*" (God knew the goat that would be a bully, that is why he gave him only one eye). This proverb suggests that disability is an insignia of moral deficit and is a signal of divine providence in providing a warning for the nondisabled. Again, the process of negative stereotyping is impossible to miss. The third pertinent factor underlining attitudes toward disability in Ghana is the quick and unexamined connection that is often made between disability and an invisible metaphysical order of things. Sometimes this has an unusual articulation, such as when nondisabled people going to engage in a major business deal stop to give alms to a disabled beggar with the injunction to "bring me luck." In other words, it is okay to extend a few pesewa of charity to a disabled beggar so long as that guarantees the success of a major project for the person extending the charity. The disabled beggar is thus seen as a talisman of fortune that may also be blamed for the collapse of good luck in such an eventuality. As we saw in chapter 1, all the foregoing attitudes have been pertinent to how persons with disability have been treated in various cultures. The interesting thing in the Ghanaian scene is how the particular collocation of such attitudes had combined to frustrate the passage of a comprehensive Disabilities Act for so long.

The occasion at the CDD was celebratory but also quite sober, for the questions that followed the talk showed that there were various areas that despite having been covered by the Act would need a great deal of cultural sensitivity to be fully actualized. What were mothers with disabled children to do when their neighbors accused them of witchcraft, for example? Sections 4 and 39 of the Act make discriminatory treatment and derogatory remarks against persons with disability a criminal act punishable by a fine, a stint in prison, or both. But how was this provision to be implemented when accusations of witchcraft were directed at anyone that appeared socially marginal, such as old women, children brought into households as servants, and cultural outsiders, as well as persons with impairments? How could accusations of witchcraft against disabled persons be separated from the social containment and disciplinary implications of such accusations that derive from the severe incoherences of the sociocultural realm in the first place? What about disability conscientization of public servants? Were they all obliged to know about the social model of disability? The Act stipulated that public workers in the education, health delivery, and police sectors would be educated and sensitized on disability issues. But what about the judicial system, as one questioner interrupted in the course of the discussion. What about the judge who was to set an interpretative precedent on a delicate disability-related case that might have implications for the future implementation of provisions of the Act? What about chiefs? Yes, the chiefs who, through the regional and national Houses of Chiefs had historically wielded so much influence on both cultural and political questions? Was it not time for the chiefs to be brought to acknowledge that they had been unwitting guardians of prejudice toward disabled persons? These and other questions made for a very lively debate and served to show that the treatment of disability issues was of major concern to a wide range of people in Ghanaian society.

I kept asking myself both then and afterward: what is the relation between *Aesthetic Nervousness* and an occasion such as this, between a discussion of the representation of disability in literature and the condition of the lives of disabled persons on the streets of the city where I grew up? What, in short, is *the* point? A subtle turn in Tobin Siebers' *The Ethics of Criticism* (1988) helps shed some light on what the point might be. He writes, concerning violence:

> *Here too I am concerned with the forms of violence that injure human beings by creating categories or ideas that risk depriving them of rights in political and psychological contexts.* . . . The problem of violence cannot be properly defined outside of an anthropological context, and the world of human beings is vertiginously complex. Violence is a human problem. It is never an infernal machine without a driver. It is never without a victim. If it may be called systematic, it is only so because it establishes languages and patterns of behaviour that can be repeated by others.
>
> (7; italics added)

It is the force of Siebers' unremitting impulse to demonstrate how literary theory and criticism cannot be separated from ethical questions that makes his book so attractive to me. And yet, as I have tried to show throughout *Aesthetic Nervousness*, the ethical core that disability implies within literary representation is rarely if ever clearly evident on casual reading. It is only a rigorous set of reading practices alive to the implications of disability that would help to give space to that ethical core. Each chapter in the study has been an illustration of what such a reading practice might look like. Among other things, it entails reading disability not as a discrete entity within the literary aesthetic domain, but as part of the totality of textual representation. In this totality, everything is linked to everything else such that in isolating a detail of disability for analysis we take it not merely as a particular detail, but as a threshold that opens up to other questions of a textual and also ethical kind. Often, this threshold effect is also the precise point at which the short-circuiting of the dominant protocols of representation reveal itself. Thus disability-as-threshold is also a signifier of textual tension. In my critical practice I have given different names to this threshold feature of disability: fulcrum, pivot, radiating point. Thus in the chapter on Toni Morrison I showed how disability acted as the hinge upon which various textual negotiations in her work take place. It is with respect to Morrison's work also that we saw the necessity for delaying final judgment on the status of disability, given the insistent invitation in her work for us to always anticipate alternatives in coming to any such judgment.

The delay in passing judgment, however, must not be taken as an excuse to defer such judgment indefinitely, for ethical questions hinge even on the process of delay. Thus it is that in discussing Samuel Beckett I suggested that the play of negation and deferral implied in his writing might be seen as being constructed around an absence, an absence discernable in the ambiguous status he gives to pain in his work. For pain, as we noted, requires a witness for its epistemological verification. All the many slips of language, the talking at cross-purposes, and the difficulties in establishing a clear frame of reference for his many impaired characters ultimately hide the fact that they ought to be in pain but are patently not. The identification of this absence of pain essentially means that we are reading against the logic of his texts themselves so as to discover where their ethical implications might reside. With the range and nuance of Beckett, this reading against the grain also means reading his work not as autonomous and disconnected from the real, but as part of the construction of reality, despite its strenuous efforts at distancing and detachment from any putative reality.

The unknotting of Beckett's textual turgidities is also pertinent to a reading of Wole Soyinka, despite the fact that he has always been one of the most explicitly political writers in African literature. For in Soyinka we saw how the force of ritual served to assimilate the disabled characters in his work to a domain of the metaphysical, thus leading to a gap being instituted between ritual and politics in the writing. Yet this gap is shown to be unsustainable, since his disabled characters are as much implicated in the process of the denomination of violence and victimhood as they are themselves objects of such violence. Their ritualization is then also a process of their romanticization as avatars of superior insight not dissimilar to the playwright's own. In this instance, the reading of disability in the work of such a highly political writer was designed to show how central disability is to his political project. This serves to correct the heavy emphasis that has been placed on the Ogun cycle in commentary on his work.

J. M. Coetzee's writing acted as a means of tying together various critical vectors that had been opened up in the three earlier writers. Of particular note is the concept of the skeptical interlocutor, first introduced in the discussion on Beckett but later elaborated in Morrison and Soyinka. For Coetzee also allowed us to raise a critical theoretical point about the nature of narrative as such: what is the link between speech and silence when silence is practically abrogated by the very ontological nature of writing? And what does it then mean when, in reading an autistic character, we are invited by the nature of narrative to read echoes into their elective silence via our shifting identification with the implied interlocutor, which is an inescapable aspect of narrative as such? How do we know when the autist is being spoken for? Thus, though the study by no means followed a teleological trajectory, it still managed to foreground a steady cluster of issues that seemed to be incrementally repeated by the various writers and that allowed particularly productive theoretical insights for the nature of narrative to be drawn from the work of Coetzee.

The shift to Robben Island and the lives of various disabled persons that had dotted its history was designed to show how much features of a critical literary reading might be used for understanding disability issues in a nonliterary context. But in this chapter, the other, larger objective was to animate these historical personages and to imagine what it might have been like to have suffered prejudice that was produced at the intersection of colonialism, class, disability, and, in the case of Krotoa, gender. How, in other words, might a reading of the fertile history of a place such as Robben Island generate a radically different perspective when pursued from the coupling of *literary* disability studies and history as opposed to plain history?

These and the many other questions that arose over the course of *Aesthetic Nervousness* help us ponder what its relationship might be to disability issues in places such as Ghana and elsewhere. For me, what emerged quite clearly from the deliberations at the CDD event was that language and cultural stereotypes are the most deadly instruments for denying the humanity of people. To provide the tools for unmasking the essentially violent dimensions of such stereotypes from a close reading of literary texts is to go some way toward at least rectifying the attitudes behind such stereotyping practices. More important, it helps to show that our ultimate obligation as literary critics must be addressing the particularities of injustice of the world in which we live. Abstractions may be necessary to school our moral sense, but in the final instance it is the nature of the social world we imagine and work for that validates our ethical dispositions. Let me close with the opening paragraph from Siebers' book, pausing only to say that the insight is highly relevant to what we do as students of literature: "The character of criticism emerges in its critical choices, and the nature of critical choice reveals that literary criticism is inextricably linked to ethics. . . . To criticize ethically brings the critic into a special field of action: the field of human conduct and belief concerning the human."

NOTES

1. Introduction: Aesthetic Nervousness

1. For a version of this view, see Chabal and Daloz (1999), and for a more elaborated version applicable to the idea of sovereignty in general, see Achille Mbembe's essay "Necropolitics," in *Public Culture* (2002).

2. For the account of social attitudes toward disability in fourteenth-century England, I draw mainly on *The Common Lot*, Margaret Pelling's fascinating book of essays on social conditions in Elizabethan England. But see also Paul Slack, *The English Poor Law, 1531–1782* (1995); and Paul Griffiths and Mark Jenner, eds., *Londinopolis* (2000) for corroborative accounts from other parts of the country. Henri Jacques Stiker's *A History of Disability* (1999) is a more Foucauldian study of disability in Europe and attempts to account for changing social attitudes to disability as they emerge from the nexus of attitudes, institutional practices, and social relations. By this genealogical means he seeks to show the degree to which twentieth-century attitudes to disability derive from and yet are sharply differentiated from what came before. His central premise is that the desire to see everyone as alike is what underlies contemporary notions of disability. This he sets out to systematically challenge. Stiker's is the best such account I can think of, and it even surpasses Foucault in focusing not only on madness but on wider questions of corporeal difference.

3. The notion of empire as a laboratory for the sharpening of various discourses in Europe is from Ann Laura Stoler (1995). On the relation be-

tween empire and criminal profiling, see Pablo Mukherjee (2003). The point about the intermeshing of metropolitan and extra-European realities is well made by various postcolonial writers such as Edward Said (1994), Robert Young (1995), and Benita Parry (2004).

4.   See the fascinating video documentary by Snyder and Mitchell, *A World Without Bodies* (2001). The scholarly literature on the Nazi extermination of people with disabilities is vast. Stefan Kuhl (1994) and Henry Friedlander (1995) provide good overview arguments, with Kuhl also looking at the contribution of debates in the American eugenics movement of the 1920s to what ultimately became the nightmare of Nazi experimentation. Ursula Hegi's *Stones from the River* (1994) presents a moving literary account of the ways in which the intersection between anti-Semitism and disablism affects the evolving consciousness of Trudi Montag, the dwarf girl who is the sensitive protagonist of the novel.

5.   David Millikan's arguments from Australia, in which he launched a robust defense of Hoddle's right to the expression of his religious beliefs regardless of how it might be offensive to others, exemplified this tendency. See http://www.shootthemessenger.com.au/u_feb_99/c_soccer.htm. Also relevant in this regard was a piece by Kevin Carey, available at http://www. g21.net/do59.htm. Kevin Carey is described on his Web page as "director of a UK charity, HumanITy, which combines rigorous social analysis with experimental field projects on learning IT skills through content creation. Educated at Cambridge and Harvard before a spell at the BBC, followed by 15 years in Third World Development, Carey offers a unique perspective on world affairs. He is a political theorist, moral philosopher, classical music critic and published poet"—clearly a well-educated, middle-class former public servant with an interest in the rest of the world, whose opinions are not to be dismissed as those of a quirky fraction.

6.   Richard Downes, letter to the editor, *The Guardian*, February 3, 1999.

7.   On first considering this point about the vertiginous fears of the nondisabled regarding disability I focused primarily on Lacan's discussion of the mirror phase and his exploration of the *imagos* of dismemberment that come up for people under psychic stress. From this, I elaborated what I termed the primal scene of the encounter between the disabled and the nondisabled, which, as I argued, was riven by constitutive emotional ambiguities. Even though I still find that perspective persuasive, in the current discussion I want to leave the contours of the psychoanalytic interpretation to one side and instead invoke the work of philosophers and disability writers who have thought and written about this matter. For my earlier argument, see "Disability and Contingency" in *Calibrations: Reading for the Social* (2003). At any rate, though I didn't know it then, the argument about Lacan and the primal scene of disability had already been quite persuasively put by Lennard Davis (1995, 140–142) and so will not be reprised here.

8.   For the discussions of the sublime and the beautiful that I have drawn upon, see Allison (2001), Crockett (2001), Ashfield and de Bolla (1996), Caruth (1988), and de Man (1990). The issue of whether the sublime triggers an ethical recognition or not is a contentious one and not yet settled on either side, but Ashfield and de Bolla provide a good account of how the ethical debates on the sublime have unfolded in British literary history from the eighteenth century onward.

9.   For particularly insightful readings of *Richard III* from a disability studies perspective, see Mitchell and Snyder (2000, 95–118) and Lennard Davis.

2.   A Typology of Disability Representation

1.   I think here mainly of Frye's *Anatomy of Criticism* (1957) and *Fables of Identity* (1963) and Erich Auerbach's *Mimesis* (1953), exemplary works of literary synthesis that combine literary history with astute close readings of texts.

2.   Sometimes the assumed sublimity of the literary text made the critic gasp for words. This is the sense one gets from R. P. Blackmur when he writes regarding Wallace Stevens's "The Death of a Soldier" that "to gloss such a poem is almost impertinent" (2003, 116). The injunction to fall silent is one that can plainly not be respected in a discussion of literary representations of disability, thus marking a necessary critical distance between the current enterprise and the work of the New Critics. "Speaking for," in terms of taking a clearly ideological position, is now as much part of the literary-critical domain as the hitherto dominant enterprise of "speaking about" the literary text and limiting oneself strictly to the domain of the text under discussion. For an astute discussion of some of the reasons for the shift in critical practices, see Andrew DuBois' introduction to *Close Reading* (2003), in which R. P. Blackmur's essay just cited is to be found.

3.   See also "Exploring the 'Hearing Line': Deafness, Laughter, and Mark Twain," Christopher Krentz's (2002) insightful essay on hearing and comedy in Twain.

4.   Rosemarie Garland Thomson (2002) also provides a helpful typology of representations in which she identifies the rhetoric of the wondrous, the sentimental, the exotic, and the realistic. Her discussion draws mainly on photographs of disabled people used for advertisements and art exhibitions in the twentieth century. The distinction to be drawn between Thomson's account and what is presented here is that there are more subtle gradations to be established in literary works. The various categories often overlap or indeed shift between more than one rhetoric, to use her word. A typology of disability representation thus has to be both suppler and more provisional, since the variety of literary expression makes it impossible to arrive

at an all-encompassing mode of explanation. See also Martin Norden (1994) for a discussion of types of representation of disability in cinema.

5.   Redactions of the tale of the Loathely Lady are to be found in various sources. Particularly well known are those told by Chaucer's Wife of Bath. The Wife of Bath's account is itself traceable to "The Weddynge of Sir Gawen and Dame Ragnell," which can be found in *Sources and Analogues of Chaucer's Canterbury Tales* (Bryan and Dempster 1941). A more modern rendition of this story is provided in Rosemary Sutcliff's *The Sword and the Circle* (1981), which itself draws upon Mallory's *Le Morte D'Arthur*. Sutcliff's story, written essentially for children, accentuates certain details of atmosphere and of the Loathely Lady's personal qualities, such as the mellifluous timbre of her voice and the class markings of her clothes. Particularly telling is the effect of the Loathely Lady's disability in almost freezing the knights' capacity for speech and gesture when she is brought to the castle. This serves as a fascinating example of the social nervousness that nondisabled people exhibit on first-time encounters with persons with disabilities, a nervousness Thomson writes of in *Extraordinary Bodies* (1997).

6.   For a riveting discussion of such cartoons, see L. Perry Curtis's *Apes and Angels: The Irishman in Victorian Caricature* (1997).

7.   To get the full value of Spivak's remarks, it is best to read her essay alongside Benita Parry's critique/response. Both pieces are helpfully anthologized in *Postcolonialism: Critical Concepts in Literary and Cultural Studies*, vol. 2, edited by Diana Brydon (2000).

8.   It has to be noted, however, that even though Dory's extreme form of short-term amnesia makes her stand out in the film, she is not the only one to carry a disability. Nemo himself has one fin smaller than the other and the character of the black-and-white fish in the dentist's aquarium has one mangled fin. He is himself a peculiar figure whose characterization combines an interplay between light and darkness. He only becomes benign after almost getting Nemo killed in one of his many fruitless plots to get himself and the other fish out of the small aquarium they have been trapped in and back into the sea.

9.   Cases in which an impairment is taken as a direct insignia of evil abound in literature: Captain Hook in Peter Pan, the much-discussed Ahab in Melville's *Moby Dick*, Zaita in Naguib Mahfouz's *Midaq Alley*, and the protagonist of Patrick Suskind's *Perfume* are just a few examples. Dreamworks' recent *Shrek 2* has an entire tavern filled with all kinds of disabled characters. The tavern is supposed to be the source of the baddies in the film (they turn out not to be so bad in the end); Captain Hook is shown playing the piano at the tavern.

10.   It is useful to recall here Irving Zola's (1987) remarks on how rare it is for detectives who use wheelchairs in detective stories to complain when faced with architectural impediments to their mobility (such as a flight of stairs, for instance). Their impairment suddenly vanishes from the ac-

count. See his "Any Distinguishing Features?—The Portrayal of Disability in the Crime-Mystery Genre."

11. Though it is difficult to make a generalization about this kind of epiphanic disability, it has to be noted that such discursive deployments of disability may be seen in various texts of a postcolonial nature, such as in Arundhati Roy's The God of Small Things around the character of Kuttapen, the doomed Velutha's brother, and in Chinua Achebe's Things Fall Apart. Achebe's Things Fall Apart is fascinating for first hinting that Okonkwo's stammer is the mark of a cultural deficit and then completely effacing that deficit while the narrative establishes his credentials as a lord of the clan. It is only at the very end, with the killing of the district administrator's messenger, that we suddenly see that his lack of verbal facility was indeed a serious deficit: he kills the messenger against the background of his gathered tribesmen coming to talk about their most recent humiliation at the hands of the white man. The descent of his machete marks for him an assertion of the masculine warrior ethic for which he had always been rewarded. But for them its descent is his final severance from a society that has changed imperceptibly due to the colonial encounter. It is only here at the climactic moment of the narrative that we see that his stammer was indeed a severe cultural deficit that would ultimately lead to his being peripheralized by the culture. The next time we encounter him, Okonkwo is hanging from a tree, a suicide. As we shall see in chapter 4, Toni Morrison's work displays a broad range of such epiphanies tied to disability.

12. See the Vellacott translation of Prometheus Bound (1961), lines 561–630.

13. Other examples of the use of disability as enigma or hermeneutical impasse can be found as variously as in Hoffman's The Sandman, Kafka's Metamorphosis, Keri Hulme's The Bone People, Athol Fugard's Master Harold and the Boys, and Coetzee's Waiting for the Barbarians, among various others. What has to be remembered is that even while illustrating different vectors of disability representation, what is central to these accounts is the enigmatic aura that surrounds the impairment, whether this is visible or otherwise. The aura is designed to generate an open-ended problem of interpretation for the characters as well as the readers. For a discussion along similar lines related to war wounded, see Amanda Claybaugh's (2005) excellent piece in the Yale Journal of Criticism, which discusses the responses to Berthold Lindau, the disabled character in Dean Howells' A Hazard of New Fortunes, itself set in the period just after the U.S. Civil War.

14. Helen Deutsch has argued that the impairments carried by writers such as Alexander Pope, Lord Byron, and Samuel Johnson, among others, gives a particular quality to their works, something that has long been denied by mainstream scholars. She elaborates her argument in Resemblance and Disgrace: Alexander Pope and the Deformation of Culture (1996); see also her piece in Snyder et al. (2002). Nancy Mairs (1996), Anne Finger (1990), Audre Lorde (1982), and others have written sensitive works of both a fic-

tional and semiautobiographical nature from the perspective of people who are disabled themselves. On the other hand, we have highly sensitive fictional works such as Wilkie Collins's *Poor Miss Finch* and Ursula Hegi's *Stones from the River* as but two examples from nondisabled writers.

3.   Samuel Beckett: Disability as Hermeneutical Impasse

1.   This production of *Endgame* ran from March 10 to May 1, 2004.

2.   Variously and respectively, Kate Bassett in the *Independent*, March 14, 2004; Michael Billington in *The Guardian*, March 11, 2004; Alistair Macauley in the *Financial Times*, March 12, 2004; and Susannah Clapp, *The Observer*, March 14, 2004.

3.   On Beckett as postmodernist/deconstructivist, see for instance Ihab Hassan, Steven Connor, Stanley Cavell, and Richard Begam, among others. On Beckett as existential humanist read through a general perspective of phenomenology, see Trevise, St. John Butler, David Hesla, and Stanton Garner, among others. Within these two broad rubrics, there are also two methodologies in evidence, the genetic and the intertextual. The genetic approach attempts to uncover the specific philosophical debts that Beckett owes to various philosophers, while the intertextual approach tries to show how close his own thought and practice has been to those of philosophers such as Derrida, Deleuze and Guattari, Badiou, Merleau-Ponty, and others. For an overview of these approaches, see Lane (2002).

4.   Indeed, others have drawn up such an inventory, but for different purposes. See, for example, Pierre Chabert (1982), Marie-Claude Hubert (1994), Katherine M. Gray (1996), and John Wall (2000). Such an inventory would include works such as *Murphy* (1938), *Waiting for Godot* (1952), *Endgame* (1957), *The Trilogy* (*Molloy, Malone Dies, The Unnamable*) (1958), *Rough for Theatre I* (1950s), *All That Fall* (1956), *Krapp's Last Tape* (1958), *Happy Days* (1961), and *Play* (1963).

5.   As Gontarski (1985, 242) notes in his analysis of Beckett's style of composition, his slow process of writing usually progresses in this fashion: after the initial image or incident is recorded (often straight from memory or the unconscious), what follows is a shaping process that includes: (1) deleting detail, explanation, and often connection; (2) rejecting, consciously destroying those artificial, manmade, extrinsic systems of chronology and causality; and (3) creating an alternative arrangement or internal relationship that will emphasize *pattern* if not *order*. Thus it would be very risky to read off any biographical details as directly pertinent to the interpretation of any of his characters. Biographical details have to remain purely speculative.

6.   For a fuller discussion of the theme of surveillance in *Molloy*, see Uhlmann (1999).

7. There is also a play on the mechanized gaze and technological interlocutor. This is combined with the compulsion to act and the necessity and terror of being seen. Thus in *Krapp's Last Tape* he hugs the tape recorder and listens to it intently as a means of interacting with different parts of himself. The tape recorder becomes both an interlocutor and a prosthesis of his own voice. Again, in *Play*, the spotlight acts as a prosthesis of the audience, but it also generates anxiety because of the impossibility of verifying the status of this technological interlocutor. The direct effect is an incitement to narrate.

8. A similar question may be posed of *Murphy*, where Murphy makes a conscious preference for mind over body yet finds himself of a necessity having to perfect repetitive rituals to calm his body in order to liberate his mind. He calls this at a point in the novel the big world versus the little world, his choice being firmly with the little world. *Murphy*, however, raises another level of difficulty because of the role of the third-person narrator, who at every turn proliferates lacunae at the level of the narrative technique, whether this has to do with the reporting of an event in the past, the description of various characters, or the unfolding of the plot. Thus it is that every level of the text seems riddled with shifting gaps, all of which are not helped by the highly dense and often Latinate register of the language of the novel in general.

9. For an overview of these and an independent allegorical reading of the play, see Jane Allison Hale's piece in Steven Connor (1992).

10. There are variant terms that are used to refer to users of wheelchairs in disability studies: "wheelchair user" and its variants "chair user" and "user of a wheelchair," to the more specific "x or y uses a wheelchair," where the emphasis is as much on the agent-user as on the wheelchair itself. In all such instances, the idea is to refer to the user in such a way as not to assimilate his or her identity to a function of the technological prosthesis, whatever that might be given the impairment. See Albrecht et al. (2001) for a range of essays that pick up and elaborate on these and other terms in disability studies. However, in the case of Hamm, the wheelchair is so much an inescapable part of his identity that it would be inadequate to say he was merely a user of the wheelchair. Everything that he does is linked to the fact that he is immobilized *and* in a wheelchair, thus my preference for the term "wheelchair bound."

11. Though this is not really the place for it, it would be interesting to contrast the dialectic of movement/immobility in *Endgame* to the one we see in Aeschylus's *Prometheus Bound*, which was touched on briefly in chapter 2. The main difference between the two plays would be in the construction of an epic topos around Prometheus's stillness, something that is then contrasted to the various entrances and exits of the other characters in the play. *Endgame* has no such epic topos, since its "geography" is entirely domestic and not given to imaginative elaborations beyond it. Furthermore,

whereas Aeschylus's play introduces a degree of geographical extension with the entry of each of the characters that come to speak to Prometheus (Oceanus, Io, and then the hated Hermes), in *Endgame* that geographical extension is, strictly speaking, not allowed, since all the characters seem to be constrained both in their physical conditions and in the reach of their imaginations. Even when "nature" outside the stage is admitted into account, it is admitted only to be undermined in its status as provider of epistemological verity or ontological sustenance.

12.   On the odd logic of necropoltics, see Achille Mbembe's 2003 essay of the same title.

13.   Recalling Shakespeare, similar doubts can be raised about Gertrude's description of Ophelia's death in *Hamlet* III.iv. As far as I can tell, it is humanly impossible to drown and sing at the same time, but this is what Gertrude claims Ophelia was doing when she drowned. Her description is obviously not solely about the death of the young woman. Apart from being a fascinating example of ekphrasis in Shakespeare, it is also clearly an attempt to deflect the responsibility for the suicide away from the mentally ill Ophelia and onto the surrounding environment. But this deflection of responsibility goes beyond that. It is also implicitly an attempt to rehabilitate insanity and to retranscribe it aesthetically as a moment of transcendence, when, as it were, the mad character of Ophelia acquires a oneness with nature. This is surely a sign of aesthetic nervousness. For further accounts of the challenges to realism imposed by disability, see Zola's (1987) account of the representation of detectives with impairments in the history of the crime/mystery novel.

4.   Toni Morrison: Disability, Ambiguity, and Perspectival Modulations

1.   The texts she pays close attention to in *Playing in the Dark* are as follows (with the disability in parentheses where relevant): Marie Cardinal, *The Words to Say It* (mental disorder, vii–xii); Willa Cather, *Sapphira and the Slave Girl* (Sapphira, slave mistress who is also a wheelchair user, 18–28); Edgar Allan Poe, *The Narrative of Arthur Gordon Pym* (31–32, 51–54); Herman Melville, *Moby Dick* (monomaniacal leg-amputee Ahab); Bernard Bailyn, *On William Dunbar* (39–44); Mark Twain, *Huckleberry Finn* ('Lizabeth, deaf-mute daughter of Jim, and the pretend-deaf duke, 54–57); Ernest Hemingway, *To Have and Have Not* (central character Harry has an amputated arm, 58, 70–80); Ernest Hemingway, *The Garden of Eden* (80–91).

2.   In fact, the device of using a narrative moment as the nodal point for the interweaving of fragmentary reflections both for the third-person narrator and for individual characters in the narrative is a distinctive feature of many of Morrison's novels, at least in those since *Song of Solomon*, when

the device becomes most prominent. Thus, in *Song of Solomon* we have the opening sequence with the suicide of the man from the insurance company who attempts to "fly" off the ledge of the building. This initial moment becomes an intersecting point for various others over the course of the narrative. In *Beloved*, we have Sethe's terrible choice as such a moment, and *Love* returns to the time of Heed's marriage to Cosey as the foundational ground upon which several characters try to recall the past and reframe their own present circumstances. Sometimes, as in the contradictory accounts that Milkman gets from his father and mother about the cause of the coldness in their marriage, the business of the bones that hang from the rafters of Pilate's house, or the events surrounding the Ruby men's invasion of the convent, the nodal story becomes the point of hermeneutical impasse for the characters, leading to multiple and contradictory interpretations and the general breakdown of communication among them. For the reader, the process of making meaning of what we read requires a vigilance similar to what we see in the case of Violet in *Jazz*, who when walking has to pay particular attention to the cracks in the pavement so that she does not slip into them (23; see also *The Bluest Eye*, 35–36). Is it the case, then, that from the very narrative devices Morrison deploys she is suggesting that we are all subjects of a hermeneutical delirium in our quest for meaning?

3.   The image of bird's wings also operates as the signal of possession in Sethe's case in *Beloved*. When the four horsemen come to seize her and her children, Sethe is suddenly possessed by an ungovernable feeling that is captured in the image of hummingbirds: "Little hummingbirds stuck needle beaks right through her headcloth into her hair and beat their wings. And if she thought anything, it was No. No. Nono. Nonono. Simple. She just flew" (163).

4.   Several critics have commented on Eva's deity-like functions, among them Hortense Spillers (2003, 112), for whom Eva behaves "as though she were herself the sole instrument of divine inscrutable will."

5.   The conflicting issues that parents have toward their children with disabilities is amply discussed by social workers and disability scholars. For a representative view on this, see Wiess (1994) and Read (2000).

6.   Even though the novel does not tell us what exactly is on Plum's mind and thus does not give us enough to properly evaluate the reason for his drug habit, it would not be excessive to compare him to Shadrack, the only other returnee soldier the narrative gives us. Having himself suffered from harrowing experiences in the war, Shadrack returns to Medallion a recluse, living on the outskirts of the community in a hut. He is generally considered to be mentally disabled. Shadrack institutes an annual National Suicide Day, which takes place every January 3 since 1920. With his bell, the disheveled prophet annually rouses the community to the sense of an ending on this special day until, at the end of the novel, it marks a

true apocalypse: several people die in a landslide amid melting ice within a giant tunnel (160–162). In this way, Shadrack is discursively aligned with Plum as a witness to the sense of an ending that, in one case, is articulated through an annual communal ritual and, in another, is completely internalized and only expressed through a desire for self-destruction. For a discussion of the sense of an ending in modern literature, see Frank Kermode (1968).

7.   Sethe's notion of rememory may fruitfully be understood within the framework provided by Teresa Brennan in her book *The Transmission of Affect* (2004). Brennan argues that complex affects (love, hate) are not merely made up of emotions but also involve judgment. Thus she is able to elaborate the concept of affective transmission to argue that individual identity is far from self-contained, but is rather porous and inherently transgressed by the affects of others. In the case of Sethe's rememory, the transmitted affect is necessarily communal rather than merely individual, since the implication that Sethe raises is that the negative affect has leaked into history itself and saturated the moment of its leakage, thus reorienting it as a granulated moment. On the relationship between trauma and interpretation, see Cathy Caruth (1996); also, with respect to the evaluation of history in the present and the general concept of granulated reality see Quayson (2003, 76–82, 125–135).

8.   On epiphanies in literature, see Martin Bidney's *Patterns of Epiphany* (1997).

9.   In this regard, it would be interesting to compare Baby Suggs's contemplation of primary colors to William Blake's implied questioning of the inherent contradictions within God's creation in his poem "Tyger." For the question that Blake poses has no answer: "What immortal hand or eye / dare frame thy fearful symmetry?" This question is not dissimilar to that implicitly posed by Baby Suggs's retreat: "God puzzled her and she was too ashamed of Him to say so. Instead she told Stamp she was going to bed to think about the colors of things. . . . Strangers and familiars were stopping by to hear how it went one more time, and suddenly Baby declared peace. She just up and quit. By the time Sethe was released she had exhausted blue and was well on her way to yellow" (177).

5.   Wole Soyinka: Disability, Maimed Rites, and the Systemic Uncanny

1.   On the Ogun heroic ideal, see Soyinka's own discussion in *Myth, Literature, and the African World* (1975). Also, see Ketu Katrak (1986) and Quayson (1997, 67–78).

2.   My discussion of Greek terms here is drawn from G. E. R. Lloyd's *In the Grip of Disease: Studies in the Greek Imagination* (2003).

3. It is true that at the end of the play the chief priest and the rest of the community feel not a sense of elation and freedom but one of despair and foreboding. Guilt has taken the place of joy and a feeling of liberation. And yet there is something dissatisfying even about this, because Eman is not given any energetic poetic lines that would stick in the mind (at least not of this reader). We are then not wrong to assume that the community's feeling of guilt is more because of the frayed and difficult ritual process.

4. In Freud's account, the blurring of the boundary between the mechanical and the physical is one of the main ways of producing the sense of *unheimlich*. See his well-known essay on "The Uncanny" (1919). Also, see Neil Hertz (1985). We shall return to Freud later in the chapter.

5. It might also be possible to cast Goyi as some sort of marionette, but I must admit that this is purely speculative, as there is no evidence from existing accounts of performances of the play that he has ever been cast in such a way. However, the thematic possibilities that this might open up are quite enticing.

6. The most extended discussion of biopower is of course that provided by Foucault in *Discipline and Punish* and *The History of Sexuality*. But see also Giorgio Agamben's *Homo Sacer* (1998), for the relationship between biopower, notions of the sacred, and the constitution of political sovereignty.

7. The threat of violence that never quite breaks out to the surface until the very end is a characteristic device in Soyinka's drama; the best examples of this are *The Road* and *Kongi's Harvest*, two plays that, as we have seen, also close on a note of enigmatic open-endedness.

8. I elaborate more fully on a view of uncanny as the retranscription of an inchoate sense of systemic disorder in my chapter on literature, history, and South Africa's TRC, in Quayson (2003, chap. 4). See also Quayson, "Symbolization Compulsions: Testing a Psychoanalytic Concept Through African Literature" (2004).

9. The best historical contexts for understanding the nature of the systemic uncanny are those to do with war, the rumors of war, and generalized social upheaval. The Rwandan genocide and the events in the months following the September 11 attacks in New York are cases in point. But I write this a day after the July 7 suicide bombings in London, in which at least thirty-seven people were killed and several more injured. All media reports spoke of the fear and uncertainty unleashed by the bombing. For good discussions on violence, trauma, and the uncanny, see the essays in Robben and Suarez-Oroco (2000). And for a fascinating discussion specifically dealing with instances of the endemic chaos and incoherence of African life that may bring forth the sense of the systemic uncanny as I describe it here, see Mbembe (2001, chaps. 3–4) and Chabal and Daloz (1999).

10. For the pitfalls of literary psychoanalysis, especially its attempt to set up a proximity between the author and his or her work, see Brooks (1988).

11. We may also find further corroboration for this argument about the centrality of disability to his work from looking at his poetry. Poems such as "Abiku" (an inspiration behind Okri's *The Famished Road*) and the more recent "Doctored Vision" (2002) both encapsulate the ways in which disability generates a creative payout for him.

6. J. M. Coetzee: Speech, Silence, Autism, and Dialogism

1. It is also important to note with respect to *Disgrace* and *Foe* that the inarticulacy of the disabled characters in those novels is also used to raise not just the problem of interpersonal meaning-making but the additionally complex one of the veridical processes implied in the genre of the detective thriller, a genre that both novels gesture toward in subtle and as yet unaccounted for ways.

2. Films such as *Rain Man* (dir. Barry Levinson, 1988), *Silent Fall* (dir. Bruce Beresford, 1994), and *Mercury Rising* (dir. Harold Becker, 1998) all serve to illustrate some of these features of autism. However, beyond the sentimental and emotionally epiphanic value of the autist to such filmic representation is whether it is possible to discern features of autism that are endemic to the very texture of the various levels of narrative and filmic discourse within which the autistic spectrum is represented (i.e., spanning character, narratorial perspective, and the relationship between narration in general and the representation of the autist).

3. The definition of autism and the list of features are adapted from Simon Baron-Cohen (2000) as well as from numerous personal conversations I have had with him on the subject.

4. The following list, compiled originally by Stuart Murray at the University of Leeds, shows the potential for such a framework of interpretation in helping us to reread certain well-known literary texts:

Charles Dickens—*Barnaby Rudge* (1841)
Hermann Melville—"Bartleby, the Scrivener" (1853)
Joseph Conrad—*The Secret Agent* (1907)
William Faulkner—*The Sound and the Fury* (1929)
Gertrude Stein—*The Autobiography of Alice B. Toklas* (1933)
John Steinbeck—*Of Mice and Men* (1937)
Ken Kesey—*One Flew Over the Cuckoo's Nest* (1972)
Anita Desai—*Clear Light of Day* (1980)
Keri Hulme—*The Bone People* (1983)
Doris Lessing—*The Fifth Child* (1988)
Sue Miller—*Family Pictures* (1990)
Pauline Melville—*The Ventriloquist's Tale* (1997)
Nick Hornby—*About a Boy* (1998)
David Lodge—*Thinks . . .* (2001)

Simon Armitage—*Little Green Man* (2001)
Elizabeth Moon—*Speed of Dark* (2003)
Jill Dawson—*Wild Boy* (2004)
Eli Gottlieb—*The Boy Who Went Away* (2004)
We might also add several of Beckett's characters to this list: Molloy, Winnie, Murphy, Clov, Krapp, and Vladimir and Estragon all illustrate aspects of the autistic spectrum.

5. The last point is very persuasively put by James Berger in terms of the implicit social autism of the Swindon of the novel. See his fascinating piece "Alterity and Autism: Mark Haddon's Curious Incident in the Neurological Spectrum" (2005).

6. The point about Magda's narrativity is put succinctly by Brian Macaskill in his fine essay "Charting J. M. Coetzee's Middle Voice: *In the Heart of the Country*": "*In the Heart of the Country* can also be said to constitute—inside and out—an act of agency that seeks to speak between incommensurable imperatives. . . . Coetzee writes Magda into being both as a 'real' person and as paper entity, shaping her—and allowing her to shape herself—between the demands of the verisimilitude valued by historical materialism and the discursive play practised by poststructural theories of language. The 'internal' characteristics of Magda's voice thus reflect the 'external' situation whereby she is made to speak—by a writer conscious of and embroiled by competing notions of appropriate speech" (1998, 73).

7. Coetzee's *Disgrace* falls into the category of the truth-and-reconciliation genre of literary writing that has been evident in South Africa since the end of apartheid. Like Gillian Slovo's *Red Dust*, Jane Taylor and William Kentridge's *Ubu and the Truth Commission*, Ivan Vladislavic's "The Fugu Eaters," Mike Nicol's *The Ibis Tapestry*, Achmat Dangor's *Bitter Fruit*, and Sindiwe Magona's *Mother to Mother*, it revisits questions of the reconstitution of identities within a postapartheid era that is none the less saturated with claims of the traumatic past. Some of these texts (Slovo, Magona, Nicol, Taylor and Kentridge) reflect either directly or indirectly upon the work of the TRC itself, sometimes thematizing its institutional apparatus as part of the fabric of the works themselves. In Coetzee's *Disgrace*, the process of truth and reconciliation resides in the background to the unfolding crises of the lives of the characters. Contrastively, with Dangor's *Bitter Fruit* we are left in no doubt that the life crises of the characters are to be directly connected to the presence or absence of truth and reconciliation. Both *Bitter Fruit* and *Disgrace* focus on rape events as a means of thematizing political violence, yet they differ dramatically in the status that the event is given for the constitution of present-day senses of the self. *Disgrace* mutes the effect of the rape while *Bitter Fruit* intensifies its disruptive qualities. The two thus represent different conceptualizations of trauma and their effect on the constitution of identities after apartheid.

8.   It is instructive to contrast Paul Rayment's "transgressive" and ultimately unrequited desire for a nondisabled woman to what we find in the relationship between the Magistrate and the blind Barbarian Girl in *Waiting for the Barbarians* (1980). There, the Magistrate cannot consummate his sexual desire for the girl until he has actually restored her to her own people through what can only be described as a discombobulating rite of geographical passage. His efforts had been toward restoring her to a wholeness that lies beyond the traumatic history that has scarified her body and blinded her eyes: "I am with her not for whatever raptures she may promise or yield but for other reasons, which remain as obscure to me as ever. Except that it has not escaped me that in bed in the dark the marks her torturers have left upon her, the twisted feet, the half-blind eyes, are easily forgotten. Is it then the case that is the whole woman I want, that my pleasure in her is spoiled until these marks on her are erased and she is restored to herself; or is it the case (I am not stupid, let me say these things) that it is the marks on her which drew me to her but which, to my disappointment, I find, do not go deep enough? Too much or too little: is it she I want or the traces of a history her body bears?" (64). This then suggests that the disability short-circuits desire, in this case precisely because its genealogy is traceable to the regime of state-sponsored violence and torture to which the Magistrate has inadvertently subscribed by having been such a dutiful servant of the Empire. The point is that in both *Waiting for the Barbarians* and *Slow Man* the disability produces a structure of impossibility either for the disabled contemplating an erotic encounter with a nondisabled or a nondisabled contemplating something similar with the disabled.

9.   Derek Attridge sets out the main terms of the debate around the interpretation of Michael K. He is either to be taken as a metaphor of an overarching political condition or as a character that precisely refuses metaphorization. The readings that these two viewpoints generate seem in Attridge's view to be diametrically opposed and sometimes contentiously so. See particularly "Against Allegory" in *J. M. Coetzee and the Ethics of Reading* (2004).

10   For more examples of his incapacity to interpret questions and what people say to him, see also 48, 51, 64, and 78, among others.

11.   Other examples of this partially realized interlocutor may be found on 79, 89, and 140, among others.

12.   Graham Pechey has helpfully pointed out that there may be a very important characterological intertext to Michael K in South African literature and elsewhere. He suggests that the motif of sleep is also found in the opening paragraphs of Schreiner's *The Story of an African Farm* and also with reference to her character Waldo, who is also sleepy, earthbound, and a keeper of ostriches, or "birds without flight," as Pechey points out. He also suggests that Coetzee must almost certainly have been thinking of

7. THE REPEATING ISLAND 227

one of Rilke's Orpheus sonnets, in which sleep is rescued from its knee-
jerk association with death and linked instead to the receptivity of life.
Pechey, personal communication.

13. On locusts, see Exodus 10:4, 12–13; Deut. 28:38; 1 Kings 8:37, Psalms
78:46, 105:34, and 109:23, among various others. Manna is most famously
associated with the Israelites fleeing from Egypt (Exodus 16), but see also
Joshua 5:10–12 and John 6:31, 48–51 for New Testament interpretations.
Sparrows and other birds abound in biblical stories, the most pertinent
source for the doctor's views being Christ's parable in Matt. 10:19–33.

7. The Repeating Island: Race, Difference, Disability, and the
Heterogeneities of Robben Island's History

1. I want to say a very special thanks to Harriet Deacon, the foremost historian of Robben Island, who generously shared with me her own insights
and indeed some of her own material when I approached her for advice on
writing this chapter. The chapter is heavily dependent on a reading of her
wide-ranging work on Robben Island, and I want to highlight here how
significant this work has been in challenging the current orthodoxy that
links the island solely to its more recent political past.

2. This sentiment and others like it are to be found in the collection of Tambo's speeches, edited by Adelaide Tambo (1987).

3. See Saul Dubow's *Racial Segregation and the Origins of Apartheid in South
Africa* (1989) for a good discussion. More specifically in terms of the general theoretical view on embodiment, I take my cue from the insightful
work of Elizabeth Grosz, particularly her *Volatile Bodies* (1994).

4. For disability in Fugard, it would be best to turn to *Master Harold and the
Boys*, where the white Hally's father is crippled, an alcoholic, and also a
racist. The difficult father-son relationship is only partially offset by the
positive role that Hally tries to provide for Sam, one of the black characters. With respect to Robben Island, it has inspired mainly protest and
prison literature such as that of Dennis Brutus (1968, 1973) as well as several autobiographies, the most well-known ones being those by Govan
Mbeki (1991), Nelson Mandela (1994), and Ahmed Kathadra (2005),
among various others. As far as I can tell, Fugard's play is the only one
piece of creative writing that actually takes Robben Island itself as the primary setting on which to place the action.

5. The phrase "normal society" is bound to strike a jarring note, given the
fact that under the colonial expropriation of land and property normality
was strictly speaking abrogated and could only be regained through various forms of struggle. Normality then can only be seen in as far as it was
tied to an articulation of freedom. Colonial and apartheid Cape society
was in that sense more normal than the culture of Robben Island, but

completely abnormal under the impress of colonial domination. And colonial domination itself produced variegated standards of normality for the Europeans and the natives they ruled over.

6.   For a further elaboration and expansion of Hegel's idea of the interrelationship of the social universal to the family as the ground of moral relations, see Honneth (1996).

7.   De Villiers' *Robben Island: Out of Reach, Out of Mind* (1971) is a blatantly hagiographic account of the first Dutch commander van Riebeeck and the establishment of the early European settlement. The attitude de Villiers expresses toward the locals is sometimes quite shocking, and yet by the same token he gives an unflinching account of some of the brutal conditions existing among the settlers themselves. I try to read between the lines of his account, as it were, to gain a sense of the inescapable shadow that even such a blatantly celebratory account allows us to discern about the nature of early colonialism at the Cape.

8.   Autshumato was not the first to be taken away by the English for training. An earlier Khoikhoi man called Coree had been kidnapped by the English in 1613 and taken to England. On his return a year later he was supposed to act as their intermediary and promote their interests. He was not cooperative, and it is reported that he died in 1626 at the hands of Dutch sailors for refusing to give them food. See Penn (1996, 12–13) and Elphick (1985, 78–82).

9.   *Journal of Van Riebeeck*, 1:103. Hereafter, *JVR*. Many other references were made to Autshumato in the journal and they were all uniformly of a suspicious nature. He was deeply mistrusted by the settlers, not least because he seemed to be undisguisedly in pursuit of his own interests. For further such references, see *JVR* 1:76, 1:104, 1:119, and 1:183, among various others.

10.   There have been various speculations as to why Krotoa was brought to live with the van Riebeecks, but the most persuasive I have found has been that advanced by Julia C. Wells (1998), who argues that it was her uncle Autshumato who gave Krotoa to the van Riebeecks, seeing that she was an "orphan" and that her presence in their household would strengthen his relationship with them. Wells also points out that van Riebeeck had two nieces of a similar age as Krotoa living with him. One of these, Eva Van Opdorp, was years later to take in Krotoa's children while she was incarcerated on Robben Island. Wells' account may also explain Krotoa's strong attachment to Autshumato, whom she often defended against the negative opinions of the settlers.

11.   *JVR* 2:328.

12.   *JVR* 2:404–405, 3:1.

13.   *JVR* 2:406.

14.   *JVR* 3:71–78, 3:83–85, 3:91.

15.   Wells (1998) provides a more positive spin to the relationship between Pieter and Krotoa, reading in it the first example of a viable if bumpy inter-

racial relationship in South African history. What she is not quite able to explain is why, despite his marriage to Krotoa, Pieter was able to justify going on slave-hunting expeditions, one of which led to his untimely death.

16. Leibbrandt (1900–1902, 1:80–81); Malherbe (1990, 48).
17. Leibbrandt (1900–1902, 1:252; 1:266–267).
18. Leibbrandt (1900–1902, 2:209).
19. JVR 2:307, 2:309.
20. JVR 3:70–75, 3:77–80.
21. JVR 2:4.
22. JVR 2:342–343; also 3:307–308.
23. I should quickly add that I don't interpret the term "tragedy" as implying defeat or victimhood. It is much more complicated than that. I provide my view on tragedy in relation to the life and times of Ken Saro-Wiwa. See "African Postcolonial Relations Through a Prism of Tragedy" in Quayson (2003).
24. On the links between disease, the notion of contagion, and race in South African and other contexts, see variously M. W. Swanson (1977), Gussow (1989), Timothy Burke (1996), and Sander Gilman (1985), among others.
25. The Cape had been under British rule from 1795 through 1803 and then again from 1806 through 1910, when it joined the Union of South Africa.
26. From "Memorandum by the Under Colonial Secretary on the subject of the Leper Settlement on RI" (August 29, 1893), PRO, CO 48/522. Thanks to Harriet Deacon for this reference and for sharing with me her forthcoming piece on Franz Jacobs.
27. September 1893, letter 94: from Henry B. Loch to Lord Marquis as a report on conditions on Robben Island. PRO, CO 48/522.
28. Ibid.

BIBLIOGRAPHY

Primary Texts

Beckett, Samuel. 1986. *The Complete Dramatic Works*. London: Faber. (Main texts referred to: *Waiting for Godot, Endgame, Krapp's Last Tape*, and *Play*)
——. 1936. *Murphy*. New York: Grove Press, 1957.
——. 1958. *The Trilogy (Molloy, Malone, The Unnamable)*. New York: Grove Press.
Coetzee, J. M. 1977. *In the Heart of the Country*. London: Penguin.
——. 1980. *Waiting for the Barbarians*. London: Penguin.
——. 1983. *Life and Times of Michael K*. London: Penguin.
——. 1987. *Foe*. London: Penguin.
——. 2002. *Disgrace*. London: Vintage.
——. 2003. *Elizabeth Costello: Eight Lessons*. New York: Secker and Warburg.
——. 2005. *Slow Man*. New York: Secker and Warburg.
Morrison, Toni. 1970. *The Bluest Eye*. New York: Holt, Rinehart & Winston.
——. 1974. *Sula*. New York: Knopf.
——. 1977. *Song of Solomon*. New York: Knopf.
——. 1987. *Beloved*. New York: Knopf.
——. 1998. *Paradise*. New York: Knopf.
Soyinka, Wole. 1973–1974. *Collected Plays*. 2 vols. Oxford: Oxford University Press. (Vol. 1 contains *A Dance of the Forests, The Swamp Dwellers, The Strong*

Breed, *The Road*, and *The Bacchae of Euripides*. Vol. 2 contains *The Lion and the Jewel*, *Kongi's Harvest*, and *Madmen and Specialists*.)
——. 1975. *Death and the King's Horseman*. London: Methuen.

References

Abrahams, Yvette. 1996. "Was Eva Raped? An Exercise in Speculative History." *Kronos: Journal of Cape History* 23: 3–21.
Adams, Rachel. 2001. *Sideshow U.S.A.: Freaks and the American Cultural Imagination*. Chicago: University of Chicago Press.
Adorno, Theodor. 1985. "Trying to Understand *Endgame*." In *Samuel Beckett*, ed. Harold Bloom, 51–81. New York: Chelsea House.
Aeschylus. 1961. *Prometheus Bound and Other Plays*. Trans. Philip Vellacott. London: Penguin.
Agamben, Giorgio. 1998. *Homo Sacer: Sovereign Power and Bare Life*. Trans. Daniel Heller-Roazen. Stanford, Calif.: Stanford University Press.
Albrecht, Gary L. 2002. "American Pragmatism, Sociology, and the Development of Disability Studies." In *Disability Studies Today*, ed. C. Barnes et al., 18–37. Cambridge: Polity Press.
Albrecht, Gary L., Katherine D. Sleeman, and Michael Bury, eds. 2001. *Handbook of Disability Studies*. London: Sage.
Allison, Henry E. 2001. *Kant's Theory of Taste: A Reading of the Critique of Aesthetic Judgment*. Cambridge: Cambridge University Press.
Altaman, Marbara M. 2001. "Disability Definitions, Models, Classification Schemes, and Applications." In *Handbook of Disability Studies*, ed. G. Albrecht et al., 97–122. London: Sage.
Amuta, Chidi. 1983. "The Nigerian Civil War and the Evolution of Nigerian Literature." *Canadian Journal of African Studies* 17, no. 1: 85–100.
——. 1986. "The Ideological Content of Wole Soyinka's Writings." *African Studies Review* 29, no. 3: 43–54.
Ashfield, Andrew, and Peter de Bolla. 1996. *The Sublime: A Reader in British Eighteenth-Century Aesthetic Theory*. Cambridge: Cambridge University Press.
Attridge, Derek. 2004. *J. M. Coetzee and the Ethics of Reading: Literature in the Event*. Chicago: Chicago University Press.
Attwell, David, ed. 1992. *Doubling the Point: Essays and Interviews*. Cambridge, Mass.: Harvard University Press.
——. 1993. *J. M. Coetzee: South Africa and the Politics of Writing*. Berkeley: University of California Press.
Auerbach, Erich. 1953. *Mimesis: The Representation of Reality in Western Literature*. Princeton, N.J.: Princeton University Press.
Baines, Graham. 1990. "The Origins of Urban Segregation: Local Government and the Residence of Africans in Port Elizabeth, c. 1835–1865." *South African Historical Journal* 22: 61–81.

Bakhtin, Mikhail. 1984. *Problems of Dostoevsky's Poetics*. Ed. and trans. Caryl Emerson. Manchester: Manchester University Press.

Bapsi, Sidhwa. 1991. *Cracking India*. Minneapolis: Milkweed Editions.

Barnes, Colin, Mike Oliver, and Len Barton, eds. 2002. *Disability Studies Today*. Cambridge: Polity Press.

Baron-Cohen, Simon. 2000. "Is Asperger's Syndrome Necessarily a Disability?" *Development and Psychopathology* 12: 489–500.

Begam, Richard. 1996. *Samuel Beckett and the End of Modernity*. Stanford, Calif.: Stanford University Press.

Belmonte, Michael. 2005. "Human, but More So: What the Autistic Brain Tells Us About the Process of Narrative." Paper presented at conference on "Autism and Representation: Writing, Cognition, Disability." Available online at http://www.case.edu/affil/sce/Texts_2005/representingautism/html.

Benitez-Rojo, Antonio. 1996. *The Repeating Island: The Caribbean in Postmodern Perspective*. 2nd ed. Durham, N.C.: Duke University Press.

Bennett, A., ed. 1978. *Recent Advances in Community Medicine*. London: Heinemann.

Berger, James. 2005. "Alterity and Autism: Mark Haddon's *Curious Incident* in the Neurological Spectrum." Paper presented at conference on "Autism and Representation: Writing, Cognition, Disability." Available online at http://www.case.edu/affil/sce/Texts_2005/representingautism/html.

Bérubé, Michael. 1996. *Life as We Know It: A Father, a Family, and an Exceptional Child*. New York: Pantheon Books.

Bidney, Martin. 1997. *Patterns of Epiphany: From Wordsworth to Tolstoy, Pater, and Barrett Browning*. Carbondale, Ill.: Southern Illinois Press.

Blackmur, R. P. 2003. "Examples of Wallace Stevens." In *Close Reading: The Reader*, ed. Frank Lentricchia and Andrew Du Bois, 111–135. Durham, N.C.: Duke University Press.

Bloom, Harold, ed. 1985. *Samuel Beckett*. New York: Chelsea House.

——, ed. 1990. *Toni Morrison*. New York: Chelsea House.

Boulter, Jonathan. 1998. "'Speak No More': The Hermeneutical Function of Narrative in Samuel Beckett's *Endgame*." In *Samuel Beckett: A Casebook*, ed. J. Jeffers, 39–62. New York: Garland Publishing.

Bourdieu, Pierre. 1991. *Language and Symbolic Power*. Cambridge, Mass.: Harvard University Press.

Braddock, David L., and Susan L. Parish. 2001. "An Institutional History of Disability." In *Handbook of Disability Studies*, ed. G. Albrecht et al., 11–68. London: Sage.

Brennan, Teresa. 2004. *The Transmission of Affect*. Ithaca, N.Y.: Cornell University Press.

Briganti, Chiara. 1988. "'A Bored Spinster with a Locked Diary': The Politics of Hysteria in *In the Heart of the Country*." In *Critical Essays on J. M. Coetzee*, ed. S. Kossew, 84–99. New York: G. K. Hall.

Brooks, Peter. 1988. "The Idea of a Psychoanalytic Literary Criticism." In *The*

Trials of Psychoanalysis, ed. Francois Meltzer, 145–159. Chicago: Chicago University Press.

Brutus, Dennis. 1968. *Letters to Martha and Other Poems*. London: Heinemann.

——. 1973. *A Simple Lust: Selected Poems*. London: Heinemann.

Bryan, William Frank, and Germaine Dempster, eds. 1941. *Sources and Analogues of Chaucer's Canterbury Tales*. Chicago: Chicago University Press.

Brydon, Diana. 2000. *Postcolonialism: Critical Concepts in Literary and Cultural Studies*. 5 vols. New York: Routledge.

Burke, Timothy. 1996. *Lifebuoy Men, Lux Women: Commodification, Consumption, and Cleanliness in Modern Zimbabwe*. Durham, N.C.: Duke University Press.

Butler, Lance St. John. 1984. *Samuel Beckett and the Meaning of Being: A Study in Ontological Parable*. London: Macmillan.

Caruth, Cathy. 1988. "The Force of Example: Kant's Symbols." *Yale French Studies* 74: 17–37.

Chabal, Patrick, and Jean-Pascal Daloz. 1999. *Africa Works: Disorder as Political Instrument*. Oxford: James Currey; Bloomington: Indiana University Press.

Chabert, Pierre. 1982. "The Body in Beckett's Theatre." *Journal of Beckett Studies* 8: 23–28.

Claybaugh, Amanda. 2005. "The Autobiography of a Substitute: Trauma, History, Howells." *Yale Journal of Criticism* 18, no. 1: 45–65.

Coetzee, Carli. 1998. "Krotoa Remembered: A Mother of Unity, A Mother of Sorrows?" In *Negotiating the Past: The Making of Memory in South Africa*, ed. S. Nuttal and C. Coetzee, 112–119. Oxford: Oxford University Press.

Coetzee, J. M. 1988. *White Writing: On the Culture of Letters in South Africa*. New Haven, Conn.: Yale University Press.

Cohn, Bernard. 1987. *An Anthropologist Among Historians and Other Essays*. Oxford: Oxford University Press.

Connor, Steven. 1992. *Waiting for Godot and Endgame—Samuel Beckett*. New York: St. Martin's Press.

Corker, Mairian, and Sally French, eds. 1999. *Disability Discourse*. Buckingham: Open University Press.

Crockett, Clayton. 2001. *A Theology of the Sublime*. London: Routledge.

Cunningham, David. 2002. "Trying (Not) to Understand: Adorno and the Work of Beckett." In *Beckett and Philosophy*, ed. R. Lane. London: Palgrave.

Curtis, L. Perry. 1997. *Apes and Angels: The Irishman in Victorian Caricature*. Washington, D.C.: Smithsonian Institution Press.

Dangor, Achmat. 2001. *Bitter Fruit*. Cape Town: Kwela.

Davis, Lennard J. 1995. *Enforcing Normalcy: Disability, Deafness, and the Body*. London: Verso.

——. 2002. "Who Put the *The* in The Novel?" In *Bending Over Backwards: Disability, Dismodernism, and other Difficult Positions*, 79–101. New York: New York University Press.

De Man, Paul. 1990. "Phenomenality and Materiality in Kant." In *The Textual*

Sublime, ed. H. Silverman and G. Aylesworth, 87–108. Albany, N.Y.: SUNY Press.

De Villiers, Simon A. 1971. *Robben Island: Out of Reach, Out of Mind.* Cape Town: C. Struik.

Deacon, Harriet. 1994. "Leprosy and Racism at Robben Island." *Studies in the History of Cape Town* 7: 54–83.

——. 1996a. *The Island: A History of Robben Island, 1488–1990.* Cape Town: David Philip.

——. 1996b. "Racial Segregation and Medical Discourse in Nineteenth-Century Cape Town." *Journal of Southern African Studies* 22, no. 2: 287–308.

——. 2001. "Racism and Medical Science in South Africa's Cape Colony in the Mid- to Late Nineteenth Century." *Osiris*, 2nd ser., 15: 190–206.

——. 2003. "Patterns of Exclusion on Robben Island, 1654–1992." In *Isolation: Places and Practices of Exclusion*, ed. C. Strange and A. Bashford, 153–172. London: Routledge.

Deutsch, Helen. 1996. *Resemblance and Disgrace: Alexander Pope and the Deformation of Culture.* Cambridge, Mass.: Harvard University Press.

——. 2002. "Exemplary Aberration: Samuel Johnson and the English Canon." In *Disability Studies: Enabling the Humanities*, ed. S. Snyder et al., 197–210. New York: MLA.

Douglas, Mary. 1966. *Purity and Danger.* London: Routledge, 2004.

Dovey, Teresa. 1988. *The Novels of J. M. Coetzee: Lacanian Allegories.* Cape Town: A. D. Donker.

——. 1996. "Waiting for the Barbarians: Allegory of Allegories." In *Critical Perspectives on J. M. Coetzee*, ed. G. Huggan and S. Watson, 138–151. London: Macmillan.

Dubow, Saul. 1989. *Racial Segregation and the Origins of Apartheid in South Africa, 1919–1936.* London: Macmillan.

Durkheim, Emile. 1912. *Elementary Forms of Religious Life.* Trans. Karen E. Fields. New York: Free Press, 1995.

Ellison, Ralph. 1992. *Invisible Man.* New York: Modern Library.

Elphick, Richard. 1985. *Khokhoi and the Founding of White South Africa.* Johannesburg: Ravan Press.

Elphick, Richard, and Robert Shell. 1979. "Intergroup Relations: Khokhooi, Settlers, Slaves, and Free Blacks, 1652–1795." In *The Shaping of South African Society, 1652–1840*, ed. R. Elphick and H. Giliomee, 184–242. Middletown, Conn.: Wesleyan University Press.

Ezeigbo, Akachi T. 1991. *Fact and Fiction in the Literature of the Nigerian Civil War.* Lagos: Unity Publishing.

Foucault, Michel. 1977. *Discipline and Punish.* Trans. Alan Sheridan. New York: Vintage, 1995.

——. *The History of Sexuality.* 1978. Trans. Robert Hurley. New York: Vintage, 1990.

Freud, Sigmund. 1919. "The Uncanny." In *Standard Edition of the Complete Psy-*

chological Works of Sigmund Freud, trans. under the general editorship of James Stratchey in collaboration with Anna Freud, assisted by Alix Stratchey and Alan Tyson, vol. 17. London: Hogarth.

———. 1926. *Beyond the Pleasure Principle*. In *Standard Edition of the Complete Psychological Works of Sigmund Freud*, vol. 18. London: Hogarth.

———. 1938. *Moses and Monotheism*. In *Standard Edition of the Complete Psychological Works of Sigmund Freud*, vol. 23. London: Hogarth.

Friedlander, Henry. 1995. *The Origins of Nazi Genocide: From Euthanasia to the Final Solution*. Charlottesville: University of North Carolina Press.

Frye, Northrop. 1957. *Anatomy of Criticism: Four Essays*. Oxford: Oxford University Press.

———. 1963. *Fables of Identity: Studies in Poetic Mythology*. New York: Harcourt and Brace.

Fugard, Athol. 1993. *The Island*. In *Township Plays*, 193–227. Oxford: Oxford University Press.

Garland, Robert. 1995. *The Eye of the Beholder: Deformity and Disability in the Graeco-Roman World*. Ithaca, N.Y.: Cornell University Press.

Garner, B. Stanton, Jr. 1994. "Beckett, Merleau-Ponty, and the Phenomenological Body." In *Bodied Spaces: Phenomenology and Performance in Contemporary Drama*, 18–38. Ithaca, N.Y.: Cornell University Press.

Gates, Henry Louis, Jr. 1988. *Signifying Monkey: A Theory of Afro-American Literary Criticism*. Oxford: Oxford University Press.

Genette, Gerard. 1980. *Narrative Discourse: An Essay in Method*. Trans. Jane E. Lewin. Ithaca, N.Y.: Cornell University Press.

Gilman, Sander. 1985. *Difference and Pathology: Stereotypes of Sexuality, Race, and Madness*. Ithaca, N.Y.: Cornell University Press.

Goffman, Erving. 1959. *Stigma: Notes on the Management of Spoiled Identity*. New York: Simon and Schuster.

Gontarski, S. E., ed. 1986. *On Beckett: Essays and Criticism*. New York: Grove Press.

Gray, Katherine M. 1996. "Troubling the Body: Toward a Theory of Beckett's Use of the Human Body Onstage." *Journal of Beckett Studies* 5, no. 1/2: 1–17.

Griffiths, Paul, and Mark S. R. Jenner. 2000. *Londinopolis: Essays in the Cultural and Social History of Early Modern England*. Manchester: Manchester University Press.

Grosz, Elizabeth. 1994. *Volatile Bodies: Towards a Corporeal Feminism*. Bloomington: Indiana University Press.

———. 1996. "Intolerable Ambiguity: Freaks as/at the Limit." In *Freakery: Cultural Spectacles of the Extraordinary Body*, ed. R. Thomson, 55–66. New York: New York University Press.

Gussow, Zachary. 1989. *Leprosy, Racism, and Public Health: Social Policy in Chronic Disease Control*. Boulder, Colo.: Westview Press.

Haddon, Mark. 2003. *The Curious Incident of the Dog in the Night-Time*. London: Jonathan Cape.

Hampate Ba, Amadou. 1999. *The Fortunes of Wangrin*. Trans. Aina Pavolini Taylor. Bloomington: Indiana University Press.

Harper, Stephen. 2003. *Insanity, Individuals, and Society in Late-Medieval English Literature: The Subject of Madness*. Lewiston, Me.: The Edwin Mellen Press.

Hays, Peter. 1971. *The Limping Hero: Grotesques in Literature*. New York: New York University Press.

Head, Dominic. 1997. *J. M. Coetzee*. Cambridge: Cambridge University Press.

Hegel, G. W. F. 1998. "Tragedy as Dramatic Art." In *Tragedy*, ed. John Drakakis and Naomi Conn Liebler, 23–52. London: Longman.

Hegi, Ursula. 1994. *Stones from the River*. New York: Scribner.

Hertz, Neil. 1985. *The End of the Line: Essays on Psychoanalysis and the Sublime*. New York: Columbia University Press.

Hesla, David. 1971. *The Shape of Chaos: An Interpretation of the Art of Samuel Beckett*. Minneapolis: University of Minnesota Press.

Heywood, Annemarie. 2001. "The Fox's Dance: The Staging of Soyinka's Plays." In *Perspectives on Wole Soyinka: Freedom and Complexity*, ed. B. Jeyifo, 130–138. Jackson: University Press of Mississippi.

Hillyer, Barbara. 1993. *Feminism and Disability*. Norman: Oklahoma University Press.

Hirsch, Marianne. 1989. *The Mother/Daughter Plot: Narrative, Psychoanalysis, Feminism*. Bloomington: Indiana University Press.

Holmes, Martha Stoddard. 2000. *Fictions of Affliction: Physical Disabilities in Victorian Culture*. Ann Arbor: University of Michigan Press.

———. 2002. "The Twin Structure: Disabled Women in Victorian Courtship Plots." In *Disability Studies: Enabling the Humanities*, ed. S. Snyder, 222–233. New York: MLA.

Honneth, Axel. 1995. *The Struggle for Recognition: The Moral Grammar of Social Conflict*. Cambridge: Polity Press, 1995.

Hubert, Marie-Claude. 1994. "The Evolution of the Body in Beckett's Theater." *Journal of Beckett Studies* 4, no. 1: 55–65.

Huggan, Graham, and Stephen Watson, eds. 1996. *Critical Perspectives on J. M. Coetzee*. London: Macmillan.

Hutcheon, Linda, and Michael Hutcheon. 1996. *Opera: Desire, Disease, and Death*. Lincoln: University of Nebraska Press.

Ingstad, Benedicte, and Susan Reynolds Whyte, eds. 1995. *Disability and Culture*. Berkeley: University of California Press.

Jeffers, Jennifer M. 1998. "A Place Without an Occupant: Krapp's Rhizome Identity." In *Samuel Beckett: A Casebook*, ed. J. Jeffers, 63–79. New York: Garland Publishing.

Jeyifo, Biodun. 2004. *Wole Soyinka: Politics, Poetics, and Postcolonialism*. Cambridge: Cambridge University Press.

Kane, Leslie. 1984. *The Language of Silence: On the Unspoken and the Unspeakable in Modern Drama*. London: Associated University Presses.

Kant, Immanuel. 1960. *Observations on the Feeling of the Beautiful and Sublime*. Trans. John T. Goldthwait. Berkeley: University of California Press.

——. 1987. *Critique of Judgment.* Trans. Werner Pluhar. Indianapolis: Hackett.

Kathadra, Ahmed. 2005. *Memoirs.* Johannesburg: Stuik.

Katrak, Ketu. 1986. *Wole Soyinka and Modern Tragedy: A Study of Dramatic Theory and Practice.* New York: Greenwood Press.

Keith, Lois, ed. 1994. *"What Happened to You?": Writing by Disabled Women.* London: Women's Press.

Kermode, Frank. 1968. *The Sense of an Ending.* Oxford: Oxford University Press.

Klein, Melanie. 1997. *Envy and Gratitude and Other Works, 1946–1963.* London: Vintage.

Knowlson, James. 1996. *Damned to Fame: The Life of Samuel Beckett.* New York: Touchstone.

Knowlson, James, and John Pilling. 1979. *Frescoes of the Skull: The Later Prose and Drama of Samuel Beckett.* London: John Calder.

Kossew, Sue, ed. 1998. *Critical Essays on J. M. Coetzee.* New York: G. K. Hall.

——. 1998. "'Women's Words': A Reading of J. M. Coetzee's Women Narrators." In *Critical Essays on J. M. Coetzee,* ed. S. Kossew, 166–179. New York: G. K. Hall.

Krentz, Christopher. 2002. "Exploring the 'Hearing Line': Deafness, Laughter, and Mark Twain." In *Disability Studies: Enabling the Humanities,* ed. S. Snyder et al., 234–247. New York: MLA.

Kuhl, Stefan. 1994. *The Nazi Connection: Eugenics, American Racism, and German National Socialism.* Oxford: Oxford University Press.

Lacan, Jacques. 1948. "Aggressivity in Psychoanalysis." In *Écrits,* trans. Alan Sheridan. London: Routledge, 1995.

——. 1949. "The Mirror Stage as Formative of the Function of the I as Revealed in Psychoanalytic Experience." In *Écrits,* trans. Alan Sheridan. London: Routledge, 1995.

Lane, Richard, ed. 2002. *Beckett and Philosophy.* London: Palgrave.

Leibbrandt, H. C. V., ed. 1900–1902. *Precis of the Archives of the Cape of Good Hope.* 5 vols. Cape Town: J. C. Juta.

Lee, Harper. 1960. *To Kill a Mockingbird.* Philadelphia: J. B. Lippincott.

Lentricchia, Frank, and Andrew Du Bois. 2003. *Close Reading: The Reader.* Durham, N.C.: Duke University Press.

Lindfors, Bernth. 1996. "Ethnological Show Business: Footlighting the Dark Continent." In *Freakery: Cultural Spectacles of the Extraordinary Body,* ed. R. Thomson, 207–218. New York: New York University Press.

Linton, Simi. 1998. *Claiming Disability: Knowledge and Identity.* New York: New York University Press.

Lloyd, G. E. R. 2003. *In the Grip of Disease: Studies in the Greek Imagination.* Oxford: Oxford University Press.

Macaskill, Brian. 1998. "Charting J. M. Coetzee's Middle Voice: *In the Heart of the Country.*" In *Critical Essays on J. M. Coetzee,* ed. S. Kossew, 66–83. New York: G. K. Hall.

Magona, Sindiwe. 2000. *Mother to Mother.* London: Beacon.

Mahfouz, Naguib. 1992. *Midaq Alley*. Trans. Trevor Le Gassick. New York: Anchor Books.

Malherbe, V.C. 1990. *Krotoa, Called 'Eva': A Woman Between*. Cape Archives 19. Cape Town: Centre for African Studies.

Mandela, Nelson. 1994. *Long Walk to Freedom*. London: Jonathan Cape.

Marback, Richard. 2004. "The Rhetorical Space of Robben Island." *Rhetoric Society Quarterly* 34, no. 2: 7–21.

Mbeki, Govan. 1991. *Learning from Robben Island*. Oxford: James Currey.

Mbembe, Achille. 2002. *On the Postcolony*. Berkeley: University of California Press.

——. 2003. "Necropolitics." *Public Culture* 15, no. 1: 11–40.

Melville, Herman. 1851. *Moby Dick*. New York: Norton, 2002.

Merleau-Ponty, Maurice. 1962. *The Phenomenology of Perception*. Trans. Colin Smith. London: Routledge and Kegan Paul.

——. 1964. *The Primacy of Perception*. Evanston, Ill.: Northwestern University Press.

Mitchell, David T., and Sharon L. Snyder. 2000. *Narrative Prosthesis: Disability and the Dependencies of Discourse*. Ann Arbor: University of Michigan Press.

Morrison, Toni. 1992. *Playing in the Dark: Whiteness and the Literary Imagination*. Cambridge, Mass.: Harvard University Press.

Mukherjee, Pablo. 2003. *Crime and Empire: The Colony in Nineteenth-Century Fictions of Crime*. Oxford: Oxford University Press.

Murphy, Robert. 1990. *The Body Silent*. New York: Norton.

Nabokov, Vladimir. 1995. "Signs and Symbols." In *Collected Short Stories*. London: Penguin.

Ndebele, Njabulo S. 1994. *South African Literature and Culture: Rediscovery of the Ordinary*. Manchester: Manchester University Press.

Nicol, Mike. 1988. *The Ibis Tapestry*. New York: Alfred A. Knopf.

Norden, Martin. 1994. *The Cinema of Isolation: A History of Physical Disability in the Movies*. New Brunswick, N.J.: Rutgers University Press.

Obafemi, Olu. 1992. *Nigerian Writers on the Nigerian Civil War*. Ilorin: J. Olu Olatiregun Company.

Oliver, Michael. 1990. *The Politics of Disablement*. London: Macmillan.

Ondaatje, Michael. 1992. *The English Patient*. London: Bloomsbury.

O'Sullivan, Ellie. 1994. "The Visit." In *"What Happened to You?": Writing by Disabled Women*, ed. L. Keith, 13–17. London: Women's Press.

Parry, Benita. 1996. "Speech and Silence in the Fictions of J.M. Coetzee." In *Critical Perspectives on J.M. Coetzee*, ed. G. Huggan and S. Watson, 37–65. London: Macmillan.

——. 2000. "Problems in Current Theories of Colonial Discourse." In *Postcolonialism: Critical Concepts in Literary and Cultural Studies*, ed. Diana Bryden, 2: 714–747. New York: Routledge.

——. 2004. *Postcolonial Studies: A Materialist Critique*. London: Routledge.

Pelling, Margaret. 1998. *The Common Lot: Sickness, Medical Occupations, and the Urban Poor in Early Modern England*. London: Longman.

Penn, Nigel. 1996. "Robben Island, 1488–1805." In *The Island: A History of Robben Island, 1488–1990*, by H. Deacon, 9–32. Cape Town: David Philip.

Pierre-Vernant, Jean. 1980. *Myth and Society in Ancient Greece*. Trans. Janet Lloyd. New York: Zone Books.

Pilling, John, ed. 1990. *The Cambridge Companion to Samuel Beckett*. Cambridge: Cambridge University Press.

Porter, Roy. 2002. *Madness: A Brief History*. Oxford: Oxford University Press.

Propp, Vladimir. 1958. *Morphology of the Folktale*. Trans. Laurence Scott. Bloomington: Indiana University Press.

Quayson, Ato. 1997. *Strategic Transformations in Nigerian Writing: Samuel Johnson, Amos Tutuola, Wole Soyinka, and Ben Okri*. Oxford: James Currey; Bloomington: Indiana University Press.

———. 2003. *Calibrations: Reading for the Social*. Minneapolis: Minnesota University Press.

———. 2004. "Symbolization Compulsions: Testing a Psychoanalytic Category on Postcolonial African Criticism." *University of Toronto Quarterly* 73, no. 2: 754–772.

Read, Janet. 2000. *Disability, the Family, and Society: Listening to Mothers*. Buckingham: Open University Press.

Ricks, Christopher. 1993. *Beckett's Dying Words*. Oxford: Clarendon.

Robben, Antonio C. G. M., and Marcelo M. Suarez-Orozco, eds. 2000. *Cultures Under Siege: Collective Violence and Trauma*. Cambridge: Cambridge University Press.

Said, Edward. 1994. *Culture and Imperialism*. New York: Knopf.

Sandblom, Philip. 1997. *Creativity and Disease: How Illness Affects Literature, Art, and Music*. New York: Marion Boyars.

Scarry, Elaine. 1985. *The Body in Pain: The Making and Unmaking of the World*. New York: Oxford University Press.

Siebers, Tobin. 1998. *The Ethics of Criticism*. Ithaca, N.Y.: Cornell University Press.

———. 2002. "Tender Organs, Narcissism, and Identity Politics." In *Disability Studies: Enabling the Humanities*, ed. S. Snyder et al., 40–55. New York: MLA.

Slack, Paul. 1995. *The English Poor Law, 1531–1782*. Cambridge: Cambridge University Press.

Slovo, Gillian. 2000. *Red Dust*. London: Virago.

Snyder, Sharon, and David Mitchell. 2001. *A World Without Bodies*. Video documentary. Syracuse: Program Development Associates.

Snyder, Sharon L., Brenda Jo Brueggemann, and Rosemarie Garland Thomson, eds. 2002. *Disability Studies: Enabling the Humanities*. New York: MLA.

Soyinka, Wole. 1975. *Myth, Literature, and the African World*. Cambridge: Cambridge University Press.

Spillers, Hortense J. 2003. *Black, White, and in Colour: Essays on American Literature and Culture*. Chicago: Chicago University Press.

Spivak, Gayatri. 2000. "Three Women's Texts and a Critique of Imperialism." In *Postcolonialism: Critical Concepts in Literary and Cultural Studies*, ed. Diana Bryden, 2:694–713. New York: Routledge.

Stiker, Henri-Jacques. 1997. *A History of Disability*. Trans. William Sayers. Ann Arbor: University of Michigan Press. First published in French in 1982.

Stoler, Ann Laura. 1995. *Race and the Education of Desire: Foucault's History of Sexuality and the Colonial Order of Things*. Durham, N.C.: Duke University Press.

Suskind, Patrick. 1986. *Perfume: The Story of a Murderer*. Trans. John E. Woods. New York: Knopf.

Sutcliff, Rosemary. 1981. *The Sword and the Circle: King Arthur and the Knights of the Round Table*. London: Bodley Head.

Swanson, M. W. 1977. "The Sanitation Syndrome: Bubonic Plague and Urban Native Policy in the Cape Colony, 1900–1909." *Journal of African History* 18: 387–410.

Swartz, Sally. 1999. "Lost Lives: Gender, History, and Mental Illness in the Cape, 1891–1910." *Feminism and Psychology* 9, no. 2: 152–158.

Tagliaferri, Aldo. 1985. "Beckett and Joyce." In *Samuel Beckett*, ed. H. Bloom, 247–261. New York: Chelsea House.

Tambo, Oliver. 1987. "Mandela and Nehru." In *Preparing for Power: Oliver Tambo Speaks*, comp. and ed. Adelaide Tambo, 193–200. London: Heinemann.

Taylor, Jane, and William Kentridge. 1998. *Ubu and the Truth Commission*. Cape Town: University of Cape Town Press.

Thiher, Allen. 1999. *Revels in Madness: Insanity in Medicine and Literature*. Ann Arbor: University of Michigan Press.

Thom, H. B., ed. 1954. *Journal of Jan van Riebeeck*. 3 vols. Cape Town: A. A. Balkema.

Thompson, Robert Faris. 1983. *Flash of the Spirit: African and Afro-American Art and Philosophy*. New York: Random House.

Thomson, Rosemarie Garland, ed. 1996. *Freakery: Cultural Spectacles of the Extraordinary Body*. New York: New York University Press.

——. 1997. *Extraordinary Bodies: Figuring Physical Disability in American Culture and Literature*. New York: Columbia University Press.

——. 2002. "The Politics of Staring: Visual Rhetorics of Disability in Popular Photography." In *Disability Studies: Enabling the Humanities*, ed. S. Snyder et al., 56–75. New York: MLA.

Trezise, Thomas. 1990. *Into the Breach: Samuel Beckett and the Ends of Literature*. Princeton, N.J.: Princeton University Press.

Turner, Victor. 1967. *The Forest of Symbols*. Ithaca, N.Y.: Cornell University Press.

——. 1982. *From Ritual to Theatre*. New York: Performing Arts Journal Publications, 1982.

Uhlmann, Anthony. 1999. *Beckett and Poststructuralism*. Cambridge: Cambridge University Press.

UN Landmine Monitor Report. 1999.

Van Gennep, Arnold. 1908. *The Rites of Passage*. Trans. Monika B. Vizedom and Gabriele L. Caffe. London: Routledge and Kegan Paul, 1960.

Vandenbroucke, Russell. 1985. *Truths the Hands Can Touch*. New York: TCG.

Vaughan, Megan. 1991. *Curing Their Ills: Colonial Power and African Illness*. Cambridge: Polity Press.

Vladislavic, Ivan. 1998. "The Fugu-Eaters." In *A Writing Life: Celebrating Nadine Gordimer*, ed. Andries Oliphant, 200–206. London: Viking.

Wall, John. 2000. "Murphy, Belacqua, Schopenhauer, and Descartes: Metaphysical Reflections on the Body." *Journal of Beckett Studies* 9, no. 2: 21–61.

Wasserman, David. 2001. "Philosophical Issues in the Definition and Social Response to Disability." In *Handbook of Disability Studies*, ed. G. Albrecht et al., 219–251. London: Sage.

Wells, Julia, C. 1998. "Eva's Men: Gender and Power in the Establishment of the Cape of Good Hope, 1652–74." *Journal of African History* 39, 417–437.

Wendell, Susan. 1996. *The Rejected Body: Feminist Philosophical Reflections on Disability*. London: Routledge.

Wetmore, Kevin J., Jr. 2002. *The Athenian Sun in an African Sky*. Jefferson, N.C.: McFarland.

Wiess, Meira. 1994. *Conditional Love: Parent's Attitudes Toward Handicapped Children*. Westport, Conn.: Bergin and Garvey.

Williams, David. 1996. *Deformed Discourse: The Function of the Monster in Mediaeval Thought and Literature*. Montreal: McGill Queen's University Press.

Williams, Gareth. 2001. "Theorizing Disability." In *Handbook of Disability Studies*, ed. G. Albrecht et al., 123–144. London: Sage.

Williams, Raymond. 1977. *Marxism and Literature*. Oxford: Oxford University Press.

Wills, David. 1995. *Prosthesis*. Stanford, Calif.: Stanford University Press.

Wood, P., and N. Bradley. 1978. "An Epidemiological Appraisal of Disablement." In *Recent Advances in Community Medicine, No. 1*, ed. A. E. Bennett, 149–174. London: Heinemann.

Worton, Michael. 1994. "*Waiting for Godot* and *Endgame*: Theatre as Text." In *The Cambridge Companion to Beckett*, ed. J. Pilling, 67–87. Cambridge: Cambridge University Press.

Young, Robert. 1995. *Colonial Desire: Hybridity in Theory, Culture, and Race*. London: Routledge.

Zipes, Jack. 1979. *Breaking the Magic Spell: Radical Theories of Folk and Fairy Tales*. Austin: University of Texas Press.

Zola, Irving. 1987. "'Any Distinguishing Features?'—The Portrayal of Disability in the Crime-Mystery Genre." *Policy Studies Journal* 15, no. 3: 487–513.

INDEX

CPSIA information can be obtained
at www.ICGtesting.com
Printed in the USA
JSHW031356010621
15421JS00007B/128